8 9r —

HIPPOCRENE LANGUAGE STUDIES

SAUDI ARABIC BASIC COURSE

Margaret K. Omar

HIPPOCRENE BOOKS
New York

Originally compiled in 1975 by Margaret K. Omar of the Foreign Service Institute, Department of State.

Hippocrene paperback edition, 1994.

For information, address:
HIPPOCRENE BOOKS, INC.
171 Madison Avenue
New York, NY 10016

ISBN 0-7818-0257-1

Printed in the United States of America.

INTRODUCTION

There are three major groups of dialects in Saudi Arabia--Hijazi, spoken on the western coast, in Jidda, Taif, and the holy cities of Mecca and Medina; Najdi, spoken in and around Riyadh, in the north central part of the country; and Shargi, spoken in the oil-rich eastern region. While the Najdi dialect enjoys prestige by virtue of its conservatism and relative closeness to Classical Arabic and the fact that it is the dialect of the royal family, the Hijazi dialect is used throughout the country for government and commercial purposes, and has become the most widely-understood dialect in the Arabian Peninsula. The Hijazi dialect is not "pure" Saudi Arabic, and reflects recent borrowings from other dialects, especially Egyptian, Jordanian and Palestinian; for this reason, sometimes one word or expression was selected from several which may be heard, and sometimes alternative expressions are introduced, since two or even three forms may be in frequent use.

Since there is no "standard" Hijazi dialect, this book reflects the dialect as spoken in Jidda. Whenever forced to choose between language usage in the other Hijazi cities and that of Jidda, the Jidda usage was given preference. A few of the most common words from Najdi and from other cities are introduced for recognition and identified as such. There has also been a preference for "modern" words and structures, despite the fact that this sometimes means rejecting an older, more "Saudi" usage. This dialect has been designated "urban" Hijazi to distinguish it from Bedouin dialects also native to the Hijaz region.

No doubt Saudi instructors will find that, depending on their place of origin, they may wish to substitute words or alter certain forms used in this text. The student should follow the model of his instructor.

The pronunciation of some sounds in Hijazi is variable. There are three interdental consonants (variations of 'th') which may be pronounced as they are in Classical Arabic and in Najdi, as for example in /thalaatha/, or as they are in Egyptian and Palestinian, which would be /talaata/. Since the latter type of pronunciation is more common in Jidda, it will be presented. This is discussed further in the Pronunciation section.

After completion of this book, the student should have attained a "working" proficiency in the language (approximately S-2 level by the FSI rating system). In other words, the student will be able to satisfy routine social demands and limited business requirements, carry on conversations regarding a wide range of general subjects (asking directions, ordering a meal, giving personal information, making purchases, etc.), and comprehend speech about such subjects at a normal rate of speed. This book will provide a student with all the basic grammatical structures of the dialect, so that he will be ready to proceed on his own to acquire the speed and new vocabulary which lead to real fluency.

Design of the Book

The book is divided into 50 lessons. Each lesson (beginning with Lesson 4) has the following parts:

Dialogue. The dialogues have been kept short and were designed to be practical and worth memorizing. Each dialogue should be memorized for recitation and practice among the students.

Structure Sentences. In each lesson, certain words and grammatical structures are presented. Structures which did not appear in the dialogue will be illustrated in these sentences. Structure sentences serve the purpose of linking the dialogue sentences, which are necessarily limited in type, with the grammatical explanations coming up in the Grammatical Notes. They contain examples of new structures used in a sentence context.

Grammatical Notes. New structures are presented and explained, with examples.

Vocabulary Notes. Included in this section are only the new words which need the illustration of additional forms (for example, the present tense of a verb, or the plural of a noun). Words which are clear from their presentation elsewhere in the lesson will not be repeated here. The student is held responsible for all new vocabulary regardless of where it appears in a lesson, although it is recognized that some words are more essential for the students' own production than others. The instructor will determine which words should be learned for production and which are sufficient for the student to recognize passively.

Drills. New words and structures are drilled by substitution, by the transformation of sentences (for example, from affirmative to negative), by questions and answers, and by translation. The part of a model sentence which is to be substituted is underlined.

Situations. These are typical situations, with the sentences given in English, which the student should be able to say in Arabic after he has mastered the lesson. This section may be used as a self-test at the end of every lesson.

Cultural Notes. Where appropriate, comments on speech attitudes, situational behavior, or social etiquette are presented.

Every tenth lesson is a review lesson.

In addition to the 50 lessons, the book contains a series of appendices dealing with specialized vocabulary, social expressions, gestures, and Saudi names. There is also a glossary and an index of grammatical structures.

ACKNOWLEDGEMENTS

I owe thanks to many persons for their assistance in the preparation of this book. I am indebted to Dr. Mahmoud Sieny of the University of Riyadh for his help in all stages of the project. His dissertation, "The Syntax of Urban Hijazi Arabic", was an important source of grammatical information; it is the only scientifically-designed linguistic study of this dialect.

I appreciate the assistance of Mr. Charles Cecil and Mr. Hamdi Rida of the American Embassy in Jidda in helping me meet Saudis who provided me with language information. I thank my informants, among them Mr. Younis Ishaq, Mr. Talal Qusti, and Mr. Mustafa Darwish, all of Jidda, and especially Mrs. Ayesha Al-Marzouki. I also thank Captain Stephen Franke of the U.S. Army, Fort Bragg, for his useful comments.

Finally I express appreciation to the family of Badr El-Din Negm El-Din of Jidda, for their kind hospitality during my two stays there.

ABBREVIATIONS AND SYMBOLS

(m)	masculine
(f)	feminine
(p)	plural
C	consonant
V	vowel
C_1	initial consonant of a verb root
C_2	medial consonant of a verb root
C_3	final consonant of a verb root
lit.	literally (i.e., literal translation)

GRAMMATICAL TERMS

Most grammatical terms used here are defined as they are introduced. Listed below are a few other general terms which the student should know:

classicism. A word or expression which is borrowed from Classical Arabic. Classicisms will be identified as such.

colloquial. Arabic as it is spoken (as opposed to the written variety of Arabic). Colloquial words are usually slightly modified from Classical or written Arabic and vary considerably from one dialect to another.

conjugate. To list all forms of a verb for the various persons, for example, 'I go, he goes', etc.

decline. To list the various forms of a noun or adjective, for number ('book, books') or gender ('waiter, waitress'). Most nouns in colloquial Arabic are declined for number and gender.

idiom, idiomatic. An expression which is not part of the regular language pattern, and which must be accepted as it is without trying to explain its structure. Idioms will always be identified as such.

literal translation. The word-for-word translation which often does not sound natural in another language. For example, 'Good morning' in Arabic is literally translated as 'the morning of the goodness'. It is better to think of "equivalent translations" when learning a foreign language.

modal word. A helping word which is used with verbs to form a phrase, for example, 'should': 'I should go, we should try', etc.

modify. To refer to or describe another word in the sentence, for example, the adjective 'big' modifies the noun 'tree' in the sentence, 'The tree is big.'

prefix. A grammatical form attached to the beginning of a word, for example 'un-' as in 'unable'.

suffix. A grammatical form attached to the end of a word, for example, '-ing' as in 'going'.

transitive verb. A verb which takes an object, for example, 'hit': 'Bob hit Bill.' In this sentence, 'Bill' is the object of the verb. An intransitive verb does not take an object, for example, 'live'.

PRONUNCIATION

The Transcription System

The following is a list of the symbols used in the transcription of the sounds of Saudi Arabic and their approximate equivalents in English. It was decided to write this textbook using a transcription system rather than the Arabic alphabet because the alphabet cannot accurately represent the pronunciation of all words in the dialect (some consonant and vowel distinctions would be missing) and the instructor or student may be tempted to pronounce the word in the classical way if it is spelled the same. The Arabic alphabet has been added, however, as a supplement to the dialogues, drills, and some vocabulary lists, and is intended for use by the native-speaking instructor. The spelling of some words has been changed to reflect colloquial speech.

It should be borne in mind that Arabic and English sounds rarely correspond exactly, and the correct Arabic pronunciation is to be learned from the instructor.

Arabic Letter	Symbol	Approximate English Equivalent
ء	'	the catch in the throat between the vowels of oh-oh
ا	a, aa	ranges from a in cat to a in father; may be long or short
ب	b	b in bet
د	d	d in dead
ض	ḍ	not in English; d pronounced with the back of the tongue raised
	ee	ai in bait; usually occurs as a long vowel
ف	f	f in fee
ق	g	g in get
غ	gh	not in English; somewhat like a Parisian r but harsher
ه	h	h in head
ح	H	not in English; similar to h, but strongly whispered from deep in the throat
ي	i, ii	if short, i in bit, except at the end of words; at the end of a word or when long, ee in meet
ج	j	j in jet
ك	k	k in king
ل	l	l in let
ل	ł	l in ball
م	m	m in man
ن	n	n in net
	oo	oa in coat; usually occurs as a long vowel
ق	q	not in English; like the c in cool but farther back in the throat

Arabic Letter	Symbol	Approximate English Equivalent
ر	r	not in English; a tongue-tip trill as in Italian or Spanish
س	s	s in sit
ص	ṣ	not in English; s pronounced with the back of the tongue raised
ش	š	sh in ship
ت	t	t in tip
ط	ṭ	not in English; t pronounced with the back of the tongue raised
و	u,uu	if short, u in put, except at the end of words; at the end of a word or when long, oo in cool
و	w	w in wet
خ	x	not in English; ch in German acht
ي	y	y in yet
ز	z	z in zero
ظ	ẓ	not in English; z pronounced with the back of the tongue raised
ع	9	not in English; voiced equivalent of H; pronounced by tightening muscles deep in the throat

The symbol /´/ over a vowel indicates that the syllable containing that vowel is stressed.

The Consonants

The consonants drilled here will be those which are different from English. Words used are all real Arabic words, but they will not be translated, since the meanings are not relevant for the drills.

1. /'/ is the sound produced when the breath is stopped in the throat and then released. This sound occurs in English before vowels, such as in the expression oh-oh. It is easy for English-speakers to produce, but in Arabic you must become accustomed to using it in the middle and end of words, as well as in the beginning. Since the sound is automatically at the beginning of a word which starts with a vowel, it will not be marked in the transcription.

insaan	انسان
awwal	اول
sa'al	سأل
mas'ala	مسألة
la'	لاء

2. /H/ is pronounced by tightening the muscles in the middle of the throat so that a harsh H results. It sounds like a whisper and is produced without any voice.

Habb	حب	ṣubuH	صبح	Haal	حال
raaH	راح	ṣaHiiH	صحيح	aHwaal	احوال
aHad	احد	marHaba	مرحبا	aHmad	احمد

Contrasts between /h/ and /H/:

hamal	Hamal	همل	حمل
hal	Haal	هل	حال
minha	minHa	منها	منحة
taah	saaH	تاه	ساح
nahar	naHal	نهر	نحل
ahlan	aHsan	اهلا	احسن

3. /9/ is the voiced counterpart of the /H/. It is pronounced by tightening the muscles deep in the throat, while using the voice, and results in a sort of strangled sound.

9arabi	عربي	saa9a	ساعة	da9wa	دعوة
9ala	على	ma9aaya	معايه	raaji9	راجع
ma9a	مع	baa9	باع	raaj9a	راجعة

Contrasts between /'/ and /9/:

aala	9ala	آلة	على
sa'al	saa9ad	سأل	ساعد
aadaab	9aada	آداب	عاد
iid	9iid	ايد	عيد

Contrasts between /h/ and /9/:

haada	9aada	هادا	عادة
mahmuul	ma9muul	مهمول	معمول
haadi	9aadi	هادي	عادي
šahar	ša9ar	شهر	شعر

Contrasts between /H/ and /9/:

saamiH	saami9	سامح	سامع
balaH	bala9	بلح	بلع
Haal	9aal	حال	عال
minHa	min9a	منحة	منعة

Contrasts between /i9/ and /9a/:

saami9	saam9a	سامع	سامعة
saabi9	saab9a	سابع	سابعة
ţaali9	ţaal9a	طالع	طالعة
raaji9	raaj9a	راجع	راجعة

4. /x/ is pronounced by raising the back of the tongue to the position for /k/, but without blocking the air passage. It results in a friction sound, and is voiceless.

xeer	aaxir	خير	آخر
axuuya	xalli	اخويّ	خلّي
muxx	xamsa	مخ	خمسة

Contrasts between /k/ and /x/:

kaaf	xaaf	كاف	خاف
kaan	xaan	كان	خان
akuun	axu	اكون	اخو
sakan	suxun	سكن	سخن

Contrasts between /H/ and /x/:

Haal	xaal	حال	خال
Haram	xaram	حرم	خرم
ṣaHan	saxar	صحن	سخر

5. /gh/ is the voiced counterpart of /x/. It is pronounced by raising the back of the tongue to the position for /g/, but without blocking the air passage. It results in a friction sound, and is voiced.

gheer	ghaali	غير	غالي
baghdaad	abgha	بغداد	ابغى
dimaagh	ghariib	دماغ	غريب

Contrasts between /g/ and /gh/:

yibga	yibgha	يبقى	يبغى
gariib	ghariib	قريب	غريب
saayig	saayigh	سايق	سايغ
guul	ghuul	قول	غول
istiglaal	istighlaal	استقلال	استغلال

Contrasts between /x/ and /gh/:

xeer	gheer	خير	غير
xaali	ghaali	خالي	غالي
yixayyiṭ	yighayyir	يخيط	يغير
maṭbax	mablagh	مطبخ	مبلغ

6. /q/ is pronounced farther back in the throat than /k/, accompanied by tightening the muscles at the top of the throat. The back of the tongue touches the top of the throat, then pulls away suddenly. (This sound occurs only in "classicized" words; it often alternates with /g/.)

qur'aan	قرآن
al-qaahira	القاهرة
iqtiṣaad	اقتصاد

Contrasts between /k/ and /q/:

kaaf	qaaf	كاف	قاف
kamaan	qaamuus	كمان	قاموس
istikraar	istiqbaal	استكرار	استقبال

7. /r/ is pronounced by tapping the tip of the tongue against the ridge above the upper teeth. The quality of /r/ may range from "light" to "heavy". This contrast, however, rarely makes a difference in the meaning of words.

9aarif	šaari9	عارف	شارع
raaH	raadyu	راح	راديو
ḍarab	garš	ضرب	قرش
door	guruuš	دور	قروش
Haaḍir	xeer	حاضر	خير

When doubled, /rr/ is a trill, made by holding the tip of the tongue against this ridge and vibrating it.

marra	مرة
barra	برا
murr	مر
Harr	حر
xarraj	خرّج

8. Velarized Consonants.

There are five consonants which are "velarized", and contrast with their "plain" counterparts. They will be symbolized with a comma under the letter: ḍ, ṣ, ṭ, ẓ, ḷ. They differ from the "plain" consonants in that the back of the tongue is raised toward the top of the mouth while the sound is being articulated at the front of the mouth, and the result is a resonant sound. This is also known as "emphasis", and has a noticeable lowering effect on surrounding vowels in the word.

Contrasts between /d/ and /ḍ/:

raadyu	raaḍi	راديو	راضي
daal	ḍaad	دال	ضاد
9add	9aḍḍ	عد	عض
dulaar	ḍuyuuf	دولار	ضيوف

Contrasts between /t/ and /ṭ/:

tiin	ṭiin	تين	طين
tuut	ṭuub	توت	طوب
taalit	ṭaali9	ثالث	طالع
gatal	giṭaar	قتل	قطار

Contrasts between /s/ and /ṣ/:

siin	ṣiin	سين	صين
seef	ṣeef	سيف	صيف
sab9a	ṣabagh	سبعة	صبغ
xass	xaṣṣ	خس	خص
magaas	magaṣṣ	مقاس	مقص
gaas	giṣṣa	قاس	قصة

Contrasts between /z/ and /ẓ/:

zeet	ẓahar	زيت	ظهر
mazkuur	maẓbuuṭ	مزكور	مظبوط

Contrasts between /l/ and /ḷ/:

lillaah	aḷḷaah	لله	الله

9. The "TH" Consonants.

Three consonants in Classical Arabic have been changed in Hijazi pronunciation. The Classical (and Najdi) pronunciation is heard often enough, however, that the student should be aware of the reason for the variation. The correspondences are:

th as in 'this' (voiced; the phonetic symbol is ð). This is usually pronounced as d or z:

haaða ⟶ haada
asta'ðan ⟶ asta'zan

th as in 'think' (voiceless; the phonetic symbol is θ). This is usually pronounced as t or s:

θalaaθa ⟶ talaata
maθalan ⟶ masalan

th̡ , which is th (voiced), pronounced with the back of the tongue raised (the phonetic symbol is ð̣). It is usually pronounced as ẓ:

mað̣buuṭ ⟶ maẓbuuṭ

Of course this does not mean that all the occurrences of s, z, t, or d are in fact 'th' consonants; on the contrary, these consonants are relatively rare. ẓ, however, is always ð̣ in Classical Arabic.

Doubled Consonants

All consonants in Arabic may be doubled, and occur in the middle and at the end of words. In the case of sounds where friction is produced, doubling the consonant means holding it longer:

ṭili9	ṭalla9	طلع	طلّع
fihim	fahham	فهم	فهّم
daxal	daxxal	دخل	دخّل
min	sinn	من	سنّ
ṣaghiir	ṣaghghar	صغير	صغّر
kam	damm	كم	دم

Some consonants are produced by completely stopping the flow of air. These cannot be actually "doubled", but holding them before releasing them gives that impression:

katiir	kattar	كثير	كثّر
kabiir	kabbar	كبير	كبّر
makaan	makka	مكان	مكّة
baṭal	baṭṭaal	بطل	بطال
mudun	mudda	مدن	مدة
šugag	šagga	شقق	شقة

As noted above, /r/ changes its quality when doubled:

bara	barra	برى	برا
xaraj	xarraj	خرج	خرّج
daras	darras	درس	درّس

The Vowels

There are five basic vowels in Saudi Arabic; three may be long or short: /a,aa/, /i,ii/, and /u,uu/. Two usually occur as long vowels: /ee/ and /oo/ (because they came from Classical Arabic /ay/ and /aw/, so they are not fully part of the vowel system).

Note that the long vowels are held approximately twice as long as the short vowels, which affects the rhythm of the word.

1. /a,aa/. There is great variation in this vowel, ranging from the flat a of cat to the broad a of father. The pronunciation is usually predictable, and depends on the consonants around the vowel.

The broad /a/ occurs in the environment of the velarized consonants, at the end of words, and in most words which contain /r/ or /w/:

Harr	sayyaara	حر	سيارة
9arabi	waaHid	عربي	واحد
ṭayyiba	ṭaali9	طيبة	طالع
walad	raadyu	ولد	راديو

The flat /a/ occurs in any other environment:

malik	Haal	ملك	حال
xamsa	9aali	خمسة	عالي
galam	gaal	قلم	قال
kam	salaama	كم	سلامة

The quality of /a/ is not entirely predictable, however; for example, it is flat in some words which contain /r/ or /w/, such as /šaari9/ and /mawaad/. In such cases, follow the pronunciation of the instructor. There is great variation among Arabic dialects regarding the pronunciation of /a/, and the precise quality rarely affects the meaning of words.

2. /i,ii/. /i/ is pronounced like the i in bit except at the end of words; final /i/ and /ii/ are pronounced like the ee in meet, except that of course /ii/ is held for more time. Since the quality of these vowels differs, it is easy to hear and produce the difference, but remember that the long vowel must be held longer as well.

min	miin	مِن	مين
inti	iidi	انتِ	ايدي
hina	šiil	هنا	شيل
inta	ibrahiim	انتَ	ابراهيم

3. /u,uu/. /u/ is pronounced like u in put, except at the end of words; final /u/ and /uu/ are pronounced like oo in cool.

judud	ma9guul	جُدُد	معقول
ruHt	ruuHu	رحت	روحوا
mumkin	ṭuul	ممكن	طول
šuftu	suug	شفتوا	سوق

4. /ee/ is pronounced like ai in bait, but it is held longer. It is also more tense.

beet	ma9aleeš	بيت	معليش
itneen	eeš	اثنين	ايش
ṣeef	feen	صيف	فين

5. /oo/ is pronounced like the oa in coat, but it is held longer.

ṣoot	hadool	صوت	هدول
loon	9irifoo	لون	عرفوه
moot	9irifooni	موت	عرفوني

Elision

When one word ends in a vowel and the next word begins with a vowel, they may be "elided" together in rapid speech. Dropping these vowels in the text, however, may lead to confusion for the student, who would have probably dropped one of them anyway in imitation of his instructor. For this reason, elision between words will not usually be shown in the transcription; rather, each word will be presented as a whole.

ya aHmad (actually: ya Hmad)	'O Ahmad'
sana uula ibtidaa'i (actually: san uula btidaa'i)	'first grade'

Some special elisions with the definite article, /al-/, will be shown in the text. The /a-/ is dropped after a word which ends in a vowel:

ma9a + al-9eela ⟶ ma9a l-9eela 'with the family'

There are also three short prepositions which are conventionally written attached to the /al-/:

fi + al-beet ⟶ fil-beet 'in the house'

li + aţ-ţawaabi9 ⟶ liţ-ţawaabi9 'for the stamps'

bi + at-tarjama ⟶ bit-tarjama 'with the translation'

Sometimes vowels inside of words are dropped or shortened, and this will be shown in the text; for example:

raaji9 + -a ⟶ raaj9a 'returning (f)'

amrikaani + -yya ⟶ amrikaniyya 'American (f)'

LESSON 1

Dialogue

A.	Hello.	marHaba.	مرحبا ٠
	how	keef	كيف
	condition	Haal	حال
	your (m)	-ak	ـك
B.	Hello. How are you? ('How is your condition?')	marHaba. keef Haalak?	مرحبا ٠ كيف حالَك؟
	fine, good	ţayyib	طيب
	glory	al-Hamdu	الحمد
	to God	lillaah	لله
	and	w	و
	you (m)	inta	انتَ
A.	Fine, thank God. And you?	ţayyib, al-Hamdu lillaah. w inta?	طيب الحمد لله ٠ وانت؟
	I	ana	انا
B.	I'm fine [too], thank God.	ana ţayyib, al-Hamdu lillaah.	انا طيب الحمد لله ٠
A.	It's good to see you. (lit., 'Welcome!')	ya hala.	يا هلا ٠
	welcome	ahlan	اهلا
	to you (m)	biik	بيك
B.	I'm glad to see you, too. (lit., 'Welcome to you.')	ahlan biik.	اهلا بيك٠

Grammatical Notes

1. You will note that the English translation is not always the exact equivalent of the Arabic expression. "Free", rather than "literal" translations in English will sometimes be used, to make the English more natural. The literal Arabic can be understood from the broken-up words preceding sentences.

2. Arabic has different forms for feminine singular and for plural. Most dialogues will be presented in the masculine singular form, and the other variations will occur in drills. Feminine and plural are marked by various sets of suffixes added to the masculine form; there are different suffixes for different parts of speech.

3. Sentences like /keef Haalak/, 'How is your condition?', and /ana ţayyib/, 'I am fine', are examples of "equational sentences". An equational sentence is a simple type of sentence which has no verb. The subject is "equated" with the predicate, and the translation in English uses 'am', 'is', or 'are'.

4. The definite article, 'the', is /al-/ in Arabic, prefixed to a noun or adjective. It is not always translated in English. In rapid speech, the vowel may be lost when the preceding word ends in a vowel (see Classroom Expressions, below.)

5. The /wu/, 'and', may be reduced to /w/ or even /u/ when followed by a word which begins with a vowel.

6. If a word has a long vowel, it is stressed; if more than one, the last long vowel is stressed.

imtiHáan	su9uudiyíin
Háalak	šaafóo
saláama	
wizaaráat	

If it has short vowels, a word is stressed on the second-to-last syllable in two-syllable words, and the third-to-last syllable in all others.

ínta	9ála
ṭáyyiba	húwwa
mádrasa	múškila
ma9rífatak	kútub

If a word ends in a syllable which has two consonants, that syllable is stressed:

aHúbb
waṣált
atkallámt
tisa9ṭá9š

Stress is usually predictable; these general rules are sufficient to cover most cases. In words where the stress falls elsewhere, it will be marked.

Drills

1. (to a man) How are you? keef Haalak? كيف حالَك؟

Substitute:

(to a woman) How are you? keef Haalik? كيف حالِك؟

(to a group) How are you? keef Haalakum? كيف حالكم؟

2. Fine (m), thank God. ṭayyib, al-Hamdu lillaah. طيب الحمد لله .

Substitute:

Fine (f), thank God. ṭayyiba, al-Hamdu lillaah. طيبة الحمد لله .

Fine (p), thank God. ṭayyibiin, al-Hamdu lillaah. طيبين الحمد لله .

3. (to a man) And you? w inta? و انتَ؟

Substitute:

(to a woman) And you? w <u>inti</u>? و انتِ؟

(to a group) And you? w <u>intu</u>? وانتو؟

4. (to a man) I'm glad to see you. ahlan biik. اهلا بيك.

Substitute:

(to a woman) I'm glad to see you. ahlan <u>biiki</u>. اهلا بيكِ.

(to a group) I'm glad to see you. ahlan <u>biikum</u>. اهلا بيكم.

Exercise: Practice the dialogue in the feminine and plural.

Cultural Notes

1. Greetings in Arabic are important culturally, and several elaborate variations may be used (we have seen two forms of 'Welcome' already). Mastering a variety of greeting exchanges is important to establish yourself as "well-mannered". The use of these and other types of speech exchanges which have been developed for different situations is much more important in the Arab world than in America.

Useful Classroom Expressions

1. (to a group) Repeat. 9iidu. عيدوا.

2. Repeat the sentence. 9iidu l-jumla. عيدوا الجملة.

3. Repeat the word. 9iidu l-kilma. عيدوا الكلمة.

4. (to a group) Open your books. iftaHu l-kutub. افتحوا الكتب

5. (to a group) Close your books. igfilu l-kutub. اقفلوا الكتب.

LESSON 2

Dialogue

	morning	ṣabaaH	صباح
	the goodness	al-xeer	الخير
A.	Good morning. ('the morning of goodness')	ṣabaaH al-xeer.	صباح الخير.
	the light	an-nuur	النور
B.	Good morning. ('the morning of light')	ṣabaaH an-nuur.	صباح النور.
A.	How are you (m)?	šloonak?	شلونَك؟
B.	Fine, thank God.	zeen, al-Hamdu lillaah.	زين الحمد لله.
	when	mita	مِتا
	you (m) arrived	waṣalt	وصلْت
A.	When did you arrive?	mita waṣalt?	مِتا وصلت؟
B.	Yesterday.	ams.	امس.
	for	9a (9ala)	عَ - (على)
	the safety	as-salaama	السلامة
A.	Welcome back. ('Thank God for your safety')	al-Hamdu lillaah 9as-salaama.	الحمد لله عالسلامة.
	God	aḷḷaah	الله
B.	Thanks. ('May God make you safe')	aḷḷaah yisallimak.	الله يسلِّمك.

Grammatical Notes

1. The words /an-nuur/, 'the light', and /as-salaama/, 'the safety', show the definite article becoming /an-/ and /as-/ instead of /al-/. This assimilation of the /l/ to the following consonant occurs with several consonants: t, d, z, r, s, š, ṣ, ṭ, ḍ, ẓ, l, n. You will soon learn to do this automatically.

2. The alternative words for 'How are you?' and 'Fine' are used commonly in the Najd area of Arabia, around Riyadh. The words in Lesson 1 are heard throughout Arabia, but more commonly on the western coast (the Hijaz).

3. In the afternoon and evening, you say "Good evening":

masaa' al-xeer. ('the evening of goodness') — مساء الخير.

Response:

masaa' an-nuur. ('the evening of light') — مساء النور.

4. /waṣalt/ is a verb in the perfect (past) tense; it has several suffixes for various persons, but will be drilled in this lesson for feminine and plural only.

5. The expression /al-Hamdu lillaah 9as-salaama/ is used when welcoming someone back from a trip or when he has recovered from an illness. It has a standard response.

6. /9a/, 'for', is a contraction of the full word /9ala/; it may be heard in rapid speech.

7. Note that the word /aḷḷaah/, 'God', is pronounced with emphasis and a lower /a/ when alone, and it becomes non-emphatic with a higher /a/ when prefixed.

Drills

1. (to a man) How are you?	šloonak?	شلونَك؟
Substitute:		
(to a woman) How are you?	šloonik?	شلونِك؟
(to a group) How are you?	šloonakum?	شلونكم؟
2. Fine (m), thank God.	zeen, al-Hamdu lillaah.	زين الحمد لله .
Substitute:		
Fine (f), thank God.	zeena, al-Hamdu lillaah.	زينة الحمد لله .
Fine (p), thank God.	zeen,* al-Hamdu lillaah.	زين الحمد لله .
*Note that this word is not made plural.		
3. (to a man) When did you arrive?	mita waṣalt?	متا وصلتْ؟
Substitute:		
(to a woman) When did you arrive?	mita waṣalti?	متا وصلتِ؟
(to a group) When did you arrive?	mita waṣaltu?	متا وصلتوا ؟
4. (to a man) May God make you safe.	aḷḷaah yisallimak.	الله يسلمَك.
Substitute:		
(to a woman) May God make you safe.	aḷḷaah yisallimik.	الله يسلمِك.
(to a group) May God make you safe.	aḷḷaah yisallimkum.	الله يسلمكم.

Exercise: Practice the dialogue in the feminine and plural.

Useful Classroom Expressions

1.	Pardon? (I didn't understand)	na9am?	نعم؟
2.	(to a man) Say it again, please.	guul marra taanya, min faḍlak.	قول مرة ثانية من فضلَك.
3.	(to a woman) Say it again, please.	guuli marra taanya, min faḍlik.	قولي مرة ثانية من فضلِك.
4.	Slowly.	b-šweeš.	بشويش.
5.	(to a man) Do you understand?	faahim?	فاهم؟
6.	(to a woman) Do you understand?	faahma?*	فاهمة؟
7.	(to a group) Do you understand?	faahmiin?*	فاهمين؟
8.	Yes, I (m) understand.	iiwa, faahim.	ايوه فاهم.
9.	Yes, I (f) understand.	iiwa, faahma.	ايوه فاهمة.
10.	Yes, we understand.	iiwa, faahmiin.	ايوه فاهمين.
11.	No.	la'.	لاء.
12.	Correct.	ṣaHH	صح.
13.	Wrong.	ghalaṭ.	غلط.

*Note that in these words, the /i/ is dropped ("elided") before the /-a/ and /-iin/ endings.

LESSON 3

Dialogue

(Visiting a home)

peace	salaam	سلام
upon	9alee-	عليـ
you (p)	-kum	ـكم
A. Peace be upon you.	as-salaamu 9aleekum.	السلام عليكم.
B. And upon you peace. Welcome.	wu 9aleekum as-salaam. ahlan wu sahlan.	وعليكم السلام. اهلا وسهلا.
A. Thanks. ('Welcome to you')	ahlan biik.	اهلا بيك.
B. Come in.	atfaḍḍal.	اتفضل.
A. Thank you.	šukran.	شكرا.
I like	aHubb	احب
I introduce	a9arrif	اعرّف
you (m) (object)	-ak	ـك
Mr.	as-sayyid	السيد
B. I'd like to introduce you to Mr. Ahmad.	aHubb a9arrifak 9ala s-sayyid aHmad.	احب اعرفك على السيد احمد.
C. Pleased to meet you.	ahlan wu sahlan.	اهلا وسهلا.
this (m)	haada	هادا
he	huwwa	هو
from	min	من
B. This is Mr. Smith. He is American, from Chicago.	haada mistar Smith. huwwa amrikaani, min Chicago.	هادا مستر سميث. هو امركاني من شكاغو.
by	b-	بـ
acquaintance	ma9rifa	معرفة
A. I'm honored to make your acquaintance. ('by your acquaintance')	atšarraft b-ma9rifatkum.	اتشرفت بمعرفتكم.

Structure Sentences

1.	I'd like to introduce you to Mrs. Farida.	aHubb a9arrifak 9ala s-sayyida fariida.	احب اعرفك على السيدة فريدة.
2.	(to a woman) I'm honored to make your acquaintance.	atšarraft b-ma9rifatik.	اتشرفت بمعرفتِك.
3.	I'd like to introduce you (p) to Miss Amal.	aHubb a9arrifkum 9ala l-'aanisa amaal.	احب اعرفكم على الآنسة آمال.
4.	(to a woman) We're honored to make your acquaintance.	atšarrafna b-ma9rifatik.	اتشرفنا بمعرفتِك.
5.	She is American.	hiyya amrikaniyya.	هي امركانية.
6.	She is Mrs. Farida.	hiyya s-sayyida fariida.	هي السيدة فريدة.
7.	Are you Miss Amal?	inti l-'aanisa amaal?	انتِ الآنسة آمال؟
8.	I am American also.	ana amrikaani kamaan.	انا امركاني كمان.
9.	It's been a pleasure meeting you. ('happy occasion')	furṣa sa9iida.	فرصة سعيدة.

Grammatical Notes

1. /atfaḍḍal/ is used for many situations; it may mean 'Come in', 'Sit down', 'Please go first', 'Please have some (food, drink)', 'Go ahead and ask (speak)'. Literally, it means 'be preferred', and is a command form. You will see the uses of this word in future lessons.

2. The suffixes for 'you' as a direct object are the same as for possession, /-ak/, /-ik/, and /-kum/. We used these endings in the phrase /aḷḷaah yisallimak/, and now in /a9arrifak/. These endings when following a vowel have a slightly different form for two persons:

/bi-/ 'to':	/ahlan biik/	Ending:	/-k/ (m)
	/ahlan biiki/		/-ki/ (f)

The plural suffix remains the same:

/ahlan biikum/	/-kum/ (p)

The complete set of suffixes will be discussed in future lessons.

3. In Arabic, the literal expression is 'to introduce on' someone; this is an idiom.

4. When an adjective ends in /i/, the feminine ending is /-yya/:

/amrikaani/
/amrikaniyya/

The vowel /aa/ is usually shortened when the feminine ending is added, although some speakers keep it long.

5. Arabic titles, such as /as-sayyid/, /as-sayyida/, and /al-'aanisa/ are usually used with the definite article.

6. /atšarraft/ and /atšarrafna/ are actually passive verbs ('I am honored', etc.). They can be learned simply as vocabulary items at this point. This expression is more common in the Hijaz.

7. In the expression /atšarraft b-ma9rifatkum/, 'I'm honored by your acquaintance', note that the plural form may be used when speaking to one person. This is an honorific usage and shows respect. The expression /as-salaamu 9aleekum/ is used only in the plural form.

8. To ask a question which elicits a "yes" or "no" answer, simply raise your voice at the end of the sentence. Otherwise, it is a statement. (cf. Structure Sentence 7.)

9. /furṣa sa9iida/, 'happy occasion', may be used when meeting someone for the first time. The response is /ana as9ad/, 'I am happier'.

Drills

1. (to a man) Come in.	atfaḍḍal.	اتفضل.
Substitute:		
(to a woman) Come in.	atfaḍḍali.	اتفضلي.
(to a group) Come in.	atfaḍḍalu.	اتفضلوا.
2. (to a man) I'd like to introduce you to Mr. Ahmad.	aHubb a9arrifak 9ala s-sayyid aHmad.	احب اعرفَك على السيد احمد.
Substitute:		
(to a woman) I'd like to introduce you to Mr. Ahmad.	aHubb a9arrifik 9ala s-sayyid aHmad.	احب اعرفِك على السيد احمد.
(to a group) I'd like to introduce you to Mr. Ahmad.	aHubb a9arrifkum 9ala s-sayyid aHmad.	احب اعرفكم على السيد احمد.
3. He is American.	huwwa amrikaani.	هو امركاني.
Substitute:		
she	hiyya amrikaniyya.	هي امركانية.
4. (to a man) I'm honored to make your acquaintance.	atšarraft b-ma9rifatak.	اتشرفت بمعرفتَك.
Substitute:		
(to a woman) I'm honored to make your acquaintance.	atšarraft b-ma9rifatik.	اتشرفت بمعرفتِك.
(to a group) I'm honored to make your acquaintance.	atšarraft b-ma9rifatkum.	اتشرفت بمعرفتكم.

(to a group) We're honored to make your acquaintance.	atšarrafna b-ma9rifatkum.	اتشرفنا بمعرفتكم.
(to a woman) We're honored to make your acquaintance.	atšarrafna b-ma9rifatik.	اتشرفنا بمعرفتِك.
(to a man) We're honored to make your acquaintance.	atšarrafna b-ma9rifatak.	اتشرفنا بمعرفتَك.

Situations

Translate into Arabic:

1.
A. Good morning. Welcome.
B. Thank you.
A. How are you?
B. Fine, thanks, and you?
A. I, too (thank God).

2.
A. Good evening.
B. Good evening.
A. How are all of you?
B. Well, thanks. When did you all arrive?
A. Yesterday.
B. Welcome back.
A. Thanks.

3.
A. I'd like you to meet Mr. Ahmad.
B. Pleased to meet you.
C. I'm honored.
A. Please sit down (you two).
B. Are you American?
C. Yes, I am American. I am from New York.

Classroom Vocabulary

drill	tamriin	تمرين
pen	galam	قلم
book	kitaab	كتاب
piece of paper	waraga	ورقة
notebook	daftar	دفتر
examination	imtiHaan	امتحان
lesson	dars	درس

Cultural Notes

1. Arabs always give visitors a warm welcome to their home or office, and may repeat welcoming phrases over and over.

2. First names are usually used in the Arab naming system, and unless they know our system of using last names, they may call you by your first name, too. Titles are used with first names as well.

LESSON 4

Dialogue

	you (m) speak	titkallam	تتكلم
	Arabic	9arabi	عربي
	good, well	kwayyis	كويس
	where	feen	فين
	you (m) studied	darast	درست
A.	You speak Arabic well. Where did you study?	inta titkallam 9arabi kwayyis. feen darast?	انت تتكلم عربي كويس. فين درست؟
	I studied	darast	درست
	in	fi	في
	institute	ma9had	معهد
	belonging to	Hagg	حق
	government	Hukuuma	حكومة
	American	amrikiyya	امريكية
B.	I studied in an institute of the American government.	ana darast fil-ma9had Hagg al-Hukuuma l-amrikiyya.	انا درست في معهد حق الحكومة الامريكية.
A.	How long?	gaddeeš?	قديش؟
	approximately	Hawaali	حوالي
	six	sitta	ستة
	months	šuhuur	شهور
B.	About six months.	Hawaali sitta šuhuur.	حوالي ستة شهور.
	only	bass	بس
	not	muu	مو
	possible	mumkin	ممكن
A.	Only [that]? It's not possible!	bass? muu mumkin!	بس؟ مو ممكن!
	well	ṭayyib	طيب
	with	ma9a	مع
B.	Well, goodby. ('with safety')	ṭayyib, ma9a s-salaama.	طيب مع السلامة.
A.	Goodby. ('May God make you safe')	aḷḷaah yisallimak.	الله يسلمك.

Structure Sentences

1.	Where did they study?	feen darasu?	فين درسوا؟
2.	We studied in school.	darasna fil-madrasa.	درسنا في المدرسة.
3.	She studied in an institute.	darasat fi ma9had.	درست في معهد.
4.	She spoke Arabic.	atkallamat 9arabi.	اتكلمت عربي.
5.	Did you (p) speak English?	atkallamtu ingiliizi?	اتكلمتوا انكليزي؟
6.	We arrived safely.	waṣalna bis-salaama.	وصلنا بالسلامة.
7.	Where is the American institute?	feen al-ma9had al-amriiki?	فين المعهد الامريكي؟
8.	He introduced Mr. Jones to Mr. Ahmad.	9arraf mistar Jones 9ala s-sayyid aHmad.	عرّف مستر جونز على السيد احمد.
9.	How did he know?	keef 9irif?	كيف عرف؟
10.	He studied the Arabic language.	daras al-lugha l-9arabiyya.	درس اللغة العربية.

Grammatical Notes

1. /kwayyis/ may be used as 'good' or 'well'; it alternates with /ṭayyib/, and is more used in the Hijaz. It is not a Saudi word; it was borrowed from the Egyptian dialect.

2. The perfect (past) tense of the verb expresses persons by using suffixes; it is known as the "suffix" tense. One type of regular verb is represented by /daras/, 'to study', and /9irif/, 'to know'. (There is no infinitive form, so verbs are cited in the 'he' form.) Forms are based on the 'he' form, and are listed in the traditional Arabic order of conjugation:

daras	he studied	9irif	he knew	عرف	درس
darasat	she studied	9irifat	she knew	عرفت	درست
darasu	they studied	9irifu	they knew	عرفوا	درسوا
darast	you (m) studied	9irift	you (m) knew	عرفت	درست
darasti	you (f) studied	9irifti	you (f) knew	عرفتِ	درستِ
darastu	you (p) studied	9iriftu	you (p) knew	عرفتوا	درستوا
darast	I studied	9irift	I knew	عرفت	درست
darasna	we studied	9irifna	we knew	عرفنا	درسنا

Note the regular shift in stress.

The forms for 'you (m)' and 'I' are the same.

/atkallam/, 'to speak' and /9arraf/, 'to introduce', represent another type of verb, in which the middle consonant is doubled:

atkallam	he spoke	9arraf	he introduced	عرّف	اتكلم
atkallamat	she spoke	9arrafat	she introduced	عرّفت	اتكلمت
atkallamu	they spoke	9arrafu	they introduced	عرّفوا	اتكلموا
atkallamt	you (m) spoke	9arraft	you (m) introduced	عرّفت	اتكلمت
atkallamti	you (f) spoke	9arrafti	you (f) introduced	عرّفتِ	اتكلمتِ
atkallamtu	you (p) spoke	9arraftu	you (p) introduced	عرّفتوا	اتكلمتوا

atkallamt	I spoke	9arraft	I introduced	عرّفت	اتكلمت
atkallamna	we spoke	9arrafna	we introduced	عرّفنا	اتكلمنا

Note the regular shift in stress.

3. Arabic nouns are either masculine or feminine, including inanimate nouns. Almost all feminine nouns end in /-a/ and are easily recognized. (There are only a few nouns which end in /-a/ and are masculine ; this is rare.)

The adjective and verb must agree in gender and number with the noun.

(masculine)	al-ma9had al-amriiki	'the American institute'
(feminine)	al-Hukuuma l-amrikiyya	'the American government'

4. The phrase /al-Hukuuma l-amrikiyya/ is a definite noun phrase, 'the American government'. In Arabic, when the definite article /al-/ is used with the noun, it must also be used with the adjective; the literal translation would be 'the government the American'.

5. The word /Hagg/ changes if the noun it refers to is feminine or plural; it is used when referring to a definite noun.

(masculine) al-ma9had Hagg al-Hukuuma
('institute')

(feminine) al-madrasa Haggat al-Hukuuma
('school')

(plural) al-kutub Haggoon al-Hukuuma
('books')

6. The words /amriiki/ and /amrikiyya/ are used here for 'American'. /amrikaani/ and /amrikaniyya/ refer to people (and some other nouns), while /amriiki/ and /amrikiyya/ are often reserved for abstract or inanimate nouns (although some speakers use them exclusively); they are more "classical". Note that the /ii/ in /amriiki/ is shortened when the feminine suffix is added.

7. /gaddeeš/ literally means 'what amount?', and can be used in other situations as well, referring not only to time, as here, but amounts of money, length, weight, etc.

8. The word /lugha/, 'language', is feminine, so the adjective must also be feminine:

al-lugha l-9arabiyya 'the Arabic language'

When the word /lugha/ is not used, a language is cited in the masculine form:

inta titkallam 9arabi kwayyis. 'You speak Arabic well.'

The phrase, /al-lugha l-9arabiyya/, 'the Arabic language', usually refers to Classical Arabic, not the colloquial dialects.

9. There is no indefinite article in Arabic (equivalent to 'a' or 'an' in English). (cf. Structure Sentence 3.)

Vocabulary Notes

Verbs (patterned like /daras/ and /9irif/)

daras	study	9irif	know	عرف	درس
fataH	open				فتح
gafal	close				قفل
katab	write				كتب
waṣal	arrive				وصل

Languages (These words are also nationalities; add /-yya/ for the feminine ending.)

lugha	language	لغة
9arabi	Arab, Arabic	عربي
ingiliizi	English	انكليزي
faransaawi	French	فرنساوي
asbaani	Spanish	اسباني
almaani	German	الماني
ruusi	Russian	روسي

Drills

For substitution drills, parts of the drill which may be substituted will be underlined. Cue words may be in English or in Arabic. The full response in Arabic will no longer be written out.

1. Where did you (m) study Arabic? — feen darast 9arabi? — فين درست عربي؟

Substitute:

you (f)
you (p)
when
she
French
he
Spanish
where
they
you (m)
Arabic

2. I studied in an institute. — darast fi ma9had. — درست في معهد.

Substitute:

we
they
school
he
she
institute
I

3. We spoke Arabic. — atkallamna 9arabi. — اتكلمنا عربي.

Substitute:

they
German
I
Russian
he
we
Arabic

4. They arrived safely. — waṣalu bis-salaama. — وصلوا بالسلامة.

Substitute:

we
he
she
I
you (f)
you (p)
we
they

5. Mr. Robert is French. — as-sayyid Robert faransaawi. — السيد روبير فرنساوي.

Substitute:

Mrs. Marie
Miss Marie
German
Mr. Robert
Russian
Are you (m) Russian?
you (f)
Arab
I am Arab.
American
Mr. Robert
French

6. How did you (m) know this? — keef 9irift haada? — كيف عرفت هادا؟

Substitute:

you (p)
you (f)
when
you (m)
how

7. When did they close the school? — mita gafalu l-madrasa? — متا قفلوا المدرسة؟

Substitute:

open
you (m)
the institute
the books
close
you (f)
they
the school

8. Answer the questions:

Example:

min feen as-sayyid Ford? ⟶ huwwa amrikaani. — من فين السيد فورد؟ هو امركاني.

Continue, substituting:

as-sayyid Brandt
as-sayyida Farida
as-sayyid Brezhnev
as-sayyid Heath

Situations

Translate into Arabic:

1.
A. Where is John?
B. At school. He arrived yesterday.
A. Safely?
B. Yes, thank God.
A. How did you know?
B. From Ahmad.

2.
A. You speak English well.
B. I studied English in school. I studied French. too.
A. Are you from Jidda?
B. Yes, how did you know?

3.
A. Welcome. Have a chair.
B. Thanks.
A. You're welcome.
B. How long did you work in the government?
A. About six months.
B. I must be going now.
A. Go safely.
B. 'Thanks'. (response)

4.
A. Is she American?
B. Yes. I'd like to introduce you to Miss Jones.
A. I'm honored. When did you arrive?
B. Yesterday.
A. Where did you study Arabic?
B. I studied in school.

LESSON 5

Dialogue

A.	Do you speak English?	inta titkallam ingiliizi?	انت تتكلم انكليزي؟
	a little	šwayya	شويه
	much	katiir	كثير
B.	Yes, a little. Not much.	iiwa, šwayya. muu katiir.	ايوه شويه . مو كثير.
	you (m) tell	tiguul	تقول
	to me	-li	-لي
	what	eeš	ايش
	his name	ismu	اسمه
A.	Could you tell me what 'car' means in Arabic?	mumkin tigulli 'car' eeš ismu bil-9arabi?	ممكن تقوللي "كار" ايش اسمه بالعربي؟
	it means	ya9ni	يعني
B.	'Car' means /sayyaara/ in Arabic.	'car' ya9ni sayyaara bil-9arabi.	"كار" يعني سيارة بالعربي.
A.	Thank you.	šukran.	شكرا.
B.	You're welcome.	9afwan.	عفوا.

Structure Sentences

1.	He speaks Arabic well.	huwwa yitkallam 9arabi kwayyis.	هو يتكلم عربي كويس.
2.	I speak French a little.	ana atkallam faransaawi šwayya.	انا اتكلم فرنساوي شويه .
3.	She wrote in Arabic.	hiyya katabat bil-9arabi.	هي كتبَتْ بالعربي.
4.	What did they do yesterday?	eeš sawwu ams?	ايش سوّوا امس؟
5.	We wrote a lot.	katabna katiir.	كتبنا كثير.
6.	The car is here.	as-sayyaara hina.	السيارة هنا.
7.	The books are there.	al-kutub hinaak.	الكتب هناك.

Grammatical Notes

1. The imperfect (present) tense of the verb expresses persons by using mostly prefixes, sometimes prefix-suffix combinations; it is known as the "prefix" tense. Forms in the imperfect tense are also based on the 'he' form. The imperfect forms of /daras/ are /9irif/ are:

yidrus	he studies	yi9rif	he knows
tidrus	she studies	ti9rif	she knows
yidrusu	they study	yi9rifu	they know

tidrus	you (m) study	ti9rif	you (m) know
tidrusi	you (f) study	ti9rifi	you (f) know
tidrusu	you (p) study	ti9rifu	you (p) know
adrus	I study	a9rif	I know
nidrus	we study	ni9rif	we know

Note that the forms for 'she' and 'you (m)' are the same.

Verbs of the /kallam/ type:

yitkallam	he speaks	yi9arrif	he introduces
titkallam	she speaks	ti9arrif	she introduces
yitkallamu	they speak	yi9arrifu	they introduce
titkallam	you (m) speak	ti9arrif	you (m) introduce
titkallami	you (f) speak	ti9arrifi	you (f) introduce
titkallamu	you (p) speak	ti9arrifu	you (p) introduce
atkallam	I speak	a9arrif	I introduce
nitkallam	we speak	ni9arrif	we introduce

The imperfect tense is used to express action which is repetitive, e.g., 'he studies every day', and progressive, e.g., 'he is studying now'. This is further discussed in Lessons 25 and 36.

From now on, learn the perfect and imperfect tenses of these verbs together (do not guess; there may be variations in the vowels). Verbs will be cited in vocabulary lists in the 'he' form only.

2. By comparing words which share the same type of meaning, we notice that Arabic retains the same combination of consonants in the words, but changes vowel patterns and adds suffixes and prefixes. These inter-related patterns are predictable in Arabic and form categories of words. For example, /daras/, /yidrus/, and /madrasa/ (a school is a 'place of study') share the consonants /d-r-s/. Similarly, /atkallam/, /yitkallam/ and /kilma/ share /k-l-m/, and /katab/ is related to /kutub/, 'books'.

The three consonants on which most words are built are called the "root" of the word. The "root-pattern" system is basic to understanding how words are formed in Arabic, and will be expanded upon as we come to new categories. Keeping this principle in mind will help you guess and remember the meanings of many words.

3. To say 'in Arabic' or 'in English', etc., a phrase with /b-/ is used, and the definite article:

/bil-9arabi/	'by the Arabic'
/bil-ingiliizi/	'by the English'

This is an idiom.

4. /mumkin/ is an adjective meaning 'possible', introduced in the last lesson. It may also be used with a verb in the imperfect tense to mean 'Could you...?' or 'You may...', and as a form for a polite request, 'Would you...?'.

mumkin tigulli?	Could you tell me?
mumkin ti9arrif John 9ala aHmad?	Would you [please] introduce John to Ahmad?

5. Note that /tiguul/, 'you (m) tell', becomes /tigul-/ in combination with /-li/. This shortening of the vowel is explained in Lesson 7.

6. /9afwan/ may also mean 'sorry' or 'pardon', as used when interrupting or correcting someone, after coughing, etc.

Vocabulary Notes

Regular verbs (a)

daras, yidrus	study	درس يدرس
fataH, yiftaH	open	فتح يفتح
gafal, yigfil	close	قفل يقفل
katab, yiktub	write	كتب يكتب
waṣal, yiwṣal	arrive	وصل يوصل

Regular verbs (i)

9irif, yi9rif	know	عِرِف يعرِف

Verbs with doubled medial consonant

atkallam, yitkallam	speak	اتكلم يتكلم
9arraf, yi9arrif	introduce	عرّف يعرّف

Drills

1. Given the cue word in the imperfect tense, change it to perfect, and vice versa:

yiktub	يكتب
yiftaH	يفتح
nigfil	نقفل
yi9rifu	يعرفوا
tiwṣali	توصلي
adrus	ادرس
darasat	درست
katabtu	كتبتوا
(inta) gafalt	(انتَ) قفلتْ
waṣalna	وصلنا
fataHu	فتحوا
(ana) 9irift	(انا) عرفت

2. You (m) speak English well. — inta titkallam ingiliizi kwayyis. — انت تتكلم انكليزي كويس

Substitute:

you (f)
you (p)
I
know
Arabic
he
she
English
speaks
you (m)

3. Can you(m) speak Arabic? — mumkin titkallam 9arabi? — ممكن تتكلم عربي؟

Substitute:

we
French
they
I

he
Arabic
she
you (m)

4. Would you (m) introduce John to Ahmad? — mumkin ti9arrif John 9ala aHmad? — ممكن تعرّف جون على احمد ؟

Substitute:

Would you (f) introduce John to Ahmad?
May I introduce John to Ahmad?
May I introduce you (m) to Ahmad?
May we introduce you (m) to Ahmad?
May John introduce you (m) to Ahmad?

5. He talked a lot. — atkallam katiir. — اتكلم كثير.

Substitute:

we
she
a little
they
in Arabic
I
a lot in Arabic
he
a lot

6. How do you (m) open this? — keef tiftaH haada? — كيف تفتح هادا؟

Substitute:

close
write
you (f)
I
you (p)
know
close
we
open
you (m)

7. Given the sentence in the masculine, change it to feminine:

šloonak? — شلونَك؟
aḷḷaah yisallimak. — الله يسلمك.
atfaḍḍal. — اتفضل.
huwwa s-sayyid Jones. — هو السيد جونز.
ana amrikaani. — انا امركاني.
haada Haggi. — هادا حقي.
daras 9arabi. — درس عربي.

Situations

1.
A. Do you know his name?
B. No. What is his name?
A. Ahmad. He is from the government.
B. When did he arrive?
A. In the evening.

2.
A. Can you tell me where John is?
B. At school.
A. Does he know English?
B. Not much...he's German.
A. I understand.

3.
A. I know English a little.
B. Good. You speak well.
A. Thanks. Where is the car?
B. Here. The car belongs to the American government.
A. Well, goodby.
B. Goodby.

4.
A. I'm American.
B. Welcome. From where in America?
A. From New York. Have you heard of New York?
(literally, 'Do you know New York?')
B. Yes, a little.
A. How did you arrive from the school?
B. By car.

LESSON 6

Dialogue

A.	Welcome. Come in.	ahlan. atfaḍḍal.	اهلا. اتفضل.
B.	Thank you. ('I thank you (m)')	aškurak.	اشكرك.
A.	Excuse me...	9afwan...	عفوا...
B.	Go ahead.	atfaḍḍal.	اتفضل.
A.	What is your name?	eeš ismak?	ايش اسمَك؟
	name	ism	اسم
B.	My name is John Smith.	ismi John Smith.	اسمي جون سميث.
	(word for direct address)	ya	يا
A.	Welcome, John.	ahlan wu sahlan ya John.	اهلا وسهلا يا جون.

Structure Sentences

1.	They studied a lot.	humma darasu katiir.	هم درسوا كثير.
2.	We know Mr. Smith well.	iHna ni9rif mistar Smith kwayyis.	احنا نعرف مستر سميث كويس.
3.	He knows us, too.	huwwa yi9rifna kamaan.	هو يعرفنا كمان.
4.	I know him a little.	ana a9rifu šwayya.	انا اعرفه شويه.
5.	Excuse me (to a group).	9an iznakum.	عن اذنكم.
6.	What's her name?	eeš ismaha?	ايش اسمها؟
7.	Where is their car?	feen sayyaarathum?	فين سيارتهم؟
8.	This is our school.	haadi madrasatna.	هادي مدرستنا.
9.	We thank you all.	nuškurkum.	نشكركم.

Grammatical Notes

1. /aškurak/ is a variation for 'thank you'. It can be conjugated as a verb in the imperfect tense, and the person endings at the end can be varied. It is most often used in the 'I' and 'we' forms.

2. The full set of personal pronouns is:

he	huwwa	هو
she	hiyya	هي
they	humma	هم
you (m)	inta	انتَ
you (f)	inti	انتِ
you (p)	intu	انتو
I	ana	انا
we	iHna	احنا

Personal pronouns are used most often in equational sentences, for example:

huwwa amrikaani.	He is an American.
hiyya hina.	She is here.

They may be used with verbs, but it is not necessary; their use may also make the sentence sound emphatic:

keef Haalak?	How are you?
keef Haalak inta?	How are <u>you</u>?

Do not overuse pronouns; you will notice that they are needed less in Arabic than in English.

3. Several types of pronouns in Arabic are suffixed to the end of words. Their forms may vary slightly, depending on the shape of the word to which they are suffixed.

A. <u>The Direct Object Pronouns</u> are:

him	-u	yi9rifu	He knows him.	يعرفه
her	-ha	yi9rifha	He knows her.	يعرفها
them	-hum	yi9rifhum	He knows them.	يعرفهم
you (m)	-ak	yi9rifak	He knows you (m).	يعرفَك
you (f)	-ik	yi9rifik	He knows you (f).	يعرفِك
you (p)	-kum	yi9rifkum	He knows you (p).	يعرفكم
me	-ni	yi9rifni	He knows me.	يعرفني
us	-na	yi9rifna	He knows us.	يعرفنا

<u>Modifications</u>:

(1) After a word which ends in two consonants, or which has a long vowel in the last syllable, /-a-/ is inserted before suffixes which begin with a consonant: /-ha/, /-hum/, /-kum/, /-ni/, /-na/:

9irift	I knew; you (m) knew	9iriftaha	I knew her.	عرفتها
		9iriftahum	I knew them.	عرفتهم
		9iriftakum	I knew you (p).	عرفتكم
		9iriftani	You (m) knew me.	عرفتني
		9iriftana	You (m) knew us.	عرفتنا

(2) After a word which ends in a vowel, that vowel is lengthened and stressed before adding suffixes. In addition, a change occurs in the three suffixes which begin with a vowel, /-u/, /-ak/, /-ik/:

9irifna	we knew	9irifnáa	We knew him.	عرفناه
		9irifnáahum	We knew them.	عرفناهم
		9irifnáaha	We knew her.	عرفناها
yi9rifu	they know	yi9rifúu	They know him.	يعرفوه
		yi9rifúuni	They know me.	يعرفوني
		yi9rifúukum	They know you (p).	يعرفوكم
		yi9rifúuk	They know you (m).	يعرفوك
		yi9rifúuki	They know you (f).	يعرفوكِ

Note that the 'him' form is expressed by lengthening whichever vowel occurs, and switching stress to that syllable.

The distinction between 'you (m)' and 'you (f)' is made by the forms /-k/ and /-ki/.

(3) The verb form for 'they' in the perfect changes to the base form with /oo/ at the end, when used before suffixes, for example, /9irifoo-/:

9irifu	they knew	9irifoo	They knew him.	عرفوه
		9irifooha	They knew her.	عرفوها
		9irifoohum	They knew them.	عرفوهم
		9irifook	They knew you (m).	عرفوكْ
		9irifooki	They knew you (f).	عرفوكِ
		9irifookum	They knew you (p).	عرفوكم
		9irifooni	They knew me.	عرفوني
		9irifoona	They knew us.	عرفونا

B. <u>The Possessive Pronouns</u> are:

his	-u	galamu	his pen	قلمه
her	-ha	galamha	her pen	قلمها
their	-hum	galamhum	their pen	قلمهم
your (m)	-ak	galamak	your (m) pen	قلمَك
your (f)	-ik	galamik	your (f) pen	قلمِك
your (p)	-kum	galamkum	your (p) pen	قلمكم
my	-i	galami	my pen	قلمي
our	-na	galamna	our pen	قلمنا

These suffixes are the same as the direct object pronoun suffixes, except for the 'my' form.

<u>Modifications</u>:

(1) For these suffixes also, when a word ends in two consonants or has a long vowel in the last syllable, /-a/ is inserted before those which begin with a consonant: /-ha/, /-hum/, /-kum/, /-na/:

ism	name	ismaha	her name	اسمها
		ismahum	their name	اسمهم
		ismakum	your (p) name	اسمكم
		ismana	our name	اسمنا
Haal	condition	Haalaha	her condition	حالها
		Haalahum	their condition	حالهم
		Haalakum	your (p) condition	حالكم
		Haalana	our condition	حالنا

(2) When a noun is feminine and ends in /-a/, a /-t-/ is inserted before the suffixes, resulting in /-at-/ before the suffix. The second-to-last syllable (before the /t/) is stressed.

madrasa	school	madrasátu	his school	مدرسته
		madrasátha	her school	مدرستها
		madrasáthum	their school	مدرستهم
		madrasátak	your (m) school	مدرستَك
		madrasátik	your (f) school	مدرستِك
		madrasátkum	your (p) school	مدرستكم
		madrasáti	my school	مدرستي
		madrasátna	our school	مدرستنا

ma9rifa	acquaintance	ma9rifátak	your m) acquaintance	معرفتَك
		ma9rifátik	your (f) acquaintance	معرفتِك
		ma9rifátkum	your (p) acquaintance	معرفتكم

(3) When a noun ends in a vowel (other than the /-a/ of the feminine), the suffixes are the same as those of direct object pronouns after nouns ending in a vowel (see modification 2, on page 24) with the exception of the 'my' form, which is /-yya/:

kursi	chair	kursii	his chair	كرسيه
		kursiiha	her chair	كرسيها
		kursiihum	their chair	كرسيهم
		kursiik	your (m) chair	كرسيكْ
		kursiiki	your (f) chair	كرسيكِ
		kursiikum	your (p) chair	كرسيكم
		kursiyya	my chair	كرسيّ
		kursiina	our chair	كرسينا

While this appears to be a great amount of material, with a little practice, you will see that relatively few variations need to be kept in mind. The main points of difference are:

1. If the word ends in two consonants or has a long vowel in the last syllable, add /-a-/ before the suffixes which begin with a consonant.

2. If the word ends in a vowel (other than the /-a/ of the feminine), lengthen it for 'him' or 'his', and use /-k/ and /-ki/ for 'you' and 'your' (m,f).

3. Remember to use /-at-/ after feminine nouns, before possessive endings.

4. Note the difference between /-ni/, 'me', and /-i/, 'my'.

4. /ya/ is called the "vocative particle"; it is used before a name or title to indicate that the speaker is addressing that person (similar to old English usage of "O", as in "O Lord..."). It may also be used with a noun, to mean a casual 'hey!', as in 'hey boy!'

Note that when using /ya/, a title does not have /al-/:

ya sayyid John
ya aHmad
ya aanisa

5. The three pronouns for 'this' are:

haada	this (m)	هادا
haadi	this (f)	هادي
hadool	these	هدول

Vocabulary Notes

Masculine nouns		Feminine nouns			
galam	pen	ghurfa	room	قلم	غرفة
kitaab	book	ţarabiiza	table	كتاب	طربيزة
baab	door	saa9a	watch, clock	باب	ساعة
kursi	chair	sayyaara	car	كرسي	سيارة
		maaşa	desk		ماصة

Drills

1. I thank you (m). — aškurak. — اشكرك.

Substitute:

We thank you (m).
We thank you (f).
We thank you (p).
I thank you (p).
I thank you (f).
I thank them.
I thank you (m).

2. With your (m) permission. — 9an iznak. — عن اذنك.

Substitute:

your (f)
your (p)

3. He knows his name. — huwwa yi9rif ismu. — هو يعرف اسمه.

Substitute:

Does he know his name?
my name
He knows your (m) name.
she
her name
they
our name
you (p)
you (f)
my name
he
his name

4. Where is their car? — feen sayyaarathum? — فين سيارتهم؟

Substitute:

our car
his car
her car
her desk
my desk
my watch
her watch
your (m) watch
your (m) book
her book
her room
your (f) room
their room
their table
your (p) table
your (p) chair
my chair
his chair
his car
your (p) car
their car

5. He knew him. huwwa 9irifu. هو عرفه

Substitute:

She knew him.
She knew me.
They knew me.
They knew you (m).
They knew you (f).
I knew you (f).
We knew you (f).
We knew them.
We knew you (f).
She knew you (f).
She knew him.
He knew him.

6. I opened it. ana fataHtu. انا فتحته .

Substitute:

We opened it.
They opened it.
They opened them.
He opened them.
He closed them.
You (f) closed them.
You (m) closed them.
I closed them.
I closed it.
I opened it.

7. Given the cue word in Arabic, respond, saying 'This is a ____', and translate into English:

Example:

galam ⟶ haada galam. قلم ← هادا قلم.
sayyaara ⟶ haadi sayyaara. سيارة ← هادي سيارة.

Continue:

ṭarabiiza طربيزة
kursi كرسي
saa9a ساعة
kutub كتب
kitaab كتاب
maaṣa ماصة
baab باب
madrasa مدرسة
as-sayyid Smith السيد سميث
al-'aanisa Jones الآنسة جونز

8. Given the cue phrase in English, respond, saying 'This is _____', 'These are ______':

Example:

my books ⟶ hadool kutubi. هدول كتبي.
his car ⟶ haadi sayyaaratu. هادي سيارته .

Continue:

her room
Is this your (m) pen?
his watch?
your (m) chair?
These are their books.
Are these your (p) books?
This is my chair.
my school
Is this your (f) car?
his name?
These are our books.
their room
my desk

Situations

1.
A. Excuse me, is this your car?
B. Yes, it belongs to me.
A. Do these books belong to you too?
B. Yes, they are Arabic books.

2.
A. Can you open the door a little?
B. Is this too much?
(literally, 'Is this much?')
A. No, that's good. (literally, 'This is good.') Thanks.
B. You're welcome.

3.
A. Where is Ahmad?
B. Pardon?
A. Do you know where Ahmad is?
B. In his room.
A. Is this his watch?
B. No, his watch is on the table.

4.
A. (To a girl) Excuse me, are you American?
B. Yes, I'm from New York.
A. Did you study Arabic?
B. Yes, a little.
A. How long?
B. Six months.
A. You speak well.
B. Thanks.

LESSON 7

Dialogue

(Going through a doorway)

A.	Go ahead.	atfaḍḍal.	اتفضل.
B.	No, you go ahead.	la', atfaḍḍal inta.	لا، اتفضل انت.
	first	al-awwal	الاول
A.	You first.	inta l-awwal.	انت الاول.
	OK	ṭayyib	طيب
	thanked (m)	maškuur	مشكور
B.	OK, thanks...('you (m) are thanked')	ṭayyib, maškuur...	طيب مشكور...
	family	9eela	عيلة
A.	How's the family?	keef al-9eela?	كيف العيلة؟
	wife	zawja	زوجة
	children	awlaad	اولاد
	they greet	yisallimu	يسلموا
	on you (m)	9aleek	عليك
B.	My wife and children are fine, thank God. They greet you.	zawjati w awlaadi ṭayyibiin, al-Hamdu lillaah, yisallimu 9aleek.	زوجتي واولادي طيبين الحمد لله يسلموا عليك.
	after	ba9d	بعد
	necessary	laazim	لازم
	I take leave	asta'zin	استأذن
	now	al-Hiin	الحين
A.	With your permission, I must be going now. ('take leave now')	ba9d iznak, laazim asta'zin al-Hiin.	بعد اذنك لازم استأذن الحين.
B.	It's early!	badri!	بدري!
	by God (oath)	waḷḷah	ولله
A.	No, (by God), I must.	la', waḷḷah, laazim.	لا، ولله لازم.
B.	Go ahead.	atfaḍḍal.	اتفضل.

Structure Sentences

1.	He told me his name.	galli ismu.	قاللي اسمه.
2.	She told us where her house is.	gaalatlana feen beetaha.	قالتلنا فين بيتها.
3.	I must write to my family.	laazim aktub li-9eelati.	لازم اكتب لعيلتي.
4.	I thank you (p). ('You (p) are thanked.')	intu maškuuriin.	انتو مشكورين.
5.	We must arrive early.	laazim niwṣal badri.	لازم نوصل بدري.
6.	They arrived first.	humma waṣalu l-awwal.	هم وصلوا الاول.
7.	They greeted me.	sallamu 9alayya.	سلموا عليّ.
8.	I greeted them (i.e., shook hands) and then left.	sallamt 9aleehum w asta'zant.	سلمت عليهم واستأذنت.
9.	May I use your car?	mumkin asta9mil sayyaaratak?	ممكن استعمل سيارتك؟
10.	Yes, you (m) can use it.	iiwa, mumkin tista9milha.	ايوه ممكن تستعملها.
11.	Have you (m) seen Ahmad?	šuft aHmad?	شفت احمد؟
12.	I went home.	ruHt al-beet.	رحت البيت.

Grammatical Notes

1. /maškuur/ may be translated into English as 'thank you', although it literally means 'thanked' and is an adjective. The feminine and plural are regular: /maškuura/,/maškuuriin/. Note that the adjective refers to the person who is thanked, not the speaker.

2. /9eela/ is translated 'family'; it usually refers to one's immediate family--either spouse and children, or parents, brothers and sisters if one is unmarried. The word /ahl/ is also used to mean immediate family or wife; it more often refers to the extended family.

3. /yisallimu 9aleek/, literally, 'they greet on you (m)', is an idiomatic expression, and is often added when commenting about someone else; it is part of the formula and may not be meant literally. It is common to respond to this with /aḷḷaah yisallimhum/ (or the response conjugated for the appropriate person).

4. The preposition /9ala/, 'on', may take possessive pronoun suffixes, which are formed in the regular way for a word ending in a vowel. The 'base' form to which suffixes are added is /9alee-/. Note that the 'I' form is irregular:

9alee	on him	عليه
9aleeha	on her	عليها
9aleehum	on them	عليهم
9aleek	on you (m)	عليكْ
9aleeki	on you (f)	عليكِ
9aleekum	on you (p)	عليكم
9alayya	on me	عليّ
9aleena	on us	علينا

5. /laazim/, 'necessary', may be used with verbs in the imperfect tense to mean 'must' or 'it is necessary...'. /laazim/ and /mumkin/ are examples of 'modals' or helping words which are used with verbs in the imperfect tense, and are quite numerous in Arabic.

6. /al-Hiin/, 'now', alternates freely with /daHHiin/, the latter being more urban and more common on the western coast.

7. Indirect object pronouns are used with the preposition /l-/, 'to', 'for', and are suffixed to the verb. The forms change slightly depending on the form of the verb. Basic forms are:

Indirect Object Pronouns:

to him (for him)	-lu
to her (for her)	-laha
to them (for them)	-lahum
to you (m) (for you)	-lak
to you (f) (for you)	-lik
to you (p) (for you)	-lakum
to me (for me)	-li
to us (for us)	-lana

These forms occur with a verb which ends in a consonant. Note that the words are stressed on the second-to-last syllable:

Perfect

(katab)

katáblu	He wrote to him.	كتبله
katabláha	He wrote to her.	كتبلها
katabláhum	He wrote to them.	كتبلهم
katáblak	He wrote to you (m).	كتبلك
katáblik	He wrote to you (f).	كتبلك
katablákum	He wrote to you (p).	كتبلكم
katábli	He wrote to me.	كتبلي
katablána	He wrote to us.	كتبلنا

(katabat)

katabátlu	She wrote to him.	كتبتله
katabatláha	She wrote to her.	كتبتلها
(etc.)		

Imperfect

(yiktub)

yiktúblu	He writes to him.	يكتبله
yiktubláha	He writes to her.	يكتبلها
yiktubláhum	He writes to them.	يكتبلهم
(etc.)		

(tiktub)

tiktúblu	She writes to him.	تكتبله
tiktubláha	She writes to her.	تكتبلها
(etc.)		

(aktub)

aktúblu	I write to him.	اكتبله
aktubláha	I write to her.	اكتبلها
(etc.)		

(niktub)

niktúblu	We write to him.	نكتبله
niktubláha	We write to her.	نكتبلها
(etc.)		

Modifications:

(1) When the verb ends in two consonants, an /a/ is placed before the suffix. The first /a/ in the four long suffixes is dropped; they become /-lha/, /-lhum/, /-lkum/ and /-lna/.* Note that stress also shifts.

(katabt)

katabtálu	You (m) wrote to him; I wrote tó him.	كتبتله
katabtálha	You (m) wrote to her; I wrote to her.	كتبتلها
katabtálhum	You (m) wrote to them; I wrote to them.	كتبتلهم
katábtalak	I wrote to you (m).	كتبتلك
katábtalik	I wrote to you (f).	كتبتلك
katabtálkum	I wrote to you (p).	كتبتلكم
katábtali	You (m) wrote to me.	كتبتلي
katabtálna	You (m) wrote to us.	كتبتلنا

*There is a widely-used alternative form in which the suffix begins with /-all-/. This will be noted for your recognition only, not for learning. (It is more common in north Hijaz):

katabtállu	كتبتلّه
katabtállaha	كتبتلّها
katabtállahum	كتبتلّهم
katabtállak	كتبتلّك
katabtállik	كتبتلّك
katabtállakum	كتبتلّكم
katabtálli	كتبتلّي
katabtállana	كتبتلّنا

(2) When a verb ends in a vowel, that vowel is lengthened and stressed:

Perfect

(katabu)*

kataboolu	They wrote to him.	كتبوله
kataboolaha	They wrote to her.	كتبولها
kataboolahum	They wrote to them.	كتبولهم
kataboolak	They wrote to you (m).	كتبولك
kataboolik	They wrote to you (f).	كتبولك
kataboolakum	They wrote to you (p).	كتبولكم

katabooli	They wrote to me.	كتبولي
kataboolana	They wrote to us.	كتبولنا

*Remember the rule about changing the vowel to /oo/ (rule 3, page 25.)

Imperfect

(yiktubu)

yiktubuulu	They write to him.	يكتبوله
yiktubuulaha	They write to her.	يكتبولها
(etc.)		

(tiktubi)

tiktubiilu	You (f) write to him.	تكتبيله
tiktubiilaha	You (f) write to her.	تكتبيلها
(etc.)		

(tiktubu)

tiktubuulu	You (p) write to him.	تكتبوله
tiktubuulaha	You (p) write to her.	تكتبولها
(etc.)		

These processes are repetitive and become automatic with a little use; you will not have to give them active thought for long. When in doubt, use the basic forms; you will still be understood.

8. Verbs on the pattern of /gaal/, 'he said', appear to have only two consonants, although the long vowel in the middle covers another "root" consonant, a /w/ or /y/. Which consonant it is usually becomes evident in the imperfect tense. These verbs are "hollow" verbs, and there are three possible patterns:

A.			B.			C.		
gaal	yiguul	'say'	jaab	yijiib	'bring'	naam	yinaam	'sleep'
(root: g-w-l)			(root: j-y-b)			(root: n-w-m)		

Type (A) has a short /u/ in some person forms; type (B) has short /i/, and type (C) may have /u/ or /i/. Type (C) is rare.

(A)	huwwa	gaal	yiguul	يقول	قال
	hiyya	gaalat	tiguul	تقول	قالت
	humma	gaalu	yiguulu	يقولوا	قالوا
	inta	gult	tiguul	تقول	قلتْ
	inti	gulti	tiguuli	تقولي	قلتِ
	intu	gultu	tiguulu	تقولوا	قلتوا
	ana	gult	aguul	اقول	قلتْ
	iHna	gulna	niguul	نقول	قلنا
(B)	huwwa	jaab	yijiib	يجيب	جاب
	hiyya	jaabat	tijiib	تجيب	جابت
	humma	jaabu	yijiibu	يجيبوا	جابوا
	inta	jibt	tijiib	تجيب	جبتْ
	inti	jibti	tijiibi	تجيبي	جبتِ
	intu	jibtu	tijiibu	تجيبوا	جبتوا
	ana	jibt	ajiib	اجيب	جبتْ
	iHna	jibna	nijiib	نجيب	جبنا

(C)	huwwa	naam	yinaam	ينام	نام
	hiyya	naamat	tinaam	تنام	نامت
	humma	naamu	yinaamu	يناموا	ناموا
	inta	numt	tinaam	تنام	نُمتْ
	inti	numti	tinaami	تنامي	نمتِ
	intu	numtu	tinaamu	تناموا	نمتوا
	ana	numt	anaam	انام	نمتْ
	iHna	numna	ninaam	ننام	نمنا

9. Hollow verbs shorten their long vowel before a suffix which begins with /l/ (the indirect object):

gaal + -li ⟶ galli   He told me.

tiguul + -li ⟶ tigulli   You (m) tell me.

10. Verbs like /asta'zan/, 'to take leave', and /asta9mal/, 'to use', are composed of a base verb with a prefix /-sta-/ which varies slightly, depending on the tense and person:

huwwa	asta'zan	yista'zin	يستأذن	استأذن
hiyya	asta'zanat	tista'zin	تستأذن	استأذنت
humma	asta'zanu	yista'zinu	يستأذنوا	استأذنوا
inta	asta'zant	tista'zin	تستأذن	استأذنتْ
inti	asta'zanti	tista'zini	تستأذني	استأذنتِ
intu	asta'zantu	tista'zinu	تستأذنوا	استأذنتوا
ana	asta'zant	asta'zin	استأذن	استأذنتْ
iHna	asta'zanna	nista'zin	نستأذن	استأذنا
		(root: '-z-n)		
huwwa	asta9mal	yista9mil		استعمل
hiyya	asta9malat	tista9mil		استعملت
	(etc.)	(root: 9-m-l)		

11. /beet/ means 'house', but in certain expressions is better translated into English as 'home':

al-beet	the house
raaH al-beet	He went to the house. He went home.
fil-beet	in the house at home

12. Note that /raaH/, 'to go', is used with a direct object:

raaH al-beet.   He went [to] the house.

Vocabulary Notes

Hollow verbs

gaal, yiguul (gult)	say	قال يقول (قلت)
raaH, yiruuH (ruHt)	go	راح يروح (رحت)
šaaf, yišuuf (šuft)	see	شاف يشوف (شفت)
kaan, yikuun (kunt)	be	كان يكون (كنت)
jaab, yijiib (jibt)	bring	جاب يجيب (جبت)
naam, yinaam (numt)	sleep	نام ينام (نمت)

/-sta-/ verbs

asta'zan, yista'zin استأذن يستأذن	take leave, ask permission
asta9mal, yista9mil استعمل يستعمل	use

Masculine nouns			Feminine nouns			Plural nouns		
ahl	اهل	family	9eela	عيلة	family	awlaad	اولاد	children*
zawj	زوج	husband	zawja	زوجة	wife			
walad	ولد	son	bint	بنت	daughter			

*Another common word for 'children' is /bazuura/.

Drills

1. Give the appropriate response to the cue sentence.

Example:

aHmad yisallim 9aleek. ⟶ allaah yisallimu. احمد يسلم عليك. ← الله يسلمه

Continue:

humma yisallimu 9aleek. هم يسلموا عليك.
zawji yisallim 9aleek. زوجي يسلم عليك.
zawjati tisallim 9aleeki. زوجتي تسلم عليكِ.
awlaadi yisallimu 9aleekum. اولادي يسلموا عليكم.
waladi yisallim 9aleek. ولدي يسلم عليك.

2. I must be going now. laazim asta'zin al-Hiin. لازم استأذن الحين.

Substitute:

we
early
I
now
they
he

3. May I use your (m) book? mumkin asta9mil kitaabak? ممكن استعمل كتابك؟

Substitute:

this (m)
the word
we
this (f)
his book
she
I
your (m) book

4. I went home. ruHt al-beet. رحت البيت.

Substitute:

she
to school
they
early
we
you (f)
there
he
often ('much')
home
I

5. You (m) must go early. laazim tiruuH badri. لازم تروح بدري.

Substitute:

I
now
we
to school
he
they
there
you (f)
you (m)
early

6. I saw him at home. šuftu fil-beet. شفته في البيت

Substitute:

I saw her
she saw me
they saw me
we saw them
he saw him
you (m) saw them?
you (f) saw them?
you (f) saw him?
you (p) saw him?
I saw him

7. He brought his son. jaab waladu. جاب ولده.

Substitute:

He brought his family.
He brought them.
I brought them.
Did you (f) bring them?
Did you (f) bring the children?
Did you (f) see the children?
Did they see the children?

8. He excused himself early. huwwa asta'zan badri. هو استأذن بدري.

Substitute:

I
we
she
used the car
the pen
we
he

9. Translate the following sentences:

You (m) must see Ahmad.
You (m) must bring your son.
You (p) must bring your son.

We must see him often ('much').
They must go now.
I must bring my book.
I may bring my book.
I may say the word.
He may say the sentence.
He may sleep there.
He must be here.
You (m) must sleep now.
You (m) must see Ahmad.

Situations

1.
A. May I introduce my wife to you?
B. With pleasure. How do you do? (literally, 'Welcome')
C. (wife) I'm honored. Excuse me, what is your name?
B. Mr. Ahmad. When did you arrive here?
C. Yesterday.
A. We arrived from New York.

2.
A. Where are the children?
B. At home. My son went home early.
A. Does he speak Arabic?
B. A little. He studied it in school.
A. With your permission, I must leave now.
B. Go ahead.

3.
A. Did you greet him?
B. Yes, I greeted him. I know him well. And his family.
A. Where are they from?
B. From here. I know where their house is.

4.
A. What did you (p) do in school?
B. We wrote in Arabic. I wrote my name in English, too.
A. Is the school good?
B. Yes, it's good.
A. Can you close the door please?
B. OK.
A. Thanks.
B. You're welcome.

Cultural Notes

1. Arabs are extremely conscious of "manners" and "politeness" as they define these concepts. Among good manners is the attempt, even if merely in form, to have others precede you through a doorway. You, as an American, will seldom win--give in graciously and go first, but only after a token gesture of declining.

2. The act of "greeting" someone is also essential to good manners. It could be considered offensive if you forget to greet someone even in a large crowd, or in an office where you are visiting a co-worker, for example. Sometimes you see the casual "Goodby everybody" type of leave-taking, but just as often, people say goodby to everyone individually before they leave, with a few polite phrases and a handshake.

3. The word /zawjati/, 'my wife', is not used as freely in Arabic as in English, especially when talking to another man. Instead, /al-9eela/, 'the family', or /al-jamaa9a/, 'the group', may be substituted. It is considered too direct for you to inquire about someone's wife; try "How is your family?" instead.

4. /waḷḷah/, 'by God', is an example of an oath used for emphasis. Oaths are used frequently, and there are many varieties. You will recognize them because they begin with /wa-/, here translated as 'I swear by...', followed by a religious reference such as 'By God'.

LESSON 8

Dialogue

A.	Muhammad!	ya muHammad!	يا محمد!
B.	Yes?	na9am.	نعم.
	I ask	as'al	اسأل
	question	su'aal	سؤال
A.	May I ask a question?	mumkin as'al su'aal?	ممكن اسأل سؤال؟
B.	Go ahead.	atfaḍḍal.	اتفضل.
	that (m)	hadaak	هداك
	man	rijjaal	رجال
A.	Who is that man?	miin hadaak ar-rijjaal?	مين هداك الرجال؟
	not	ma	ما
	I know	adri	ادري
	not	muu	مو
B.	I certainly don't know. He's not from here.	waḻḻah ma adri. huwwa muu min hina.	ولله ما ادري. هو مو من هنا.
A.	I don't know either.	ana kamaan ma adri.	انا كمان ما ادري.

Structure Sentences

1.	I took the money.	axadt al-fuluus.	اخذت الفلوس.
2.	Who is that lady?	miin hadiik as-sitt?	مين هديك الست؟
3.	Where are those people from?	min feen haadolaak an-naas?	من فين هادولاك الناس؟
4.	Where are your brothers?	feen axwaanak?	فين اخوانك؟
5.	The boy asked about you (p).	al-walad sa'al 9annakum.	الولد سأل عنكم.
6.	The boy asked about you (p).	al-walad sa'al 9aleekum.	الولد سأل عليكم.
7.	They left.	mišyu.	مشيوا.

Grammatical Notes

1. /na9am/ means 'yes' in Classical Arabic, and is often used to acknowledge being spoken to. If used as a question, /na9am?/, it means 'pardon, please repeat what you said'.

2. The three pronouns for 'that' are:

hadaak	that (m)	هداك
hadiik	that (f)	هديك
hadolaak	that (p)	هدولاك

They may be used alone; when used to modify a noun, the noun must be definite (this also applies to the words for 'this, these'). The pronoun may be used before or after the noun.

hadaak ar-rijjaal	that man
ar-rijjaal hadaak	that man
hadiik as-sitt	that lady

3. /muu/, 'not', and its variations are used to negate an equational sentence or a predicate. The full set of forms is:

huwwa	muu (mahu)	مو
hiyya	mahi	مهي
humma	mahum	مهم
inta	manta*	منت
inti	manti	منتِ
intu	mantu	منتو
ana	mana	منا
iHna	maHna	محنا

huwwa muu min hina.	He is not from here.
hiyya mahi amrikaniyya.	She is not American.
haada muu mumkin.	This is not possible.
haada muu laazim.	This is not necessary.

*Alternative forms in common use in northern Hijaz are:

inta	mannak	منّك
inti	mannik	منّك
intu	mannakum	منّكم
ana	manni	منّي
iHna	manna	منّا

/ma/ is used with verbs; it will be discussed further in Lesson 17.

4. /kamaan/ means 'also' in affirmative sentences, and 'either' in negative sentences (this is a problem of translation due to English structure; in Arabic, you simply say 'I don't know too'.)

5. /sa'al/ and /axad/ are examples of verbs which contain the glottal stop /'/ as a root consonant. You will note that /axad/ is slightly irregular in the imperfect tense (the /'/ is replaced by a vowel):

sa'al	سأل	yis'al	يسأل	(root: s-'-l)
axad	أخذ	yaaxud	ياخذ	(root: '-x-d)

6. /9an/, 'about, regarding', when suffixed with a pronoun, has the base form /9ann-/:

9annu	about him	عنه
9annaha	about her	عنها
9annahum	about them	عنهم
9annak	about you (m)	عنّك
9annik	about you (f)	عنّك
9annakum	about you (p)	عنكم
9anni	about me	عنّي
9annana	about us	عنّنا

7. Verbs like /diri/ and /mišī/ which end in /-i/ have a special form for certain perfect suffixes:

huwwa	diri	دري	miši	مشي
hiyya	diryat	دريت	mišyat	مشيت
humma	diryu	دريوا	mišyu	مشيوا
inta	diriit	دريت	mišiit	مشيت
inti	diriiti	دريتي	mišiiti	مشيتي
intu	diriitu	دريتوا	mišiitu	مشيتوا
ana	diriit	دريت	mišiit	مشيت
iHna	diriina	درينا	mišiina	مشينا

8. /sa'al/, 'to ask', may be used with /9an/ or /9ala/ (see Structure Sentences 5 and 6).

Vocabulary Notes

Nouns

rijjaal	man	رجّال
sitt	lady, woman	ست
walad	boy, son	ولد
bint	girl, daughter	بنت
axx*	brother	اخ
uxt	sister	أخت
abb*	father	اب
umm	mother	ام
axwaan	brothers, brothers and sisters	اخوان
axwaat	sisters	اخوات

*The forms for 'brother' and 'father' are irregular when used with pronouns; the base forms become /axu-/ and /abu-/:

axuu	his brother	abuu	his father
axuuha	her brother	abuuha	her father
axuuhum	their brother	abuuhum	their father
axuuk	your (m) brother	abuuk	your (m) father
axuuki	your (f) brother	abuuki	your (f) father
axuukum	your (p) brother	abuukum	your (p) father
axuuya	my brother	abuuya	my father
axuuna	our brother	abuuna	our father

Verbs

diri, yidri (diriit)	know	دري يدري (دريت)
miši, yimši (mišiit)	go	مشي يمشي (مشيت)
axad, yaaxud	take	اخذ ياخذ
sa'al, yis'al	ask	سأل يسأل

Place Names

(Note that some place names in Arabic contain the definite article /al-/)

jidda	Jidda	جدة
ar-riyaaḍ	Riyadh	الرياض
makka	Mecca	مكة
al-madiina	Medina	المدينة
aṭ-ṭaayif	Taif	الطايف
tabuuk	Tabuk	تبوك
aẓ-ẓahraan	Dhahran	الظهران
ad-dammaam	Dammam	دمام
al-xobar	Al-Khobar	الخبر

Drills

1. May I ask a question? — mumkin as'al su'aal? — ممكن اسأل سؤال؟

Substitute:

huwwa	هو
iHna	احنا
axad haada	اخذ هادا
humma	هم
hiyya	هي
al-kitaab	الكتاب
al-kursi	الكرسي
hadaak	هداك
ana	انا
sa'al su'aal	سأل سؤال

2. Who is that man? — miin hadaak ar-rijjaal? — مين هداك الرجال؟

Substitute:

sitt	ست
naas	ناس
bint	بنت
walad	ولد
haada	هادا
awlaad	اولاد
sitt	ست
rijjaal	رجال
hadaak	هداك

3. He is not American — huwwa muu amrikaani. — هو مو امركاني.

Substitute:

here
she
French
my sister
Saudi
from Taif
he
from Medina
from Mecca
American

4. This is not possible.   haada muu mumkin.   هادا مو ممكن.

Substitute:

much
necessary
early
a sentence
my watch
my brothers and sisters
a school
my school
her pen
possible

5. I don't know where he is from.   ma adri huwwa min feen.   ما ادري هو من فين.

Substitute:

when she arrived
who they are
where the notebook is
how long he studied English
what her name is
who these belong to

6. Given the sentence in the affirmative, change it to negative:

inta min hina?   انتَ من هنا؟
intu faahmiin?   انتو فاهمين؟
hiyya almaniyya.   هي المانية.
al-madrasa Haggat al-Hukuuma.   المدرسة حقة الحكومة.
haada laazim.   هادا لازم.
ahli fir-riyaaḍ.   اهلي في الرياض.

Situations

1.
A. This is my book.
B. Pardon me. It belongs to this girl. Your book isn't here.
A. Maybe Ahmad took it. He was here.
B. I don't know. I can ask him.
A. Please.

2.
A. Good morning.
B. Good morning. Welcome back.
A. Thanks.* How is your family?
B. Well, thank God. My brothers and sisters send their greetings.
A. Thanks.*

*These are, of course, not literal translations of the appropriate Arabic responses.

3.
A. Where is his brother from?
B. I don't know; not from here.
A. Maybe he's from Riyadh. What's his name?
B. Ahmad.
A. Where does he study now?
B. In a government school.

LESSON 9

Dialogue

A.	Hello.	ahlan.	اهلا.
B.	Hello. We've missed you.	ahlan, waHaštana.	اهلا. وحشتنا.
	more	aktar	اكثر
	health	ṣiHHa	صحة
A.	I've missed you, too. ('you more') How is your health?	w inta aktar. keef ṣiHHatak?	وانتَ اكثر. كيف صحتَك؟
	conditions	aHwaal	احوال
	if God wills	in šaa' aḷḷaah	ان شاء الله
B.	Fine, and how are you (p)? Fine, I hope? ('Fine, if God wills?')	ṭayyib, wu keef aHwaalakum? ṭayyibiin, in šaa' aḷḷaah?	طيب وكيف احوالكم؟ طيبين ان شاء الله؟
	happy	mabsuuṭ	مبسوط
A.	Fine, thanks.	mabsuuṭiin, al-Hamdu lillaah.	مبسوطين الحمد لله.
B.	I must be going now.	laazim asta'zin daHHiin.	لازم استأذن دحّين.
	you reach the morning	tiṣbaH	تصبح
A.	OK, good night. ('May you reach morning well')	tiṣbaH 9ala xeer.	تصبح على خير.
B.	Good night. ('And you are among those people')	w inta min ahlu.	وانت من اهله.

Structure Sentences

1.	This man is happy.	haada r-rijjaal mabsuuṭ.	هادا الرجال مبسوط.
2.	This girl is not happy.	haadi l-bint mahi mabsuuṭa.	هادي البنت مهي مبسوطة.
3.	These people are not happy.	hadool an-naas mahum mabsuuṭiin.	هدول الناس مهم مبسوطين.
4.	I am tired.	ana ta9baan.	انا تعبان.
5.	This woman is tired.	haadi s-sitt ta9baana.	هادي الست تعبانة.
6.	We are tired.	iHna ta9baaniin.	احنا تعبانين.
7.	This woman is pretty.	haadi s-sitt Hilwa.	هادي الست حلوة.
8.	These woman are pretty.	hadool as-sittaat Hilwiin.	هدول الستات حلوين.

9.	This boy is big.	haada l-walad kabiir.	هادا الولد كبير.
10.	These boys are big.	hadool al-awlaad kubaar.	هدول الاولاد كبار.
11.	The chairs are pretty.	al-karaasi Hilwa.	الكراسي حلوة.
12.	The chairs are pretty.	al-karaasi Hilwiin.	الكراسي حلوين.

Grammatical Notes

1. The plural form of nouns cannot be predicted in Arabic. Some take as the plural suffix /-iin/ (the regular masculine plural, used for most males or mixed gender, especially professions), or /-aat/(the regular feminine plural, for most females or inanimate nouns). But at least half have a "broken" plural, which consists of changed vowel patterns among the root consonants. These are hard to predict, and must be learned one by one as you come to them. Some examples, using nouns learned thus far:

/-iin/ plural	/-aat/ plural		Broken plural	
			waraga, awraag	اوراق
(no examples	imtiHaan, imtiHaanaat	امتحانات	jumla, jumal	جمل
yet)	lugha, lughaat	لغات	kitaab, kutub	كتب
	sitt, sittaat	ستات	tamriin, tamaariin	تمارين
	Hukuuma, Hukuumaat	حكومات	galam, aglaam	اقلام
	saa9a, saa9aat	ساعات	daftar, dafaatir	دفاتر
	ţarabiiza, ţarabiizaat	طربيزات	dars, duruus	دروس
	sayyaara, sayyaaraat	سيارات	ma9had, ma9aahid	معاهد
			madrasa, madaaris	مدارس
	(almost regular:)		baab, abwaab	ابواب
			ghurfa, ghuraf	غرف
	bint, banaat	بنات	walad, awlaad	اولاد
	kilma, kalimaat	كلمات	rijjaal, rijaal	رجال
			su'aal, as'ila	أسئلة
			Haal, aHwaal	احوال
			ism, asaami	اسامي
			9eela, 9awaayil	عوايل

From now on, irregular noun plurals will be given with the singular form. Regular plurals will simply be marked as /-iin/ or /-aat/ after the singular form.

2. In Arabic, the adjective always matches the noun it modifies in gender and number (see examples in the Structure Sentences). Thus:

mabsuuţ	happy	(m)	مبسوط
mabsuuţa		(f)	مبسوطة
mabsuuţiin		(p)	مبسوطين
ta9baan	tired	(m)	تعبان
ta9baana		(f)	تعبانة
ta9baaniin		(p)	تعبانين
ţayyib	good	(m)	طيب
ţayyiba		(f)	طيبة
ţayyibiin		(p)	طيبين
maškuur	thanked	(m)	مشكور
maškuura		(f)	مشكورة
maškuuriin		(p)	مشكورين

Note that if the adjective has the form CVCVC (single consonants and short vowels), it will lose the second vowel before the suffixes:

wiHiš	bad (m)	وحش
wiHša	(f)	وحشة
wiHšiin	(p)	وحشين

If the plural is an inanimate noun, the adjective may be used as plural or may be feminine singular (with /-a/) (see Structure Sentences 11 and 12). The latter use is considered "classicized" (see cultural note below.)

3. Most plural adjectives take the suffix /-iin/. Some, however, have a "broken" plural pattern. Broken adjective plurals are simpler than those of nouns; most of them have a predictable vowel form. If the singular pattern is:

$$C_1aC_2iiC_3$$

the plural pattern will be:

$$C_1uC_2aaC_3$$

kabiir, kubaar	big
ṣaghiir, ṣughaar	small

4. /waHaštana/, 'We missed you', is a structure expressed exactly backwards from the English expression, literally, 'You (actor) caused-to-miss us (object). It is usually used in the perfect tense, although it may be translated past or present in English.

Examples:

waHaštuuni	I missed you (p).	وحشتوني
waHaštuuna	We missed you (p).	وحشتونا
waHaštiini	I missed you (f).	وحشتيني
waHašoona	We missed them.	وحشونا
waHašatni	I miss her.	وحشتني
waHašni	I miss him.	وحشني

Vocabulary Notes

Adjectives

Broken plurals

kabiir, kubaar	big	كبير كبار
ṣaghiir, ṣughaar	small	صغير صغار
jadiid, judud	new	جديد جدد
gadiim, gudum	old	قديم قدم
ṭawiil, ṭuwaal	tall	طويل طوال
gaṣiir, guṣaar	short	قصير قصار
tagiil, tugaal	heavy	ثقيل ثقال
xafiif, xufaaf	lightweight	خفيف خفاف
laṭiif, luṭaaf	nice, pleasant	لطيف لطاف

Regular plurals

ṭayyib, -iin	good	طيب -ين
wiHiš, -iin	bad, ugly	وحش -ين
muhimm, -iin	important	مهم -ين
Hilu, -wiin	pretty	حلو -ين

Drills

1. We missed you (m). waHaštana. وحشتنا.

Substitute:

We missed her.
We missed him.
We missed them.
I missed them.
I missed you (m).
I missed you (f).
We missed you (f).
We missed you (m).

2. How is your (m) health? keef ṣiHHatak? كيف صحتَك؟

Continue:

(to a woman)
(to a group)

3. Good night. tiṣbaH 9ala xeer. تصبح على خير.

Continue:

(to a woman)
(to a group)

4. Good night (response). w inta min ahlu. وانتَ من اهله.

Continue:

(to a woman)
(to a group)

5. Given the sentence in the singular, change it to plural:

al-bint Hilwa. البنت حلوة.
as-su'aal muhimm. السؤال مهم.
as-sayyaara jadiida. السيارة جديدة.
al-kitaab tagiil. الكتاب ثقيل.
al-walad mabsuuṭ. الولد مبسوط.
haada xafiif. هادا خفيف.

6. This man is happy. haada r-rijjaal mabsuuṭ. هادا الرجال مبسوط.

Substitute:

as-sitt الست
as-sittaat الستات
ta9baan تعبان
al-walad الولد
aHmad احمد
kabiir كبير
humma هم
ṣaghiir صغير
uxti اختي
iHna احنا
inta انتَ
huwwa هو
mabsuuṭ مبسوط
inti انتِ
ṭawiil طويل

intu	انتو
gaṣiir	قصير
hiyya	هي
laṭiif	لطيف
ar-rijjaal	الرجال
mabsuuṭ	مبسوط

7. The chairs are pretty. <u>al-karaasi</u> <u>Hilwiin</u>. الكراسي حلوين.

Substitute:

kursi	كرسي
xafiif	خفيف
kutub	كتب
kitaab	كتاب
muhimm	مهم
as-su'aal	السؤال
kwayyis	كويس
as-saa9a	الساعة
wiHiš	وحش
al-ghurfa	الغرفة
Hilu	حلو
al-aglaam	الاقلام
hadool	هدول
jadiid	جديد
al-karaasi	الكراسي
Hilu	حلو

<u>Situations</u>

1.
A. Have you seen your brother?
B. No, I miss him very much.
A. Where is he now?
B. He is in the government.
A. You have to introduce him to me.
B. I will. (literally, 'if God wills')

2.
A. Good evening.
B. Good evening.
A. Can you tell me, who are these people?
B. I don't know. I can ask my father; he knows them.
A. Please. Thank you. ('You are thanked')
B. You're welcome.

3.
A. Is this book good?
B. No, it's very bad. It's old.
A. Who wrote it?
B. We don't know.
A. Well, I must be going. Good night.
B. Good night.

<u>Cultural Notes</u>

1. There are many situations in which Classical Arabic structures may be used in speaking colloquial Arabic. Usually such "classicisms" have a colloquial equivalent, but are used for emphasis or eloquence. Whenever a classicism appears in this course, it will be noted as such.

2. /in šaa' aḷḷaah/, 'if God wills', is always used when referring to a future action. It may have numerous translations in English, depending on the situation.

LESSON 10

Review all dialogues.

Supplementary Drills

1. Can you tell me, when did you arrive? — mumkin tigulli, mita waṣalt? — ممكن تقوللي متا وصلتْ؟

Substitute:

How is he?
What is this word in Arabic?
Can I introduce you to Mr. Jones?
What is her name?
Where are your brothers and sisters?
Does he understand English?
Where is your book?
Whom did you see there?
With whom did he go?

2. May I be excused? — mumkin asta'zin? — ممكن استأذن؟

Substitute:

use this pen?
speak English?
open the car?
do that?
write the questions?
take the small chair?
see your car?

3. I asked about him. — sa'alt 9annu. — سألتْ عنه .

Substitute:

greeted the woman.
told him.
asked your father.
talked to them.
went to Riyadh.
arrived early.

(Repeat, using 'he', 'she', 'you (p)', 'we'.)

4. Answer the questions:

eeš ismak?	ايش اسمَك؟
inta min feen?	انتَ من فين؟
mita waṣalt hina?	متا وصلتْ هنا؟
inta ingiliizi?	انتَ انكليزي؟
inta titkallam 9arabi?	انتَ تتكلم عربي؟
feen darast?	فين درستْ؟
madrasaṭak Haggat al-Hukuuma?	مدرستك حقة الحكومة؟
fataHt kitaabak?	فتحتْ كتابك؟
'Notebook' eeš ismu bil-9arabi?	"نوتبوك" ايش اسمه بالعربي؟
haada galamak?	هادا قلمك؟
inta ta9baan šwayya?	انت تعبان شويه؟

LESSON 11

Dialogue

(In an office)

	you (honorific)	Haḍratak	حضرتك
A.	Who are you?	miin Haḍratak?	مين حضرتك؟
B.	My name is Abdel-Rahman.	ismi 9abd ar-raHmaan.	اسمي عبد الرحمن.
	you (m) work	tištaghil	تشتغل
A.	Where do you work?	feen tištaghil?	فين تشتغل؟
	ministry	wizaara	وزارة
	external	xaarijiyya	خارجية
B.	In the Foreign Ministry.	fi wizaarat al-xaarijiyya.	فى وزارة الخارجية.
A.	Are you Saudi?	inta su9uudi?	انت سعودي؟
	of course	ṭab9an	طبعا
B.	Yes, of course. I'm from here, from Jidda.	iiwa ṭab9an. ana min hina, min jidda.	ايوه طبعا. انا من هنا، من جدة.
A.	Welcome.	ahlan wu sahlan.	اهلا وسهلا.
B.	Thank you.	ahlan biik.	اهلا بيك.

Structure Sentences

1.	In which ministry does he work?	yištaghil fi ayy wizaara?	يشتغل في اي وزارة؟
2.	In which school do you study?	tidrus fi ayy madrasa?	تدرس في اي مدرسة؟
3.	Bring any book.	jiib ayy kitaab.	جيب اي كتاب.
4.	He is from Jidda.	huwwa jiddaawi.	هو جداوي.
5.	Where is Mecca Road?	feen ṭariig makka?	فين طريق مكة؟
6.	The American government is big.	Hukuumat amriika kabiira.	حكومة امريكا كبيرة.
7.	The Philips company is important.	šarikat filibs muhimma.	شركة فلبس مهمة.

Grammatical Notes

1. /Haḍratak/ (/Haḍratik/), literally, 'your presence', may be used as an honorific title, substituting for /inta/ or /inti/. It is often used with persons older than yourself or of high rank. You will also hear /ṭaal 9umrak/ (/ṭaal 9umrik/), literally, 'May your life be lengthened', especially in the Najd, and for royalty.

For older people, /ya 9ammi/, 'my uncle', and /ya xaalati/, 'my aunt', are commonly heard as well. An older or respected man may be addressed as /ya šeex/, 'sheikh', and it need not imply that this is an official title.

2. /aštaghal, yištaghil/, 'to work', is the most common word, but /9amal, yi9mil/ is often heard to mean 'to work, to do' (it is more classicized).

3. /ayy/, 'which', is used before a noun. It is not declined. In a question, it means 'which?', and in a statement it means 'any'.

4. /jiddaawi/ is another adjective of the /-i/ type. For a noun which ends in a vowel, /-aawi/ is suffixed to make an adjective. This pattern is used especially often for adjectives of place origin, though it is by no means limited to them. (Not all place names can be made adjectives; you say /min/ + place.)

Most of these adjectives take the /-yiin/ plural suffix (but do not generalize without seeing it first; some nationality adjectives are irregular). The feminine form is always predictable, /-yya/.

Singular		Plural (regular)		
su9uudi	سعودي	-yiin		Saudi
najdi	نجدي	-yiin		Najdi
Hijaazi	حجازي	-yiin		Hijazi
yamaani	يماني	-yiin		Yemeni
faransaawi	فرنساوي	-yiin		French
iṭaali	ايطالي	-yiin		Italian
amriiki	امريكي	-yiin		American
yabaani	يباني	-yiin		Japanese
		(irregular)		
badawi	بدوي	badu	بدو	Bedouin
9arabi	عربي	9arab	عرب	Arab
amrikaani	امركاني	amrikaan	امركان	American
turki	تركي	atraak	اتراك	Turk
asbaani	اسباني	asbaan	اسبان	Spanish
almaani	الماني	almaan	المان	German
ingiliizi	انكليزي	ingiliiz	انكليز	English
ruusi	روسي	ruus	روس	Russian
ajnabi	اجنبي	ajaanib	اجانب	foreign

5. Structures like /wizaarat al-xaarijiyya/ and /Hukuumat amriika/ are examples of nouns placed in a "construct". A construct consists of two or more nouns placed together, to express possession (or 'of' in English):

wizaara	ministry
wizaarat al-xaarijiyya	Ministry of External [Affairs] (literally, 'ministry the-external')
Hukuuma	government
Hukuumat amriika	the government of America (literally, 'government America')
ism ar-rijjaal	the man's name

More than two nouns may be placed in a construct:

ṭariig wizaarat al-xaarijiyya	road of the Foreign Ministry (literally, 'road ministry the-external')

Note that feminine nouns which end in /-a/ replace this suffix with /-at/ when part of a construct.

The entire construct phrase is either definite ('the') or indefinite ('a, an') depending on the last noun:

ism ar-rijjaal	the man's name
ism rijjaal	a man's name

The first and middle nouns cannot be marked as definite (with /al-/), but they are usually translated definite:

ṭariig al-wizaara	the road of the ministry

Proper nouns (names) and nouns which have a possessive ending are grammatically definite, so they occur only as the last item of a construct:

sayyaarat aHmad	Ahmad's car
sayyaarat axuuya	my brother's car
ṭariig makka	Mecca Road

Other examples of constructs:

haada maktab šarika.	This is a company's office.
haada maktab aš-šarika.	This is the company's office.
haadi gunṣuliyyat safaara.	This is an embassy's consulate.
haadi gunṣuliyyat as-safaara.	This is the embassy's consulate.

As a review, remember that there is an important structural difference between "constructs" and noun phrases (nouns + adjectives):

Hukuumat amriika	the government of America
al-Hukuuma l-amrikiyya	the American government (literally, 'the government the American')
šarika amrikiyya	an American company (literally, 'company American')

The constructs are patterned:

indefinite Noun + definite Noun
indefinite Noun + indefinite Noun

whereas the noun phrases are patterned:

definite Noun + definite Adjective
indefinite Noun + indefinite Adjective

Other examples:

Constructs:

maḍiinat jidda	the city of Jidda
ṭariig al-maṭaar	Airport Road
šarikat an-nuur	the light company

Noun Phrases:

as-safaara l-amrikiyya	the American Embassy
al-madrasa l-amrikiyya	the American school
al-jeeš as-su9uudi	the Saudi army

Vocabulary Notes

Nouns

Singular	Plural		
safaara	-aat	embassy	سفارة -ات
wizaara	-aat	ministry	وزارة -ات
šarika	-aat	company	شركة -ات
madiina	mudun	city	مدينة مدن
maṭaar	-aat	airport	مطار -ات
ṭariig	ṭurug	road	طريق طرق
gunṣuliyya	-aat	consulate	قنصلية -ات
maktab	makaatib	office	مكتب مكاتب

Verbs

aštaghal, yištaghil	work	اشتغل يشتغل
9amal, yi9mil	work, do	عمل يعمل

Names of Countries

amriika	America	امريكا
almaanya	Germany	المانيا
ingiltera	England	انكلترا
faraansa	France	فرانسا
asbaanya	Spain	اسبانيا
ruusya	Russia	روسيا
al-yabaan	Japan	اليبان

The ministries in Saudi Arabia are:

wizaarat al-xaarijiyya	Foreign Ministry
wizaarat ad-daaxiliyya	Interior Ministry
wizaarat al-ma9aarif	Ministry of Education (literally, 'knowledge')
wizaarat at-tijaara w aṣ-ṣinaa9a	Ministry of Commerce and Industry
wizaarat al-muwaaṣalaat	Ministry of Communications
wizaarat ad-difaa9 w aṭ-ṭayaraan	Ministry of Defense and Aviation
wizaarat al-i9laam	Ministry of Information
wizaarat az-ziraa9a	Ministry of Agriculture
wizaarat al-maaliyya	Ministry of Finance
wizaarat al-9amal w aš-šu'uun al-ijtimaa9iyya	Ministry of Labor and Social Affairs
wizaarat al-batrool w al-ma9aadin	Ministry of Petroleum and Minerals
wizaarat al-9adl	Ministry of Justice
wizaarat al-Hajj w al-awgaaf	Ministry of Pilgrimage and Endowments

In ordinary conversation, ministries with double names are usually referred to by the first title only.

Drills

1.
A. In which ministry do you work? — tištaghil fi ayy wizaara? — تشتغل في اي وزارة؟

B. In the Foreign Ministry. — fi wizaarat al-xaarijiyya. — في وزارة الخارجية.

Continue:

in the Ministry of Interior
in the Ministry of Defense
in the Ministry of Education
in the Ministry of Communications
in the Ministry of Finance
in the Ministry of Commerce
in the Ministry of Labor
in the Ministry of Information
in the Ministry of Agriculture

2.
A. Where is he from? — huwwa min feen ? — هو من فين؟

B. He's from the city of Jidda. — huwwa min madiinat jidda. — هو من مدينة جدة.

Continue:

from Taif
from the city of Riyadh
from Mecca
from the city of New York
from Medina
from Dhahran
from the city of Chicago
from Tobuk
from Dammam
from Jidda

3. I am from Jidda. — ana min jidda. — انا من جدة.

Substitute:

Germany
England
America
Spain
Russia
Japan
France

4. Given the name of the country, respond with the nationality.

Example: humma min amriika. ⟶ humma amrikaan. — هم من امريكا ← هم امركان.

Continue:

humma min almaanya. — هم من المانيا.
humma min ruusya. — هم من روسيا.
humma min faraansa. — هم من فرانسا.
humma min asbaanya. — هم من اسبانيا.
humma min al-yabaan. — هم من اليابان.
humma min ingiltera. — هم من انكلترا.
humma min amriika. — هم من امريكا.

5. They work in the school. humma yištaghilu <u>fil-madrasa</u>. هم يشتغلوا فى المدرسة.

Substitute:

an office
the light company
the airport
the Ministry of Interior
the communications office
an American company
the German embassy
Raytheon company
in Riyadh
the American consulate

6. I saw a tall man there. šuft <u>rijjaal ṭawiil</u> hinaak. شفت رجال طويل هناك.

Substitute:

a pretty chair
a big table
those pens
new books
important people
the Foreign Ministry
a good road
the old embassy
[some] foreigners
[some] Italians
[some] Bedouins

7. Given the statement in the indefinite, change it to definite:

9amal fi šarika amrikiyya.	عمل فى شركة امريكية.
haadi sayyaarat wizaara.	هادي سيارة وزارة.
hadool tamaariin dars	هدول تمارين درس
darast fi ma9had kabiir.	درست فى معهد كبير.
haadi safaarat Hukuuma.	هادي سفارة حكومة.

8. Given the sentence in the singular, change it to plural:

al-wizaara kabiira.	الوزارة كبيرة.
al-maṭaar jadiid.	المطار جديد.
al-kitaab wiHiš.	الكتاب وحش.
as-sitt gaṣiira.	الست قصيرة.
al-imtiHaan ṭayyib.	الامتحان طيب.
aṭ-ṭarabiiza ṣaghiira.	الطربيزة صغيرة.
al-bint mabsuuṭa.	البنت مبسوطة.
as-sayyaara gadiima.	السيارة قديمة.

<u>Situations</u>

1.
A. Can you (honorific) tell me, where is the Ministry of Education?
B. That's not here in Jidda. It's in Riyadh.
A. I understand, thank you.
B. You're welcome.

2.
A. There are many foreigners here.
B. Yes, they work in companies.
A. Are there French here?
B. Yes, of course. There is a French Embassy.
A. I saw Germans too.
B. Yes. You see many people in Jidda.

3.
A. Come in. When did you (p) arrive?
B. Yesterday. We arrived at the airport in the evening.
A. Welcome back.
B. Thanks. Where is your father?
A. He went to the office.
B. I hope to see him there. (literally, 'If God wills, I [will] see him there.')
A. I hope so. (literally, 'If God wills.')

LESSON 12

Dialogue

	hour	saa9a	ساعة
	how many	kam	كم
A.	Please, what time is it?	min faḍlak, as-saa9a kam?	من فضلك الساعة كم؟
	three	talaata	ثلاثة
B.	It's three o'clock.	as-saa9a talaata.	الساعة ثلاثة.
	I was late	at'axxart	اتأخرت
	very	marra	مرة
A.	I'm very late.	ana marra at'axxart.	انا مرة اتأخرت.
	but	laakin	لاكن
	still	lissa9	لسع
	early	badri	بدري
B.	A little. But it's still early. Go safely.	šwayya. laakin lissa9 badri. ma9a s-salaama.	شويه . لاكن لسع بدري. مع السلامة.
	safety	amaan	امان
A.	In the safety of God.	fi amaan illaah.	في امان الله .

Structure Sentences

1.	It's four-thirty.	as-saa9a arba9a wu nuṣṣ.	الساعة اربعة ونص.
2.	It's 1:15.	as-saa9a waHda wu rub9.	الساعة واحدة وربع.
3.	It's 7:45 ('eight minus a quarter')	as-saa9a tamanya illa rub9.	الساعة ثمانية الا ربع .
4.	I have to meet Ahmad.	laazim agaabil aHmad.	لازم اقابل احمد .
5.	He's very nice.	huwwa marra laṭiif.	هو مرة لطيف.
6.	We are very happy.	iHna marra mabsuuṭiin.	احنا مرة مبسوطين.
7.	She is very tall.	hiyya ṭawiila jiddan.	هي طويلة جدا.
8.	I have to count them.	laazim a9iddahum.	لازم اعدهم.
9.	He is still here.	huwwa lissa9 hina.	هو لسع هنا.
10.	What are you doing now?	eeš tisawwi daHHiin?	ايش تسوي دحين؟
11.	I answered him.	raddeet 9alee.	رديت عليه .

Grammatical Notes

1. Numbers one through twelve are:

waaHid (feminine, waHda)	one	واحد (واحدة)
itneen	two	اثنين
talaata	three	ثلاثة
arba9a	four	اربعة
xamsa	five	خمسة
sitta	six	ستة
sab9a	seven	سبعة
tamanya	eight	ثمانية
tis9a	nine	تسعة
9ašara	ten	عشرة
iHḍa9š	eleven	إحْدَعْش
itna9š	twelve	إثْنَعْش

2. Expressions for telling time are:

as-saa9a arba9a.	It's four o'clock.
as-saa9a sab9a.	It's seven o'clock.
as-saa9a arba9a wu nuṣṣ.	It's 4:30. ('four and a half')
as-saa9a arba9a wu rub9.	It's 4:15. ('four and a quarter')
as-saa9a arba9a illa rub9.	It's 3:45. (four minus a quarter')

Note that the feminine form /waHda/ is used to modify /saa9a/.

The expressions for 'a.m.' and 'p.m.' are:

aṣ-ṣubuH	a.m.
al-masa	p.m.
as-saa9a talaata ṣ-ṣubuH.	It's 3:00 a.m.
as-saa9a xamsa l-masa.	It's 5:00 p.m.

Without the time phrase, the expressions are:

fis-subuH	in the morning
fil-masa	in the evening

3. /marra/ is used before an adjective or verb to mean 'very'. 'Very' may also be expressed with the phrase /bil-marra/ (after the adjective) or /jiddan/ (after the adjective). /jiddan/ is classical, and the most emphatic. (cf. Structure Sentences 5, 6, and 7.)

4. /lissa9/ has several uses in Arabic. When used before a predicate (other than a verb), it means 'still':

huwwa lissa9 walad ṣaghiir.	He is still a small boy.
al-kitaab lissa9 jadiid.	The book is still new.

(Other uses of this word will be discussed in Lesson 26.)

5. /sawwa, yisawwi/, 'to make, to do', is an example of a verb which ends in a vowel. This type of verb, as well as verbs in which the last consonant is "doubled", have different suffixes in the perfect tense (similar to those we saw for /diri/ and /miši/):

Perfect (ends in /-a/)	Imperfect		
huwwa sawwa	yisawwi	يسوّي	سوّى
hiyya sawwat	tisawwi	تسوّي	سوّت
humma sawwu	yisawwu	يسوّوا	سوّوا
inta sawweet	tisawwi	تسوّي	سوّيت
inti sawweeti	tisawwi	تسوّي	سوّيتِ
intu sawweetu	tisawwu	تسوّوا	سوّيتوا
ana sawweet	asawwi	اسوّي	سوّيت
iHna sawweena	nisawwi	نسوّي	سوّينا
(doubled)			
huwwa Habb	yiHubb	يحب	حب
hiyya Habbat	tiHubb	تحب	حبت
humma Habbu	yiHubbu	يحبوا	حبوا
inta Habbeet	tiHubb	تحب	حبيت
inti Habbeeti	tiHubbi	تحبي	حبيتِ
intu Habbeetu	tiHubbu	تحبوا	حبيتوا
ana Habbeet	aHubb	احب	حبيت
iHna Habbeena	niHubb	نحب	حبينا

Doubled verbs (like /Habb/, /9add/) may have either the vowel /u/ or /i/ in the imperfect:

Habb, yiHubb
9add, yi9idd

6. /gaabal/, yigaabil/, 'to meet', is an example of a verb which contains a long /aa/:

Perfect	Imperfect		
huwwa gaabal	yigaabil	يقابل	قابل
hiyya gaabalat	tigaabil	تقابل	قابلت
humma gaabalu	yigaabilu	يقابلوا	قابلوا
inta gaabalt	tigaabil	تقابل	قابلت
inti gaabalti	tigaabili	تقابلي	قابلتِ
intu gaabaltu	tigaabilu	تقابلوا	قابلتوا
ana gaabalt	agaabil	اقابل	قابلت
iHna gaabalna	nigaabil	نقابل	قابلنا

7. /radd/, 'to answer', is used with the preposition /9ala/, 'on', before the object:

raddeet 9alee	I answered him. (literally, 'I answered on him.')
laazim nirudd 9aleeha.	We must answer her.

8. You have now had all of the major types of verbs.

Summary of Verb Conjugations

(1) Regular (a)

daras	yidrus
darasat	tidrus
darasu	yidrusu
darast	tidrus
darasti	tidrusi
darastu	tidrusu
darast	adrus
darasna	nidrus

(2) Regular (i)

9irif	yi9rif
9irifat	ti9rif
9irifu	yi9rifu
9irift	ti9rif
9irifti	ti9rifi
9iriftu	ti9rifu
9irift	a9rif
9irifna	ni9rif

(3) Weak Initial Consonant

axad	yaaxud
axadat	taaxud
axadu	yaaxudu*
axadt	taaxud
axadti	taaxudi*
axadtu	taaxudu*
axadt	aaxud
axadna	naaxud

*These forms are often shortened to /yaaxdu, taaxdi, taaxdu/.

(4) Weak Medial Consonant ("Hollow")

gaal	yiguul
gaalat	tiguul
gaalu	yiguulu
gult	tiguul
gulti	tiguuli
gultu	tiguulu
gult	aguul
gulna	niguul

jaab	yijiib
jaabat	tijiib
jaabu	yijiibu
jibt	tijiib
jibti	tijiibi
jibtu	tijiibu
jibt	ajiib
jibna	nijiib

naam	yinaam
naamat	tinaam
naamu	yinaamu
numt	tinaam
numti	tinaami
numtu	tinaamu
numt	anaam
numna	ninaam

(5) Weak Final Consonant (i)

miši	yimši
mišyat	timši
mišyu	yimšu
mišiit	timši
mišiiti	timši
mišiitu	timšu
mišiit	amši
mišiina	nimši

(6) Weak Final Consonant (a)

sawwa	yisawwi
sawwat	tisawwi
sawwu	yisawwu
sawweet	tisawwi
sawweeti	tisawwi
sawweetu	tisawwu
sawweet	asawwi
sawweena	nisawwi

(7) Final Consonant Doubled

Habb	yiHubb
Habbat	tiHubb
Habbu	yiHubbu
Habbeet	tiHubb
Habbeeti	tiHubbi
Habbeetu	tiHubbu
Habbeet	aHubb
Habbeena	niHubb

9add	yi9idd
9addat	ti9idd
9addu	yi9iddu
9addeet	ti9idd
9addeeti	ti9iddi
9addeetu	ti9iddu
9addeet	a9idd
9addeena	ni9idd

(8) Medial Consonant Doubled

9arraf	yi9arrif
9arrafat	ti9arrif
9arrafu	yi9arrifu
9arraft	ti9arrif
9arrafti	ti9arrifi
9arraftu	ti9arrifu
9arraft	a9arrif
9arrafna	ni9arrif

(9) Contain /aa/

gaabal	yigaabil
gaabalat	tigaabil
gaabalu	yigaabilu*
gaabalt	tigaabil
gaabalti	tigaabili*
gaabaltu	tigaabilu*
gaabalt	agaabil
gaabalna	nigaabil

These forms are often shortened to /yigaablu, tigaabli, tigaablu/.

(10) Contain /-sta-/

asta'zan	yista'zin
asta'zanat	tista'zin
asta'zanu	yista'zinu
asta'zant	tista'zin
asta'zanti	tista'zini
asta'zantu	tista'zinu
asta'zant	asta'zin
asta'zanna	nista'zin

Vocabulary Notes

Verbs

(hollow)

saab, yisiib (sibt)	leave behind	ساب يسيب (سبتْ)
šaal, yišiil (šilt)	carry	شال يشيل (شلتْ)

(ending in /i/)

nisi, yinsa (nisiit)	forget	نِسِي ينْسَى (نسيتْ)

(ending in /a/)

sawwa, yisawwi (sawweet)	do	سوّى يسوّي (سوّيتْ)

(doubled)

Habb, yiHubb (Habbeet)	like, love	حب يحب (حبيتْ)
radd, yirudd (raddeet)	answer	رد يرد (رديتْ)
Haŧŧ, yiHuŧŧ (Haŧŧeet)	put	حط يحط (حطيتْ)
9add, yi9idd (9addeet)	count	عد يعِد (عديت)

/aa/

gaabal, yigaabil	meet	قابل يقابل

(Other)

at'axxar, yit'axxir	be late	اتأخر يتأخر

Drills

1. One plus three equals four.	waaHid zaayid talaata yisaawi* arba9a.	واحد زايد ثلاثة يساوي اربعة.

Continue:

2 + 4	8 + 3	5 + 2
5 + 3	7 + 2	6 + 6
3 + 3	2 + 3	7 + 1

*Note the difference between /yisaawi/, 'equals' and /yisawwi/, 'he does'.

2. Three minus one equals two.	talaata naagiṣ waaHid yisaawi itneen.	ثلاثة ناقص واحد يساوي اثنين.

Continue:

4 - 1	10 - 2	12 - 8
6 - 2	11 - 6	9 - 2
9 - 4	8 - 1	11 - 3

3. It's three o'clock.	as-saa9a talaata.	الساعة ثلاثة.

Substitute:

5:30	7:30	3:45
8:00	6:00	9:00
2:15	12:00	8:45
1:45	11:15	

4. I am very late.	ana marra at'axxart.	انا مرة اتأخرت.

Substitute:

huwwa	هو
iHna	احنا
hiyya	هي
humma	هم
al-awlaad	الأولاد
ana	انا

5. This is very pretty.	haada Hilu jiddan.	هادا حلو جدا.

Substitute:

muhimm	مهم
an-naas	الناس
al-kitaab	الكتاب
aš-šarika	الشركة
gadiim	قديم
al-madiina	المدينة
haada l-baab	هادا الباب
aṭ-ṭarabiiza	الطربيزة
xafiif	خفيف
Hilu	حلو
haada	هادا

6. He is still here. huwwa lissa9 hina. هو لسع هنا.

Substitute:

important
new
she
we
tired
very tired
you (m)
small (young)
the young lady ('miss')
the company
new
car
bad
he
here

7. What did you (m) do? eeš sawweet? ايش سويت؟

Substitute:

you (f)
she
forget
he
we
like
you (p)
they
put here
he
you (p)
she
answer
you (m)
they
when
leave
she
we
you (p)
he
they

8. He carried the boy. šaal al-walad. شال الولد.

Substitute:

I
she
we
the books
you (m)
forgot
you (p)
he
left
they
you (f)
the watch

she
liked
I
they

9. What are you (m) doing? eeš tisawwi? ايش تسوّي؟

Substitute:

you (p)
she
he
you (f)
they
you (m)

Situations

1.
A. He went late.
B. I know. That's not good.
A. He arrived at 3:30, very late.
B. What time is it now?
A. 3:45.
B. Is your watch new?
A. Yes, and it's good, too.

2.
A. Excuse me, may I ask a question?
B. Of course, go ahead.
A. Where is the American Embassy?
B. You have to go from Medina Road.

3.
A. This car is brand new, right?
B. Yes. It's my brother's car.
A. It's very pretty.
B. Thanks.
A. I've missed your brother.
B. He has missed you, too. He sends you his greetings.

Cultural Notes

1. Arabs generally have a more flexible attitude about time than Americans do. While they do make appointments and attempt to keep them, frequently apologizing for being late, there is also a longer period of time within which a person may arrive late before the other person loses patience. Sometimes appointments are made for an "approximate" time; in this case, you may expect someone to come as much as an hour late.

LESSON 13

Dialogue

	you came	jiit	جيت
	kingdom	mamlaka	مملكة
A.	When did you come to the kingdom?	mita jiit al-mamlaka?	متا جيت المملكة؟
	day	yoom	يوم
	days	ayyaam	ايام
B.	Monday. Three days ago.	yoom al-itneen. gabl talaata ayyaam.	يوم الاثنين· قبل ثلاثة ايام·
	house	beet	بيت
A.	Where is your house?	feen beetak?	فين بيتَك؟
	living	saakin	ساكن
	street	šaari9	شارع
	fourteen	arba9ŧa9š	اربعتعش
B.	I live on 14th Street.	ana saakin fi šaari9 arba9ŧa9š.	انا ساكن في شارع اربعتعش·
	far	ba9iid	بعيد
A.	Is it far from here?	ba9iid min hina?	بعيد من هنا؟
	near	gariib	قريب
B.	No, it's near here.	la', gariib min hina.	لا· قريب من هنا·

Structure Sentences

1.	We came a long time ago. ('from a long time')	jiina min zamaan.	جينا من زمان·
2.	They live on Gabil Street.	humma saakniin fi šaari9 gaabil.	هم ساكنين في شارع قابل·
3.	Have you (m) been in Jidda long? ('For you much in Jidda?')	lak katiir fi jidda?	لَكْ كثير في جدة؟
4.	I have been here five days. ('For me here five days')	liyya hina xamsa ayyaam.	لِيَّ هنا خمسة ايام·
5.	She lives near our house.	hiyya saakna gariib min beetana.	هي ساكنة قريب من بيتنا·

6. She lives far from our house.	hiyya saakna ba9iid 9an beetana.	هي ساكنة بعيد عن بيتنا.
7. I took 1,000 dollars from my father.	ana axadt alf dulaar min abuuya.	انا اخذت الف دولار من ابوي.
8. What is your (m) address?	eeš 9inwaanak?	ايش عنوانك؟

Grammatical Notes

1. /jaa/, 'to come', is an irregular verb:

Perfect	Imperfect		
huwwa jaa	yiji	يجي	جا
hiyya jaat	tiji	تجي	جات
humma joo	yiju	يجوا	جوا
inta jiit	tiji	تجي	جيتْ
inti jiiti	tiji	تجي	جيتِ
intu jiitu	tiju	تجوا	جيتوا
ana jiit	aji	اجي	جيتْ
iHna jiina	niji	نجي	جينا

2. The full name of the country is /al-mamlaka l-9arabiyya s-su9uudiyya/, 'the Saudi Arabian Kingdom'. Abbreviations are often used, /al-mamlaka/ or /as-su9uudiyya/.

3. Days of the week are:

as-sabt	Saturday	السبت
al-aHad	Sunday	الاحد
al-itneen	Monday	الاثنين
at-taluut	Tuesday	التلوت
ar-rabuu9	Wednesday	الربوع
al-xamiis	Thursday	الخميس
al-jum9a	Friday	الجمعة

Saturday and Sunday are workdays; Thursday and Friday are the "weekend", since Friday is the Moslem holy day.

4. To express 'ago', /gabl/ is used before a time word:

gabl yoomeen	two days ago

/min/ is used to express 'since':

min yoom at-taluut	since Tuesday

5. /saakin/, 'living', is an "active participle", a word which acts like an adjective but is translated as a verb in English. There are several words like this in Arabic (we have met /faahim, faahma, faahmiin/); they will be discussed fully in Lesson 22.

saakin	he lives, you (m) live, I (m) live
saakna	she lives, you (f) live, I (f) live
saakniin	they live, you (p) live, we live

This is used to mean living, in the sense of 'residing', only.

6. /zamaan/, 'a long time', is used with /min/, and only with reference to past time; it can also mean 'a long time ago'.

raaH min zamaan.	He went a long time ago.
9irif min zamaan.	He knew ('found out') a long time ago.

Used with an imperfect verb, this phrase can have a present perfect translation in English:

yi9rif min zamaan.	He has known for a long time.

7. Note that /ba9iid/ and /gariib/ both are used with the preposition /min/ when followed by a location word. When /ba9iid/ is followed by a noun or pronoun, it is used with /9an/. (cf. Structure Sentences 5 and 6.)

gariib min hina	near here
ba9iid min hina	far from here
ba9iid 9an beetana	far from our house

8. /lak/ and /liyya/ are examples of the preposition /li/ being used with a pronoun. This is further discussed in Lesson 24.

9. Note that while /riyaal/ and /dulaar/ have plural forms, they remain singular when counted with a numeral:

dulaaraat katiir	many dollars
riyaalaat katiir	many riyals

xamsa dulaar	five dollars
xamsa riyaal	five riyals

10. Other numbers are:

şifir	zero	صفر
talata9š	thirteen	ثلثعش
arba9ţa9š	fourteen	اربعتعش
xamasţa9š	fifteen	خمستعش
sitta9š	sixteen	ستعش
saba9ţa9š	seventeen	سبعتعش
tamanţa9š	eighteen	ثمنتعش
tisa9ţa9š	nineteen	تسعتعش
9išriin	twenty	عشرين
talaatiin	thirty	ثلاثين
arba9iin	forty	اربعين
xamsiin	fifty	خمسين
sittiin	sixty	ستين
sab9iin	seventy	سبعين
tamaniin	eighty	ثمانين
tis9iin	ninety	تسعين
xamsa wu 9išriin	twenty-five	خمسة وعشرين
talaata w arba9iin	forty-three	ثلاثة واربعين
sab9a wu tis9iin	ninety-seven	سبعة وتسعين
(etc.)		
miyya	one hundred	مية
miyyateen*	two hundred	ميتين
miyyaat	hundreds	ميات

miyya wu xamasṭa9š	115	مية وخمستعشر
miyyateen wu xamsa wu 9išriin	225	ميتين وخمسة وعشرين
miyyateen w arba9a wu sittiin	264	ميتين واربعة وستين
(etc.)		

*A common alternate form is /miiteen/.

Higher numbers in the hundreds have special forms:

talatmiyya	300	ثلثمية
arba9miyya	400	اربعمية
xamsmiyya*	500	خمسمية
sittmiyya*	600	ستمية
sab9miyya*	700	سبعمية
tamanmiyya*	800	ثمنمية
tis9miyya*	900	تسعمية
alf	1000	الف
alfeen	2000	الفين
aalaaf	thousands	آلاف
alf wu miyyateen	1200	الف وميتين
alf wu miyya wu xamsa wu 9išriin	1125	الف ومية وخمسة وعشرين
(etc.)		

*Common alternate forms are /xumsumiyya, suttumiyya, subu9miyya, tumunmiyya, tusu9miyya/. These are borrowed from the Egyptian dialect.

malyoon	million	مليون
malyooneen	two million	مليونين
balyoon	billion	بليون
balyooneen	two billion	بليونين
malyoon wu xamsmiyya wu xamsa wu 9išriin alf wu tamanmiyya wu waaHid w arba9iin	1,525,841	مليون وخمسمية وخمسة وعشرين الف وثمنمية وواحد واربعين
malaayiin	millions	ملايين
balaayiin	billions	بلايين

These numbers take a special ending /-een/ for 'two' (this will be explained in the next lesson).

/miyya/ becomes /miyyat/ in a construct phrase:

talatmiyyat dulaar	300 dollars
miyyat alf dulaar	100,000 dollars
xamsmiyyat alf dulaar	500,000 dollars

Vocabulary Notes

beet, buyuut	house	بيت بيوت
šaari9, šawaari9	street	شارع شوارع
9inwaan, 9anaawiin	address	عنوان عناوين
gariib, gariibiin	near	قريب قريبين
ba9iid (no plural)	far	بعيد

Drills

1. Sixty plus nine equals sixty-nine. — sittiin zaayid tis9a yisaawi tis9a wu sittiin. — ستين زايد تسعة يساوي تسعة وستين.

Continue:

15 + 7	800 + 200	3000 + 779
25 + 3	450 + 450	76 + 660
41 + 6	501 + 30	840 + 30

2. When did you (m) come to the Kingdom? — mita jiit al-mamlaka? — متا جيت المملكة؟

Substitute:

you (p)
he
they
you (f)
she

3. I have been here for three days. — liyya hina talaata ayyaam. — لي هنا ثلاثة ايام.

Substitute:

5 days
7 days
10 days
6 hours
3 hours
a long time

4. Where do you (m) live? — inta feen saakin? — انتَ فين ساكن؟

Substitute:

you (f)
they
she
he
the people
your friends
Ahmad

5. He lives on 14th Street. — huwwa saakin fi šaari9 arba9ṭa9š. — هو ساكن في شارع اربعتعش.

Substitute:

Gabil Street
she
near the embassy
far from my house
they
in Saudi Arabia
we
in Taif

6. We arrived Monday. — waṣalna yoom al-itneen. — وصلنا يوم الاثنين.

Substitute:

Thursday
Tuesday
Sunday

Friday
Monday
Saturday
Wednesday

Situations

1. (on the telephone)
A. Where is your office?
B. On 22nd Street, near the French school.
A. And your address?
B. 515, 22nd Street.
A. May I come at 4:30?
B. Are you living near here?
A. No, I can take my car.
B. OK. Goodby.

2.
A. Has he been here long? ('much')
B. Yes, he came long ago.
A. Where from?
B. From Dhahran.
A. What does he do?
B. He works in an American company.
A. Is he important in the company?
B. Yes, very important.

3.
A. May I bring my friend?
B. Of course, welcome. What's his name?
A. Abdel-Rahman. He's very nice.
B. Does he speak English?
A. A little. He studied English in school for six months.

LESSON 14

Dialogue

	will	Ha-	حَ ـ
	he comes	yiji	يجي
A.	When will he come?	mita Ha-yiji?	متا حيجي؟
	after	ba9d	بعد
	week	usbuu9	اسبوع
B.	In a week, I hope. ('after a week')	ba9d usbuu9, in šaa' aḷḷaah.	بعد اسبوع ان شاء الله.
A.	Good. And your friend, Sharif?	ṭayyib. wu ṣaaHbak šariif?	طيب. وصاحبَك شريف؟
	I think	aẓunn	اظن
	weeks	asaabii9	اسابيع
B.	After about three weeks, I think.	aẓunn ba9d Hawaali talaata asaabii9.	اظن بعد حوالي ثلاثة اسابيع.
	period of time	mudda	مدة
A.	That's a long time.	haadi mudda ṭawiila.	هادي مدة طويلة.
B.	Yes, truly.	iiwa, ṣaHiiH.	ايوه صحيح.

Structure Sentences

1.	We will go after an hour.	Ha-niruuH ba9d saa9a.	حنروح بعد ساعة.
2.	We will go today.	Ha-niruuH al-yoom.	حنروح اليوم.
3.	We will go today.	raH-niruuH al-yoom.	رَحْ نروح اليوم.
4.	I studied for about two years.	darast sanateen tagriiban.	درستْ سنتين تقريبا.
5.	They are our friends.	humma aṣHaabana.	هم اصحابنا.
6.	My friend Maryam is here for a period of three days.	ṣaaHbati maryam hina li-muddat talaata ayyaam.	صاحبتي مريم هنا لمدة ثلاثة ايام.
7.	It's approximately 6:20.	as-saa9a sitta wu tult tagriiban.	الساعة ستة وثلث تقريبا.

Grammatical Notes

1. The future tense may be expressed with the imperfect verb, prefixed with /Ha-/ or /raH-/. Both prefixes are in widespread use (/Ha-/ is a borrowing from the Egyptian dialect). /Ha-/ is used throughout the Hijaz; /raH-/ is heard mostly in Jidda.

The future prefix is frequently omitted, however, and the future meaning is understood from other time words in the sentence:

mita yiwşal? yiwşal bukra.	When will he arrive? He'll arrive tomorrow.
mita Ha-yiwşal? Ha-yiwşal bukra.	When will he arrive? He'll arrive tomorrow.
mita raH-yiwşal? raH-yiwşal bukra.	When will he arrive? He'll arrive tomorrow.

The lack of distinction in usage between the imperfect and future tense is based on a grammatical concept of tense which is different from that in European languages. Perfect and imperfect tenses are technically different from past and present tenses in that they differentiate between "completed" and "incomplete" action, rather than a time frame. For this reason, the present and future tenses have blended together somewhat, with the prefixed future tense used most often for emphasis.

2. Arabic nouns have three types of "number": singular, plural, and dual. Dual nouns are marked with the suffix /-een/ (/-teen/ for feminine nouns which end in /-a/). While we will learn a few words for which the pattern /itneen/ + plural is used, the large majority of nouns are dualized:

kitaabeen	two books
saa9ateen	two watches, two hours
madrasateen	two schools

If the noun ends in a vowel and is masculine, the ending is /-yeen/:

kursiyeen	two chairs

When a dual noun takes an adjective, it remains plural:

kitaabeen judud	two new books
saa9ateen Hilwiin	two pretty watches

3. Other expression for telling time:

as-saa9a arba9a wu xamsa.	It's 4:05.
as-saa9a arba9a wu 9ašara.	Its' 4:10.
as-saa9a arba9a wu tult.	It's 4:20. ('and one-third')
as-saa9a arba9a wu nuşş illa xamsa.	It's 4:25. ('and one-half less five')
as-saa9a arba9a wu nuşş wu xamsa.	It's 4:35. ('and one-half and five')
as-saa9a xamsa illa tult.	It's 4:40. It's 20 to 5. ('five less one-third')
as-saa9a xamsa illa 9ašara.	It's 4:50. It's 10 to 5. ('five less ten')
as-saa9a xamsa illa xamsa.	It's 4:55. It's 5 to 5. ('five less five')

4. /li muddat/ is part of a construct phrase, used with time words, literally, 'for a period of', composed of /li/, 'for', and /mudda/, 'period'. It is optional, used for clarification.

5. Numbers 11 and above are followed by nouns in the singular:

iHḍa9š kitaab	eleven books
9išriin kitaab	twenty books
miyyat sana	one hundred years
arba9 wu 9išriin saa9a	twenty-four hours

6. /Hawaali/ may alternate with /tagriiban/, 'about, approximately'. /Hawaali/ is used before the time word; /tagriiban/ may be used before or after it in the sentence.

Vocabulary Notes

	Singular	Dual	Plural	
second	saaniya	saanyateen*	sawaani	ثانية ثانيتين ثواني
minute	dagiiga	dagiigateen	dagaayig	دقيقة دقيقتين دقايق
hour	saa9a	saa9ateen	saa9aat	ساعة ساعتين ساعات
day	yoom	yoomeen	ayyaam	يوم يومين ايام
week	usbuu9	usbuu9een	asaabii9	اسبوع اسبوعين اسابيع
month	šahar	šahreen*	šuhuur	شهر شهرين شهور
year	sana	sanateen	siniin, sanawaat**	سنة سنتين سنين سنوات

* Note that the second vowel is dropped before adding the dual suffix.
** The second plural is more "classical".

biẓ-ẓabṭ	exactly	بالضبط
tagriiban	approximately	تقريبا
al-yoom	today	اليوم
bukra	tomorrow	بكرة
gabl	before	قبل
ba9deen	later	بعدين
ba9d šwayya	after a little while	بعد شويه
gariib	soon	قريب
rub9 saa9a	a quarter hour	ربع ساعة
nuṣṣ saa9a	a half hour	نص ساعة

Drills

1. He will go in an hour. Ha-yiruuH <u>ba9d saa9a</u>. حيروح بعد ساعة.

Substitute:

in a week
in two years
[for a period of] a month and a half
in five minutes
today
in a little while
later
soon, I hope
before 3:00
at 2:10 exactly

2. I will come after a long time. <u>ana raH-aji ba9d mudda ṭawiila</u>. انا رحّ أجي بعد مدة طويلة.

Substitute:

we will come
we will return
soon, I hope
tomorrow

they
later
before 5:30
go
I
after a short while
in two minutes exactly
come
in a quarter hour

3. Where is your friend (m)? feen <u>ṣaaHbak</u>? فين صاحبَك؟

Substitute:

your friend (f)
your friends
my friends
his friend (m)
our friend
her friends
her friend (f)
my friend (f)
my friend (m)
your friend (m)
your (p) friends

4.
A. When will your friend come? mita yiji ṣaaHbak? متا يجي صاحبَك؟

B. My friend will come the day after tomorrow. ṣaaHbi yiji <u>ba9d bukra</u>. صاحبي يجي بكرة.

Continue asking the question, and giving the following answers:

after an hour
in about ten minutes
soon, I think
in a year
in two weeks
in a short time
today

5. Given the phrase or sentence in the singular, change it to dual:

walad ولد
walad ṣaghiir ولد صغير
šaari9 شارع
beet بيت
ba9d usbuu9 بعد اسبوع
al-maṭaar hina. المطار هنا.
jiib kursi. جيب كرسي.
darast li-muddat šahar. درست لمدة شهر.

6. Given the word or phrase in the singular, change it to plural:

dagiiga دقيقة
šaari9 ṭawiil شارع طويل
ajnabi اجنبي
šarika amrikiyya شركة امريكية
dulaar دولار

7. Please, when will you (m) go? min faḍlak, <u>mita raH-tiruuH</u>? من فضلك متا رَحْ تروح ؟

Substitute:

When will you answer them?
What time did they leave?
Which one (m) did you (m) like?
Who will we leave with?
Was he carrying much?
Did I leave my watch here?
How did they answer the question?
What did you (p) do?

Situations

1.
A. When will your friend (m) come?
B. I don't know. Soon, I hope.
A. In about a week?
B. In a week or two, I think.
A. Maybe I will come and greet him here.
B. Welcome, of course.

2.
A. When will they arrive at the airport?
B. I don't know; I have to ask.
A. What did he say?
B. At exactly 10:20. It's still early.
A. From which door will they come?
B. That one.

3.
A. Did you (p) sleep long?
B. No, we slept an hour and a quarter. Then ('later') we took the car and went to my friend Ahmad.
A. How is Ahmad? (literally, 'Ahmad, how is he?') I've missed him.
B. Fine, he sends his greetings.
A. Thanks.

LESSON 15

Dialogue

	permit me	ismaHli	إسمحلي
	post office	bariid	بريد
A.	Permit me, how do I go to the post office?	ismaHli, keef aruuH al-bariid?	اسمحلي، كيف اروح البريد ؟
	turn	luff	لف
	right	yamiin	يمين
	end	aaxir	آخر
B.	Turn right at the end of the street	luff yamiin fi aaxir aš-šaari9.	لف يمين في آخر الشارع.
A.	And then?	wu ba9deen?	وبعدين؟
	go	ruuH	روح
	traffic light	išaara	إشارة
	left	šimaal	شمال
	facing	mugaabil	مقابل
	bank	bank	بنك
B.	Go to the light and turn left. The post office is facing the bank.	ruuH lil-išaara wu luff šimaal. al-bariid mugaabil al-bank.	روح للاشارة ولف شمال. البريد مقابل البنك.
A.	Thanks. ('you are thanked')	maškuur.	مشكور.
	thanks	šukr	شكر
	duty	waajib	واجب
B.	You're welcome. ('no thanks for a duty')	la šukr 9ala waajib.	لا شكر على واجب.

Structure Sentences

1.	The school is beside the post office.	al-madrasa jamb al-bariid.	المدرسة جنب البريد.
2.	The post office is straight ahead, behind the bank.	al-bariid dughri, wara l-bank.	البريد دغري، ورا البنك.
3.	Cross the street.	9addi š-šaari9.	عدّي الشارع.
4.	The ministry is at the beginning of the street.	al-wizaara fi awwal aš-šaari9.	الوزارة في اول الشارع.

5. Cross there.   9addi min hinaak.   عدي من هناك.

Grammatical Notes

1. /luff/ and /ruuH/ are examples of the imperative (command) in Arabic.

The imperative is formed from the second person form of the imperfect verb, omitting the person prefixes:

Verb		Imperative		
laff, yiluff	(m)	luff	turn	لف
(basic form: tiluff)	(f)	luffi		لفّي
	(p)	luffu		لفّوا
9adda, yi9addi	(m)	9addi*	cross	عدي
(basic form: ti9addi)	(f)	9addi*		عدي
	(p)	9addu		عدّوا
katab, yiktub	(m)	iktub	write	اكتب
(basic form: tiktub)	(f)	iktubi		اكتبي
	(p)	iktubu		اكتبوا

*If the masculine imperative ends in /-i/, it cannot be distinguished from the feminine imperative.

Other verbs presented			
so far:	iftaH	open	افتح
(in the masculine	igfil	close	اقفل
imperative form;	i9mil	do	اعمل
feminine and plural	idrus	study	ادرس
are predictable)	itkallam	speak	اتكلّم
	9arrif	introduce	عرّف
	ista'zin	take permission	استأذن
	ista9mil	use	استعمل
	ruuH	go	روح
	šuuf	see	شوف
	naam	sleep	نام
	guul	say	قول
	jiib	bring	جيب
	is'al	ask	اسأل
	xud	take	خذ
	imši	go	امشي
	sawwi	do	سوّي
	siib	leave behind	سيب
	šiil	carry	شيل
	rudd	answer	ردّ
	Huṭṭ	put	حطّ
	insa	forget	انسَ

/ja/ has an irregular imperative:

(m) ta9aal	come		تعال
(f) ta9aali			تعالي
(p) ta9aalu			تعالوا

3. /išaara/, 'traffic light', may also refer to any type of signal.

4. When asking and giving directions, /min/ may be used in Arabic, and is usually not translated into English:

niruuH min feen?	Which way do we go?
ruuHu min hina.	Go here. Go this way.
ruuHu min hinaak.	Go there. Go that way.

Vocabulary Notes

Prepositions

mugaabil	facing	مقابل
guddaam	in front of	قدام
wara	behind	ورا
jamb	beside	جنب
foog	up; above	فوق
taHat	down; below	تحت
barra	outside	برا
juwwa	inside	جوا

Verbs

laff, yiluff (laffeet)	turn	لف يلف (لفيت)
9adda, yi9addi (9addeet)	cross	عدى يعدي (عديت)

Nouns

išaara, -aat	traffic signal	اشارة -ات
kubri, kabaari	bridge	كبري كباري
9imaara, -aat	building	عمارة -ات
bank, bunuuk	bank	بنك بنوك
waajib, -aat	duty	واجب -ات

Drills

1. Turn right at the end of the street. — luff yamiin fi aaxir aš-šaari9. — لف يمين في آخر الشارع.

Substitute:

at the beginning of the street
on that street
at Mecca Road
left
after that building
behind the bank
before the traffic signal
near the post office

2. Given the sentence in the perfect tense, change it to a command (to a man):

fataH al-baab.	فتح الباب.
sallam 9alee.	سلم عليه.
gafal al-baab.	قفل الباب.
sawwa l-waajib.	سوى الواجب.
axad as-sayyaara.	اخذ السيارة.
raaH al-maṭaar.	راح المطار.

Repeat, giving the command to a woman, to a group.

3. Then go straight. ba9deen ruuH dughri. بعدين روح دغري.

Substitute:

cross the bridge
turn left
go inside
come here
open your book
introduce your friends
use my car
take ten dollars
cross from there
do your homework (literally, 'your duty')

Repeat, giving the command to a woman, to a group.

4. The post office is facing the bank. al-bariid mugaabil al-bank. البريد مقابل البنك.

Substitute:

inside
in front of
beside
above
beside, on the right
the bridge
on the left
the building
under
outside
near

5. This car is from Germany. haadi s-sayyaara min almaanya. هادي السيارة من المانيا.

Substitute:

England
overseas (literally, 'outside')
Japan
my brother
my father
our friends

Situations

1.
A. Permit me, where is the bank building?
B. The bank building is on that street.
A. How do I go?
B. Cross the street, go to the signal, and go straight ahead. The building is at the end of the street.
A. Can I leave my car there?
B. Yes, in front of the building.

2.
A. Where is the Foreign Ministry?
B. Not far from the embassy. Go to the light and turn right.
A. Will I see it on the right?
B. No, on the left.
A. Thanks.
B. Not at all. ('No thanks for a duty')

LESSON 16

Dialogue

	say	guul	قول
	costs	yikallif	يكلف
A.	Tell me, how much does this cost?	guul, haada yikallif kam?	قول، هادا يكلف كم؟
	cheap	raxiiṣ	رخيص
	without	bala	بلا
	money	fuluus	فلوس
B.	This is cheap. No charge.	haada raxiiṣ. bala fuluus.*	هادا رخيص. بلا فلوس.
A.	So how much?	ya9ni gaddeeš?	يعني قديش؟
B.	Twenty riyals.	9išriin riyaal bass.	عشرين ريال بس.
	believable	ma9guul	معقول
	expensive	ghaali	غالي
	I give	addi	ادي
A.	Unbelievable! That's very expensive. I'll give you ten.	muu ma9guul! haada marra ghaali. ana addiik 9ašara.	مو معقول! هادا مرة غالي. انا اديك عشرة.
B.	No, no.	la', la'.	لا، لا.
	speech	kalaam	كلام
A.	How much then? Final price. ('final speech')	b-kam? aaxir kalaam.	بكم؟ آخر كلام.
	sake	xaaṭir	خاطر
B.	OK, just for you, 18.	ṭayyib, 9ašaan xaaṭrak, tamanṭa9š.	طيب عشان خاطرَك ثمنتعش.
	finished	xalaš	خلص
A.	Twelve...OK, 15 and that's it.	itna9š...ṭayyib, xamasṭa9š wu xalaṣ.	اثنعش.. طيب، خمستعش وخلص.
	congratulations ('blessed')	mabruuk	مبروك
B.	OK. Congratulations.	ṭayyib. mabruuk.	طيب. مبروك.
	bless	yibaarik	يبارك
A.	Thanks. ('May God bless you')	aḷḷaah yibaarik fiik.	الله يبارك فيك.

*A common alternative way to say this is /b-balaaš/.

Structure Sentences

1.	This is ten piastres, half a riyal.	haada b-9ašara guruuš, nuṣṣ riyaal.	هادا بعشرة قروش، نص ريال.
2.	Money is important.	al-fuluus muhimma.	الفلوس مهمة.
3.	Go for his sake.	ruuH 9ašaan xaaṭru.	روح عشان خاطره.
4.	Can you give me two riyals?	mumkin tiddiini riyaaleen?	ممكن تديني ريالين؟
5.	Congratulations on the new car.	mabruuk 9ala s-sayyaara l-jadiida.	مبروك على السيارة الجديدة.
6.	The book cost me eight dollars.	al-kitaab kallafni tamanya dulaar.	الكتاب كلفني ثمانية دولار.
7.	Its price is reasonable.	si9ru ma9guul.	سعره معقول.
8.	The price is fixed.	as-si9r maHduud.	السعر محدود.
9.	I spent a lot of money.	ṣaraft fuluus katiir.	صرفتْ فلوس كثير.
10.	Anything else? ('Any other service?')	ayy xidma taanya?	اي خدمة ثانية؟

Grammatical Notes

1. /guul/, 'tell me', is very informal. Also used is /aguul/, 'I'll tell [you]', 'hey!'.

2. /bala/, 'without', is used with inanimate objects, especially money:

raaH bala fuluus.	He went without money.

For persons, /min gheer/ is used (some speakers use this word exclusively):

raaH min gheer axuu.	He went without his brother.

3. /fuluus/, 'money', is a feminine noun, and takes feminine adjectives (except for /katiir/, which is not declined for gender or number).

4. /kam/, 'how many', and /gaddeeš/, 'how much', are interchangeable when discussing prices, but not in other situations. /b-kam/ is the most common expression for inquiring about a price.

5. The basic unit of money in Saudi Arabia is the Saudi riyal, which contains twenty piastres, each of which contains five halala.

haada b-riyaal.	This is ('costs') one riyal.
haada b-riyaal waaHid.	This is one riyal.
haada b-riyaal wu nuṣṣ.	This is one and one-half riyals.
haada b-riyaal wu garšeen.	This is one riyal and two piastres.
haada b-rub9 riyaal.	This is a quarter riyal.
haada b-riyaaleen.	This is two riyals.
haada b-xamsa riyaal.	This is five riyals.
haada b-xamasṭa9š riyaal.	This is fifteen riyals.
haada b-9ašara guruuš.	This is ten piastres.
haada b-nuṣṣ garš.	This is one-half piastre.

6. /adda, yiddi/, 'to give', is usually used with direct object pronouns (this is an idiom); its use with indirect object pronouns (with /li-/) is technically more correct, but is usually heard in Meccan speech, and is not presented here.

(some examples)

addaani	he gave me
addaahum	he gave them
addatni	she gave me
addatak	she gave you (m)
addoohum	they gave them
addeetaha	I gave her
addeenaa	we gave him

7. /9ašaan xaaṭrak/, 'for your sake', is conjugated for all persons. Note that before suffixes which begin with a vowel, the /i/ is dropped:

(Basic word: xaaṭir, 'sake')

9ašaan xaaṭru	for his sake
9ašaan xaaṭirha	for her sake
9ašaan xaaṭirhum	for their sake
9ašaan xaaṭrak	for your (m) sake
9ašaan xaaṭrik	for your (f) sake
9ašaan xaaṭirkum	for your (p) sake
9ašaan xaaṭri	for my sake
9ašaan xaaṭirna	for our sake

This is often abbreviated to /9ašaan/ + the pronoun:

9ašaanu	for him
9ašaanaha	for her
9ašaanahum	for them
9ašaanak	for you (m)
9ašaanik	for you (f)
9ašaanakum	for you (p)
9ašaani	for me
9ašaanana	for us

8. /mabruuk/ is used with the preposition /9ala/ (/9a/) to mean 'congratulations on..., for...' (cf. Structure Sentence 5).

9. /taani/ (/taanya, taanyiin/) literally means 'second', but is frequently used to mean 'other' or 'else':

ayy xidma taanya?	Any other service?

Vocabulary Notes

adda, yiddi (addeet)	give	ادى يدي (اديت)
kallaf, yikallif	cost	كلف يكلف
ṣaraf, yiṣruf	spend, exchange money	صرف يصرف
si9r, as9aar	price	سعر اسعار
riyaal, -aat	riyal	ريال -ات
garš, guruuš	piastre	قرش قروش
xidma, xadamaat	service	خدمة خدمات

bass	only	بس
ghaali, -yiin raxiiṣ, ruxaaṣ	expensive cheap	غالي-ين رخيص رخاص

Drills

1. How much does this cost? — haada yikallif kam? — هادا يكلف كم؟

Substitute:

these
those
this book
that car
these pens

2. His house cost him a lot. — beetu kallafu katiir. — بيته كلفه كثير.

Substitute:

his car
her house
my watch
the chairs
the company's car
the new airport

3. He went without money. — raaH bala fuluus. — راح بلا فلوس.

Substitute:

his brother
their son
his books
his brothers and sisters
his watch

4. I'll give you ten. — addiik 9ašara. — اديك عشرة.

Substitute:

money
he will give you (m)
she will give you (m)
she will give me
we will give them
a good price
they will give us
they must give us
a fixed price

5. I gave the man five riyals. — addeet lir-rijjaal xamsa riyaal. — اديت للرجال خمسة ريال.

Substitute:

only three piastres
he gave
we gave
eleven riyals
she gave us

her
the homework
her watch
me

6. Congratulations on the new car. — mabruuk 9ala s-sayyaara l-jadiida. — مبروك على السيارة الجديدة.

Substitute:

the new watch
the new [baby] boy
your book
the new house
the new car

Situations

1.
A. How much is this (f)?
B. Only ten riyals.
A. No, give me a reasonable price.
B. For you, nine.
A. That's very expensive.
B. That's the final price.

2.
A. His car is very big.
B. Yes, and expensive, too. He spent a lot of money.
A. Is it new?
B. Yes, he bought it from France. Oh, sorry (/9afwan/), from Germany.

3.
A. I got this pen for a half riyal.
B. Unbelievable! That's a good price. How did you do it?
A. I spoke in Arabic and he gave me the pen for that price.
B. You should get two or three.
A. Yes, maybe.

Cultural Notes

1. Much purchasing in the Arab world, especially in the "souk" (market), is made through a bargaining process. Generally, you offer back about one-half to two-thirds of the quoted price, and gradually the buyer and seller meet somewhere in the middle. Many establishments have now instituted "fixed prices", for example, grocery stores and pharmacies.

2. /mabruuk/, 'congratulations', is used much more frequently in Arabic than in English. It is used not only for "significant" occasions (a wedding, birth of a child, graduation, etc.), but also, for example, when someone has made a purchase or finished a task.

LESSON 17

Dialogue

	pleased	9ajab	عجب
A.	I like this. How much?	haada 9ajabni. b-kam?	هادا عجبني· بكم؟
	sure	mit'akkid	متأكد
B.	I'm not sure. Wait a moment. Ten riyals.	ana mana mit'akkid. istanna šwayya. 9ašara riyaal.	انا منا متأكد· استنّ شويه· عشرة ريال·
	better	aHsan	احسن
	or else	wala	ولا
	I buy	aštari	اشتري
A.	That's too much. Tell me a better price or I won't buy anything.	haada katiir. gulli si9r aHsan wala ma aštari šayy.	هادا كثير· قوللي سعر احسن ولا ما اشتري شي·
	speech	kalaam	كلام
B.	Ten riyals, that's all.	9ašara riyaal, aaxir kalaam.	عشرة ريال، آخر كلام·
	never mind	ma9aleeš	معليش
	maybe	yimkin	يمكن
A.	OK, never mind. Maybe later.	ṭayyib ma9aleeš. yimkin ba9deen, in šaa' aḷḷaah.	طيب معليش· يمكن بعدين ان شاء الله·
	you (m) want	tibgha	تبغى
B.	Do you want to see anything else?	tibgha tišuuf šayy taani?	تبغى تشوف شي ثاني؟
A.	Not now, thanks.	muu daHHiin, šukran.	مو دحين، شكرا·

Structure Sentences

1.	I want to buy an American car.	abgha aštari sayyaara amrikiyya.	ابغى اشتري سيارة امريكية·
2.	I'm sure that Ahmad went.	ana mit'akkid innu aHmad raaH.	انا متأكد انه احمد راح·
3.	He bought another watch.	aštara saa9a taanya.	اشترىَ ساعة ثانية·
4.	Come another time.	ta9aal marra taanya.	تعال مرة ثانية·
5.	I don't like these things.	haadi l-ašyaa' ma ti9jibni.	هادي الاشياء ما تعجبني·
6.	Never mind, it's not important.	ma9aleeš, muu muhimm.	معليش مو مهم·

7.	He won't want to spend a lot of money.	ma yibgha yiṣruf fuluus katiir.	ما يبغي يصرف فلوس كثير.
8.	Take this or this.	xud haada aw haada.	خذ هادا او هادا.
9.	Do you want this or this?	tibgha haada walla haada?	تبغى هادا ولا هادا؟
10.	Maybe he'll arrive early.	yimkin yiwṣal badri.	يمكن يوصل بدري.

Grammatical Notes

1. /9ajab, yi9jib/, 'to please', is used with a direct object. It is generally translated into English as 'to like', in which case its structure is the reverse of the English expression. The verb is most commonly used in the perfect tense, and may mean past or present; this may be considered idiomatic.

9ajabni.	I liked it (m). ('it pleased me')
9ajabatni.	I liked it (f). I like it (f).
9ajabooni.	I liked them. I like them.
yi9jibni.	I like him.
ti9jibni.	I like her.
yi9jibooni.	I like them.
yi9jiboona.	We like them.
haada 9ajabak?	Do you (m) like this (m)?
haadi 9ajabatak?	Do you (m) like this (f)?
humma 9ajaboo.	He likes them.

2. /innu/ 'that', is used as a "relative pronoun" to introduce a clause. It may also be used with a pronoun suffix:

innu*	that he...
innaha	that she...
innahum	that they...
innak	that you (m)...
innik	that you (f)...
innakum	that you (p)...
inni	that I...
innana	that we...

*Note that the word /innu/ may simply mean 'that' (rather than 'that he'), without referring to anything else in the sentence.

ana mit'akkid innu haada ghaali.	I am sure that this is expensive.
ana faahim innu haada ghalaṭ.	I understand that this is wrong.
ana faahim innaha jaat.	I understand that she came.
iHna mit'akkidiin innahum judud.	We are sure that they are new.

3. /wala/, /aw/, and /walla/ may all be translated 'or' in English.

/wala/ is used to mean 'or else' or 'nor' in negative statements:

...wala ma aštari šayy.	...or [else] I won't buy anything.
ma kaan fil-beet wala fil-maktab.	He was not at home nor ('or') at the office.

/aw/ is used for affirmative statements:

xud haada aw haada.	Take this or this.
addiini itneen aw talaata.	Give me two or three.

/walla/ is used for questions:

tibgha haada walla haada?	Do you want this or this?
huwwa raaH walla la'?	Did he go or not ('or no')?

It can be used with /amma/ to mean 'either...or':

amma bukra walla ba9deen.	Either tomorrow or later.
amma huwwa walla hiyya.	Either he or she.

/aw/ and /walla/ are used interchangeably by some speakers.

4. /ma/ is used as the negation word for verbs in the perfect, imperfect, and future tenses:

aHmad ma raaH.	Ahmad did not go.
ma aštari b-haada s-si9r.	I won't buy for this price.
ma sawwat šayy.	She didn't do anything.
ma gafalu l-beet.	They didn't close the house.
ma H-as'al as-su'aal haada.	I won't ask this question.
ma raH-nista9mil haadi l-fuluus.	We won't use this money.
ma Ha-yiju bukra.	They won't come tomorrow.

It is also used with /fii/, 'there is', 'there are':

fii naas katiir.	There are many people.
ma fii naas katiir.	There are not many people.
fii šayy hinaak.	There is something there.
ma fii šayy hinaak.	There isn't anything there.

5. /yibgha/, 'to want', may be used alone or as a helping verb with other verbs in a verb phrase. It is almost always used in the imperfect tense or with /kaan/:

abgha atkallam ingiliizi.	I want to speak English.
ma nibgha niftaH al-baab.	We don't want to open the door.
ma kunt abgha ašuufaha.	I didn't want to see her.
kaanu yibghu yi9arrifoo 9alayya.	They wanted to introduce him to me.

/yibgha/ is a "pure" Saudi word, and is not heard in other Arabic dialects. When speaking with foreigners or non-Saudi Arabs, Saudis may use forms taken from other dialects, such as /biddi/ (/biddak/, /biddaha/, etc.), taken from Palestinian, or /9aawiz/ (/9aawza/, /9aawziin/), taken from Egyptian.

6. /yimkin/, 'maybe', may be used alone or as a modal word with an imperfect verb (like /laazim/ and /mumkin/). It does not change form:

yimkin yiwṣal badri.	Maybe he will arrive early.
yimkin tiwṣal badri.	Maybe she will arrive early.

Vocabulary Notes

šayy, ašyaa'	thing	شي اشياء
baa9, yibii9 (bi9t)	sell	باع يبيع (بعت)
aštara, yištari (aštareet)	buy	اشترى يشتري (اشتريت)

Drills

1. I like this. ('This pleased me.')	<u>haada 9ajabni</u>.	هادا عجبني.

Substitute:

those
pleased them
pleased her
this room
pleased me
that house
pleased us
that house
pleased us
that thing
this thing

2. I don't know anything.	<u>ma a9rif</u> šayy.	ما اعرف شي.

Substitute:

huwwa	هو
humma	هم
iHna	احنا
hiyya	هي
uxti	اختي
axwaati	اخواتي
ṣaaHbi	صاحبي
intu	انتو

3. Do you (m) want to see anything else?	tibgha tišuuf šayy taani?	تبغى تشوف شي ثاني؟

Substitute:

she
you (p)
the house
he
they
this or that
you (f)

4. I want to buy a car. — abgha aštari sayyaara. — ابغى اشتري سيارة.

Substitute:

we
they
she
you (m)
the people
he
you (f)
my father
you (p)
my friends
my wife

5. He bought another watch. — aštara saa9a taanya. — اشترى ساعة ثانية.

Substitute:

another house
she
I
new car
old book
we
another table
he
they

6. I'm sure that Ahmad went. — ana mit'akkid innu aHmad raaH. — انا متأكد انه احمد راح.

Substitute:

we
she
that they went
that it is correct
he
that it (f) cost a lot
that you (m) must buy one
they
that he is good
that she is Russian

7. Tomorrow we'll buy another book. — bukra ništari kitaab taani. — بكرة نشتري كتاب ثاني.

Substitute:

many things
they buy
you (m) buy
some pens
you (p)
she
he

8. Given the sentence in the affirmative, change it to negative:

darasat 9arabi.	درست عربي.
Ha-tiwṣal ba9d bukra.	حتوصل بعد بكرة.
saab uxtu fil-beet.	ساب اخته في البيت.
ana gult haada.	انا قلت هادا.
ana adri feen humma.	انا ادري فين هم.
waHašni.	وحشني.
Haṭṭeetahum 9aṭ-ṭarabiiza.	حطيتهم عَالطربيزة.
Ha-niruuH ba9deen.	حنروح بعدين.
sibna l-ašyaa' wara l-baab.	سبنا الأشياء ورا الباب.

Situations

1.
A. How do I go to the city?
B. Cross the bridge and then straight ahead. Can you take my friend (m)?
A. Of course. We will go in my car.
B. Thanks. He wants to buy something there.

2.
A. When will you (p) go?
B. If God wills, at the end of the month. I'm not sure.
A. You should go now.
B. We want to go now, but we spent [so] much money.
A. Well, never mind.

3.
A. I want to buy those chairs. I like them.
B. Yes, we saw them yesterday and liked them, too.
A. How much do they cost?
B. I asked and the man told me a reasonable price, about thirty riyals.
A. Good, I'll take three or four.
B. Me too.

4.
A. When will your friend (f) leave?
B. I asked her but she didn't answer me.
A. I think she wants to leave on Thursday.
B. She's not sure.

LESSON 18

Dialogue

	age	9umr	عمر
A.	How old are you?	kam 9umrak?	كم عمرك؟
	holiday	9iid	عيد
	birth	miilaad	ميلاد
	coming	jayy	جي
	January	yanaayir	يناير
B.	I'm 25. My birthday will be next month, in January.	9umri xamsa wu 9išriin sana. 9iid miilaadi Ha-yikuun as-šahar al-jayy fi yanaayir.	عمري خمسة وعشرين سنة. عيد ميلادي حيكون الشهر الجي في يناير.
	older, bigger	akbar	اكبر
	born	mawluud	مولود
A.	I'm older than you. I was born in 1948. ('I am born in 1948.')	ana akbar minnak. ana mawluud fi 9aam alf wu tis9miyya wu tamanya w arba9iin.	انا اكبر منك. انا مولود في عام الف وتسعمية وثمانية واربعين.
B.	Really?	ṣaHiiH?	صحيح؟
A.	Yes, I'm two years older than you. I'm the oldest of my brothers and sisters.	iiwa, ana akbar minnak b-sanateen. ana akbar axwaani.	ايوه ، انا اكبر منك بسنتين. انا اكبر اخواني.

Structure Sentences

1.	He is three and one-half.	9umru talaata siniin wu nuṣṣ.	عمره ثلاثة سنين ونص
2.	She is eleven.	9umraha iHḍa9š sana.	عمرها احدعش سنة.
3.	My birthday is the day after tomorrow.	9iid miilaadi ba9d bukra.	عيد ميلادي بعد بكرة.
4.	Let's go next week.	yaḷḷa niruuH al-usbuu9 al-jayy.	يلله نروح الاسبوع الجي.
5.	Let's go (leave).	yaḷḷa nimši.	يلله نمشي.
6.	This is more beautiful.	haada ajmal.	هادا اجمل.
7.	She is older than her sister.	hiyya akbar min uxtaha.	هي اكبر من اختها.
8.	This is the most beautiful.	haada l-ajmal.	هادا الاجمل.
9.	This is the cheapest book.	haada l-kitaab al-arxaṣ.	هادا الكتاب الارخص.
10.	This is the cheapest book.	haada arxaṣ kitaab.	هادا ارخص كتاب.

Grammatical Notes

1. /kam/, 'how many', is followed by a singular noun:

kam sana	how many years?
kam kitaab	how many books?
kam waaHid	how many [ones]?

2. /jayy/, 'next' (literally, 'coming'), is used with time words, and agrees in gender with the noun it modifies:

al-usbuu9 al-jayy	next week
aš-šahar al-jayy	next month
yoom al-itneen al-jayy	next Monday
as-sana l-jayya	next year
as-siniin al-jayya	the coming years

3. The "foreign" months (/aš-šuhuur al-ifranjiyya/) are:

yanaayir	January	يناير
fibraayir	February	فبراير
maaris	March	مارس
abriil	April	ابريل
maayu	May	مايو
yuunya	June	يونيا
yuulya	July	يوليا
ughusṭus	August	اغسطس
sibtambar	September	سبتمبر
uktuubar	October	اكتوبر
nufambar	November	نفمبر
disambar	December	د سمبر

Arabia officially follows the Islamic calendar, with its own months (Lesson 47), but Saudis frequently use the western months when dealing with foreigners.

4. When citing a year, the number is usually preceded by /9aam/, 'the year of' (this is the classical word for 'year'). If the year is after 1900, the numbers 'one thousand and nine hundred' may be omitted:

9aam alf wu tis9miyya wu sab9a wu sittiin	1967
9aam sab9a wu sittiin	1967

5. The pattern for forming comparative adjectives is:

$aC_1C_2aC_3$

Some adjectives are slightly irregular because of the root consonants:

Base Form	Comparative	
kabiir	akbar	big, bigger; old, older
ṣaghiir	aṣghar	small, smaller
katiir	aktar	much, more
Hilu	aHla	pretty, prettier
ghaali	aghla	expensive, more expensive
muhimm	ahamm	important, more important

The comparative adjective is used alone or with /min/ (cf. Structure Sentences 6 and 7.)

To make the adjective superlative, the same form is used with the definite article /al-/, or in construct with a noun (cf. Structure Sentences 8, 9, and 10.)

These adjective forms do not change for gender and number.

6. Some adjectives cannot be made comparative with this pattern:

Base Form	Comparative	
mabsuuṭ	mabsuuṭ aktar	happy, happier

7. /mawluud/, 'born', is declined for gender and number:

(m) mawluud
(f) mawluuda
(p) mawluudiin

8. /min/, when used with pronoun suffixes, has the base form /minn-/:

minnu	from him
minnaha	from her
minnahum	from them
minnak	from you (m)
minnik	from you (f)
minnakum	from you (p)
minni	from me
minnana	from us

9. /yaḷḷa/ is used as 'let's go', 'hurry up'. It may be used alone, with an imperfect verb in the 'we' form (cf. Structure Sentences 4 and 5), or with an imperative verb.

Vocabulary Notes

jamiil, (no plural)	beautiful	جميل
galiil, -a, -iin	few	قليل -ين

Summary of adjectives:

Base Form	Comparative Form (regular)	
kabiir	akbar	اكبر
ṣaghiir	aṣghar	اصغر
katiir	aktar	اكثر
gadiim	agdam	اقدم
ṭawiil	aṭwal	اطول
gaṣiir	agṣar	اقصر
tagiil	atgal	اثقل
laṭiif	alṭaf	الطف
ba9iid	ab9ad	ابعد
gariib	agrab	اقرب
wiHiš	awHaš	اوحش
raxiiṣ	arxaṣ	ارخص
jamiil	ajmal	اجمل
ṭayyib	aṭyab	اطيب
	(irregular)	
jadiid	ajadd	اجد
xafiif	axaff	اخف
galiil	agall	اقل
muhimm	ahamm	اهم

ghaali	aghla	اغلى
Hilu	aHla	احلى
mabsuuṭ	mabsuuṭ aktar	مبسوط اكثر
ta9baan	ta9baan aktar	تعبان اكثر
ma9guul	ma9guul aktar	معقول اكثر

The word most often used as comparative for 'good' is irregular. (It comes from a classical word, /Hasan/, 'good', which is not used in this dialect.)

aHsan	better	احسن

Drills

1. How old are you (m)? — kam 9umrak? — كم عمرَك؟

Substitute:

she
they
I
you (f)
he
you (p)

2. I am 25 years old. — 9umri xamsa wu 9išriin sana. — عمري خمسة وعشرين سنة.

Substitute:

he
you (p)
you (f)
she
they

3. My birthday will be next month. — 9iid miilaadi Ha-yikuun aš-šahar al-jayy. — عيد ميلادي حيكون الشهر الجي.

Substitute:

our birthday
his birthday
next week
next Tuesday
your (f) birthday
their birthday
next Friday
my birthday
next month

4. I was born in 1948. — ana mawluud fi 9aam alf wu tis9miyya wu tamanya w arba9iin. — انا مولود في عام الف وتسعمية وثمانية واربعين.

Substitute:

she
1951
my brother
they
we
1935
he
1893

5. I am older than you (m). ana akbar minnak. انا اكبر منّك.

Substitute:

than he
younger (smaller)
more handsome
than they
than she
shorter
newer
than you (p)
better
than you (m)

6. He is older by two years. huwwa akbar b-sanateen. هو اكبر بسنتين.

Substitute:

3 years
2 weeks
17 years
8 months
5 1/2 hours
many years

7. Let's go. yaḷḷa niruuH. يلله نروح.

Substitute:

Let's do that.
Let's close the house.
(to a man) Close the door.
(to a woman) Bring the chair.
Let's go outside.
(to a group) Buy it (m).

8. This is the cheapest book. haada arxaṣ kitaab. هادا ارخص كتاب.

Substitute:

the prettiest girl
the best room
the lightest book
the longest sentence
the biggest door
the most expensive car
the nicest boy
the most important question

9. Given the adjective, change it to comparative:

al-walad gaṣiir. الولد قصير.
ana mabsuuṭ. انا مبسوط.
haada kwayyis. هادا كويس.
al-imtiHaan ṭawiil. الامتحان طويل.
al-waraga xafiifa. الورقة خفيفة.
al-maaṣa Hilwa. الماصة حلوة.
as-si9r ghaali. السعر غالي.
al-fuluus galiila. الفلوس قليلة.

Situations

1.
A. When is your son's birthday?
B. My son's birthday is next week.
A. How old is he?
B. Five. He'll be six in a week.
A. Six years? He's big!
B. Yes, older than my daughter by three years.

2.
A. What are you doing?
B. I have to go to the office.
A. Really?
B. Yes, I have to see someone ('one') there.
A. What time will he come?
B. Soon. I must excuse myself.
A. Go ahead.

3.
A. Do we have to take the car?
B. No. I think it's not necessary.
A. Can we go this way ('from here') ?
B. Of course, that's a good street. It goes to the post office and near my bank ('the bank belonging to me').
A. That's the most important thing.

LESSON 19

Dialogue

	you (m) have	9indak	عندَك
A.	How many brothers and sisters do you (m) have?	9indak kam axx w uxt?	عندك كم اخ واخت؟
B.	I have three brothers and three sisters.	9indi talaata axwaan wu talaata axwaat.	عندي ثلاثة اخوان وثلاثة اخوات.
	married	mitzawwij	متزوج
A.	Are they married?	humma mitzawwijiin?	هم متزوجين؟
	engaged	maxṭuub	مخطوب
	university	jaam9a	جامعة
B.	One sister is married and one is engaged. My brothers are in the university.	waHda min axwaati mitzawwija wu waHda maxṭuuba. axwaani fil-jaam9a.	واحدة من اخواتي متزوجة وواحدة مخطوبة. اخواني في الجامعة.
	father	waalid	والد
	mother	waalida	والدة
	present	mawjuud	موجود
A.	Are your father and mother living? ('present')	waalidak wu waalidatak mawjuudiin?	والدك ووالدتك موجودين؟
B.	Yes.	iiwa.	ايوه.

Structure Sentences

1.	I was married a year ago.	atzawwajt gabl sana.	اتزوجت قبل سنة.
2.	She has been married since last year. ('is married')	hiyya mitzawwija min al-9aam al-maaḍi.	هي متزوجة من العام الماضي.
3.	He arrived the day before yesterday.	waṣal awwal ams.	وصل اول امس.
4.	He is not alive.	huwwa muu 9aayiš.	هو مو عايش.

Grammatical Notes

1. /9ind/ is a preposition usually translated into English as the verb 'to have'. When used in this way, it takes pronoun endings:

9indaha fuluus.	She has money.
ma 9indahum šayy.	They don't have anything.

/9ind/ may also mean 'at the home of' (used like "chez" in French):

ruHt 9ind aHmad.	I went to Ahmad's house.
jaa 9indi mit'axxir.	He came to my house late.
ta9aal 9indana.	Come to our house.

2. /mitzawwij/, 'married', is an example of a "passive participle" in Arabic. This is a predictable pattern and functions like an adjective; it refers to a "state resulting from the action of a verb", and is derived from transitive verbs. Examples:

Verbs like /katab/:
Pattern: $maC_1C_2uuC_3$

katab	maktuub	written
xaṭab	maxṭuub	engaged
wajad	mawjuud	present ('found')

Other Verbs:
Pattern: /mi/ or /mu/ + imperfect verb stem

(yitzawwij)	mitzawwij
(yit'akkid)	mit'akkid

The feminine form is predictable, and the plural form is almost always the suffix /-iin/.

Not all verbs can have a passive participle; some have another passive form (Lesson 37).

3. /waalid/ and /waalida/ are honorific terms for 'father' and 'mother'. They are frequently used when referring to parents, as a sign of respect.

4. To express 'last' or past time, the word /maaḍi/, 'past', is used. It is declined to agree in gender with the noun it modifies:

al-usbuu9 al-maaḍi	last week
aš-šahar al-maaḍi	last month
as-sana l-maaḍya	last year
yoom ar-rabuu9 al-maaḍi	last Wednesday

5. /min/, 'from', is also used to mean 'since' (cf. Structure Sentence 2).

6. The use of /mawjuud/ to mean 'living' or 'present' is idiomatic; more precise is the word /9aayiš/ (/9aayša/, /9aayšiin/), 'alive'.

7. /awwal ams/, 'the day before yesterday', is an idiomatic expression.

Vocabulary Notes

Regular Pattern

mawjuud	present, found	موجود
mawluud	born	مولود
maxṭuub	engaged	مخطوب
maktuub	written	مكتوب
mafhuum	understood	مفهوم
ma9muul	done	معمول
maškuur	thanked	مشكور
maftuuH	opened	مفتوح
magfuul	closed	مقفول
ma9ruuf	known	معروف
mabsuuṭ	pleased	مبسوط
maHbuub	beloved	محبوب
ma9guul	reasonable	معقول
mabruuk	blessed	مبروك
maHduud	limited	محدود

Other Pattern

mit'axxir	late ('delayed')	متأخر
mit'akkid	certain	متأكد
mitzawwij	married	متزوج
musta9mal	used	مستعمل
atzawwaj, yitzawwij	get married	اتزوج يتزوج
at'akkad, yit'akkid	be certain	اتأكد يتأكد
jaam9a, -aat	university	جامعة -ات

Drills

1. Are they married? humma mitzawwijiin? هم متزوجين؟

Substitute:

inti انتِ
axuuk اخوك
intu انتو
inta انتَ

2. Given the verb in the perfect tense, using the passive particple:

Example: gafal al-baab. ⟶ al-baab magfuul. قفل الباب ← الباب مقفول.
Continue:
katab ad-dars. كتب الدرس.
fihim al-jumla. فهم الجملة.
9amal haada. عمل هادا.
9irif al-beet. عرف البيت.

3. My sister is engaged. uxti maxtuuba. اختي مخطوبة.

Substitute:

married
late
my father
present
alive
my mother
happy
certain

4. This is understood. haada mafhuum. هادا مفهوم.

Substitute:

well-known ('known')
written
used
reasonable
closed
done
opened

5. I was married a year ago. atzawwajt gabl sana. اتزوجت قبل سنة.

Substitute:

they
two weeks ago
she
my friend (m)
three months ago
we
years ago
he
I
a year ago

6. She has been married since last year. hiyya mitzawwija min al-9aam al-maaḍi. هي متزوجة من العام الماضي.

Substitute:

last month
last Saturday
they
last week
he
last Thursday
we
my sister
I
last year
she

7. Let's go to my house. niruuH 9indi. نروح عندي.

Substitute:

to his house
to Ahmad's house
to our house
to my sister's house
to their house
to my father's house

Situations

1.
A. Have you heard of this book?
(literally, 'Do you know this book?')
B. Yes, it's well known ('known'). It was written long ago.
A. I want to buy it.
B. It's not necessary. You can take it from me.
A. When should I bring it?
(literally, 'When do I bring it?')
B. Later, after a month or two.

2.
A. Is your brother married?
B. No, he'll be married next week.
A. Whom will he marry?
B. Abdel-Rahman's daughter. She's very young, 16 years old.
A. Really? Congratulations.
B. Thanks. (response)

3.
A. Did you go to the university today?
B. Yes, I gave them money.
A. Is the university expensive?
B. Not [too] expensive. Reasonable.
A. I want to go to the university, too.
B. When you are older, if God wills.

LESSON 20

Review last nine dialogues.

Supplementary Drills

1. I want to buy those. abgha <u>aštari hadool</u>. ابغى اشتري هدول.

Substitute:

take money from him
get married soon
go to the airport
turn left from there
speak French
cross the bridge
get something ('thing') cheaper
spend less money
use their car
see the best room
greet her

(Repeat, using 'he', 'she', 'they', 'we'.)

2. Please go early. min faḍlak, <u>ruuH badri</u>. من فضلَك روح بدري.

Substitute:

bring a small one (m)
turn behind the building
talk with those foreigners
tell him "it doesn't matter"
take them to the airport
ask at ('in') the university
give me five piastres
come a little early

(Repeat, using feminine and plural forms)

3. Who lives in this house? miin <u>saakin fi haada l-beet</u>? مين ساكن فى هادا البيت؟

Substitute:

is married, of your brothers?
gave him the best price?
went for her sake?
wrote to the army?
took the pen from him?
said today is my birthday?
lives at the end of the street?
went months ago?
was born (literally, 'is born') in 1955?

Questions

miin Haḍratak? مين حضرتَك؟
inta mitzawwij? انت متزوج ؟
axwaanak mitzawwijiin? اخوانَك متزوجين ؟
as-saa9a kam? الساعة كم؟
keef Haalak? كيف حالَك؟
inta feen saakin? انت فين ساكن؟
kam 9umrak? كم عمرَك؟
kam 9umr ṣaaHbak? كم عمر صاحبَك؟

waalidak wu waalidatak mawjuudiin?	والدَك ووالدتَك موجودين؟
sayyaaratak ghaalya?	سيارتك غالية؟
saa9atak kallafat kam?	ساعتك كلفت كم؟

Narratives

Say in Arabic:

1. I went to the bank and took a little money. Then I bought my books for school. I like my school. I think it is the biggest and best in the city. There is no school better than this [one].
(Repeat, using different person forms.)

2. I am not sure that I know where the Americans live here, but I am sure there are many. I arrived only last month, and I am still new here. My house is big and nice, and my wife and children like Jidda. We want to go to Taif and Riyadh soon, I hope. People say that the cities are far. Maybe later we will go to Dhahran and other cities in Arabia.

LESSON 21

Dialogue

(In a taxi)

	free (unoccupied)	faaḑi	فاضي
A.	Are you (m) free?	inta faaḑi?	انتَ فاضي؟
B.	Yes, get in.	iiwa, atfaḑḑal.	ايوه اتفضل.
A.	How much from here to the embassy?	b-kam min hina lis-safaara?	بكم من هنا للسفارة؟
B.	Five riyals.	xamsa riyaal.	خمسة ريال.
	enough	kifaaya	كفاية
A.	Unbelievable! Three is enough.	muu ma9guul! talaata kifaaya.	مو معقول! ثلاثة كفاية.
	let be (command)	xalli	خلي
B.	OK, let it be three.	ţayyib, xalliiha talaata.	طيب، خليها ثلاثة.
	in a hurry	mista9jil	مستعجل
	drive (command)	suug	سوق
	carefully ('at your leisure')	9ala mahlak	على مهلَك
A.	I'm in a hurry, but drive carefully.	ana mista9jil šwayya laakin suug 9ala mahlak.	انا مستعجل شويه لاكن سوق على مهلك.
B.	OK.	in šaa' aḻḻaah.	ان شاء الله.

Structure Sentences

1.	I don't have enough money.	ma 9indi fuluus kifaaya.	ما عندي فلوس كفاية.
2.	Drive slowly.	suug b-šweeš.	سوق بشويش.
3.	The taxi driver drove fast.	sawwaag at-taksi saag b-sur9a.	سواق التكسي ساق بسرعة.
4.	Do you (m) know how to drive well?	ti9rif tisuug kwayyis?	تعرف تسوق كويس؟
5.	He works as a driver.	huwwa yištaghil sawwaag.	هو يشتغل سواق.
6.	He has two drivers.	9indu itneen sawwaagiin.	عنده اثنين سواقين.
7.	We are in a hurry.	iHna mista9jiliin.	احنا مستعجلين.
8.	You must hurry.	laazim tista9jil.	لازم تستعجل.

Grammatical Notes

1. /kifaaya/, 'enough', is used after a noun, and does not change form:

talaata kifaaya.	Three are enough.
fuluus kifaaya	enough money

2. Adverbs may be formed with particle words prefixed to a noun:

9ala mahlak	carefully ('at your (m) leisure')
9ala mahlik	('at your (f) leisure')
9ala mahlakum	('at your (p) leisure')
9ala mahli	('at my leisure')
9ala mahlana	('at our leisure')

b-šweeš	slowly ('with slowness')
b-sur9a	quickly ('with speed')

Other adverbs are simply the masculine adjective:

titkallam 9arabi kwayyis.	You speak Arabic well.
šuftu katiir.	I saw him a lot ('much').

3. /aštaghal, yištaghil/, 'to work', may be used with a noun to mean 'to work as':

huwwa yištaghil sawwaag.	He works [as] a driver.

4. Some nouns, especially nouns indicating profession or nationality, are not made dual with the /-een/ suffix. They are used with /itneen/ + the plural form:

itneen sawwaagiin	two drivers
itneen ajaanib	two foreigners
itneen su9uudiyiin	two Saudis
itneen amrikaan	two Americans

Vocabulary Notes

saag, yisuug (sugt)	drive	ساق يسوق (سقت)
ištaghal, yištaghil	work	اشتغل يشتغل
asta9jal, yista9jil	hurry	استعجل يستعجل
sawwaag, -iin	driver	سواق -ين
mista9jil, -a, -iin	in a hurry	مستعجل -ين
faaḍi, -ya, -iin	free, unoccupied	فاضي - ين

Drills

1. How much from here to the embassy?	b-kam min hina <u>lis-safaara</u>?	بكم من هنا للسفارة؟

Substitute:

the bank
the American school
Mecca Road
the Foreign Ministry
the airport
the American consulate
the post office
the embassy

2. I am in a hurry. ana mista9jil šwayya. انا مستعجل شويه .

Substitute:

we
she
you (m)
they
he
you (f)
I
you (p)

3. You (m) must hurry. inta laazim tista9jil. انتَ لازم تستعجل.

Substitute:

we
you (f)
she
you (p)
I
all of us
he

4. I don't have enough money. ma 9indi fuluus kifaaya. ما عندي فلوس كفاية.

Substitute:

books
friends
chairs
clocks
children

5. Drive slowly. suug b-šweeš. سوق بشويش.

Substitute:

quickly
behind that car
carefully
my car

6. Do you know how to drive well? ti9rif tisuug kwayyis? تعرف تسوق كويس؟

Substitute:

she
they
you (f)
he
you (p)
your brother
the driver

Situations

1.
A. Taxi! Are you free?
B. Yes, get in.
A. How much from here to the bank?
B. Only six riyals.
A. OK, let's go. But drive carefully; we're not in a hurry.

2.
A. I want to go buy something. Can you take me in the car?
B. I'm sorry, I'm not free now.
A. But I don't drive, and there aren't any taxis.
B. Why do you want to go?
A. Today is my son's birthday. I have to buy him something.
B. Ask the driver.
A. Yes, I'm sure he'll go.

Cultural Notes

1. Since taxis do not have meters, it is customary to discuss the price of a trip before getting in.

LESSON 22

Dialogue

	waiting	mistanni	مستني
A.	Have you been waiting here long? ('To you long waiting here?')	lak katiir mistanni hina?	لك كثير مستني هنا؟
B.	I've been waiting here 20 minutes. ('It has been to me...')	liyya mistanni hina tult saa9a.	لي مستني هنا ثلث ساعة.
	sorry	mit'assif	متأسف
A.	I'm sorry.	ana mit'assif.	انا متأسف.
B.	It's OK. It's nothing.	ma9aleeš. ma fii šayy.	معليش. ما فيه شي.
	you (m) drink	tišrab	تشرب
	cup	finjaan	فنجان
	coffee	gahwa	قهوة
A.	Would you like to drink a cup of coffee?	tiHubb tišrab finjaan gahwa?	تحب تشرب فنجان قهوة؟
	cold	baarid	بارد
B.	Something cold, please.	šayy baarid, min faḍlak.	شي بارد من فضلك.

Structure Sentences

1.	We are waiting for them.	iHna mistanniinhum.	احنا مستنينهم.
2.	I am waiting for him.	ana mintaẓiru.	انا منتظره.
3.	He already went.	giidu raaH.	قيده راح.
4.	I am extremely sorry.	ana mit'assif bil-Heel.	انا متأسف بالحيل.
5.	Would you (f) like to come?	inti tiHubbi tiji?	انتِ تحبي تجي؟
6.	We drank a glass of tea with milk.	širibna kubbaayat šaahi bil-Haliib.	شربنا كباية شاهي بالحليب.
7.	I heard that these things are cheap.	simi9t innu l-Hajaat haadi raxiiṣa.	سمعتُ انه الحاجات هادي رخيصة.
8.	Why is he returning?	huwwa leeš raaji9?	هو ليش راجع؟
9.	We were sleeping.	kunna naaymiin.	كنا نايمين.
10.	I am not able.	ana mana gaadir.	انا منا قادر.
11.	I heard about you (m).	ana simi9t 9annak.	انا سمعت عنك.

Grammatical Notes

1. /mistanni/ and /raaji9/ are examples of the "active participle" in Arabic. The active participle has a predictable pattern for each type of verb. It is usually translated like a verb in English, but it is in fact a noun in Arabic, declined for gender and number. If the word ends in a consonant, it takes the regular feminine ending /-a/, and the /-iin/ suffix for plural. If it ends in a vowel like /-i/, it takes /-yya/ for feminine and /-iin/ for plural. For example:

raaji9	returning (m)
raaj9a	returning (f)
raaj9iin	returning (p)

Note that the /i/ is dropped before adding the feminine and plural endings.

mistanni	waiting (m)
mistanniyya	waiting (f)
mistanniin	waiting (p)

The active participle is used to express the "actor", or the "doer" of an action. It is most often used with verbs of motion (to describe going, coming, returning, etc.) and verbs of "temporary state", mental or physical (understanding, knowing, sitting, standing). Sometimes the active participle is translated as the present perfect tense in English ('have seen', 'have done'), and whether this is meant will depend on the context of the sentence.

The most easily recognized pattern is that of regular verbs like /katab/:

$C_1aaC_2iC_3$

Examples:

faahim	'understanding'
ana faahim.	I understand. ('I am understanding')
humma mahum faahmiin al-jumla.	They do not understand the sentence. ('They are not understanding')
9aarif	'knowing'
ana mana 9aarif keef aruuH.	I don't know how to go. ('I am not knowing')
iHna 9aarfiin innu jaa.	We know that he came. ('We are knowing')
raayiH	'going'
mita huwwa raayiH?	When is he going?
jayy	'coming'
ana jayy daHHiin.	I am coming now.

Note the difference between the above sentences which describe (1) a temporary state or (2) a motion, and the sentences below which use a verb to describe (1) a permanent state or ability or (2) a habitual action:

afham ingiliizi	I understand English.
a9rif aktub kwayyis.	I know how to write well.
yiruuH al-madrasa badri.*	He goes to school early.
niji hina katiir.*	We come here often ('much').

*Some speakers use the prefix /b-/ before verbs when expressing habitual or recurring action:

b-yiruuH
b-niji

Sometimes speakers of Arabic use both the active participle and the imperfect verb for certain expressions which do not clearly fit into one category or the other. The sentences may differ slightly in connotation.

9aarifu kwayyis.	I know him well. (I know all about him).
a9rifu kwayyis.	(Now) I know him well.

When used in the sense of present perfect, the phrase is often used with a form of the word /giid-/, 'already', (see note below) or other time words which give an indication that the sentence refers to recently-completed past time.

huwwa giidu šaarib šaahi.	He has already drunk tea.
huwwa waaṣil min zamaan.	He [has] arrived long ago.

Note that "hollow" verbs add /y/ in the active participle form:

raayiH	'going'
šaayif	'seeing'

Other types of verbs form the active participle by adding the prefix /m-/ or /mi-/ to the imperfect tense "base" (minus the person prefix):

Base Form	Active Participle
yisawwi	misawwi 'doing, having done'
yi9addi	mi9addi 'crossing, having crossed'
yintaẓir	mintaẓir 'waiting'

Some of these verbs also change the final vowel:

yistanna	mistanni 'waiting'

The active participle of a transitive verb may be used with a direct object (cf. Structure Sentences 1 and 2).

2. /giid-/ is used with pronoun endings and means 'already':

giidu	he already	قيده
giidaha	she already	قيدها
giidahum	they already	قيدهم
giidak	you (m) already	قيدَك
giidik	you (f) already	قيدِك
giidakum	you (p) already	قيدُكم
giidi	I already	قيدي
giidana	we already	قيدنا

It is used before verbs:

giidu raaH.	He already went.
giidi šuftu.	I already saw him.

3. More time expressions:

tult saa9a	one-third of an hour
rub9 saa9a	one-quarter of an hour

nuṣṣ saa9a	one-half hour
nuṣṣ dagiiga	one-half minute
nuṣṣ saaniya	one-half second (etc.)

4. /Haaja, Haajaat/ is another way of saying 'thing'. It alternates with /šayy/; the latter is usually preferred and is more classical.

5. /mintaẓir/, 'waiting', is used as often as /mistanni/. It is more classical.

6. /bil-Heel/, 'very much, extremely', is equivalent to /bil-marra/, and is more often used in the Najd.

7. Nouns which refer to containers or amounts are used in a construct phrase:

finjaan gahwa	a cup of coffee
kubbaayat šaahi	a glass of tea
talaata kiilu šaahi	three kilos of tea

8. /b-/ is used to mean 'with' when discussing ingredients of food or drink:

gahwa bil-Haliib	coffee with milk
šaahi b-sukkar	tea with sugar
šaahi bil-leemuun	tea with lemon

9. The verbs /Habb, yiHubb/, 'to like', and /gidir, yigdar/, 'to be able', are used as helping verbs with other verbs in a phrase:

tiHubb tišrab finjaan gahwa?	Would you (m) like to drink a cup of coffee?
tiHubbi tiji?	Would you (f) like to come?
gidir yiji badri.	He was able to come early.
ma gidirt atkallam.	I was not able to talk.

<u>Vocabulary Notes</u>

<u>Active Participles</u>

(Translations indicate the most likely usage for each word; not all active participles are used in all possible ways.)

(regular)		
saakin	is residing	ساكن
waaṣil	has arrived	واصل
daaris	has studied	دارس
kaatib	has written	كاتب
9aamil	is working	عامل
faatiH	has opened	فاتح
gaafil	has closed	قافل
saa'il	is asking	سائل
ṣaarif	has spent	صارف
raaji9	is returning	راجع
gaadir	is able	قادر
šaarib	has drunk	شارب
saami9	is hearing, has heard	سامع
(hollow)		
gaayil	has said	قايل
raayiH	is going	رايح
šaayif	is seeing	شايف
naayim	is sleeping	نايم
jaayib	is bringing	جايب
saayib	has left behind	سايب
šaayil	is carrying	شايل

(other)		
maaši	is leaving	ماشي
middi	has given	مدي
mitkallam	has spoken	متكلم
misawwi	has done	مسوّي
mi9addi	has crossed	معدّي
mintaẓir	is waiting	منتظر
mistanni	is waiting	مستني
muwaafig	is in agreement	موافق

Verbs

širib, yišrab	drink	شرب يشرب
riji9, yirja9	return	رجع يرجع
gidir, yigdar	be able	قدر يقدر
simi9, yisma9	hear	سمع يسمع
astanna, yistanna (astanneet)	wait	استنى يستنى (استنيت)
antaẓar, yintaẓir	wait	انتظر ينتظر
waafag, yiwaafig	agree	وافق يوافق

Other Words

9aṣiir	juice	عصير
Haliib	milk	حليب
moyya	water	ميّة
gahwa	coffee	قهوة
šaahi	tea	شاهي
leemuun	lemon	ليمون
sukkar	sugar	سكر
finjaan, fanaajiin	cup	فنجان فناجين
kubbaaya, -aat	drinking glass	كباية -ات
mit'assif, -a, -iin	sorry	متأسف -ين
leeš	why?	ليش

Drills

1. Have you been waiting here long? — lak katiir mistanni hina? — لك كثير مستني هنا؟

Substitute:

you (p)
she
they
he
you (f)

2. I have been here 20 minutes. — liyya hina tult saa9a. — لي هنا ثلث ساعة.

Substitute:

1/4 hour
1/2 hour
we
1/2 year
he
1/2 minute
1/2 second
she
1/3 hour
I

3. Would you like to drink a cup of coffee? — tiHubb tišrab finjaan gahwa? — تحب تشرب فنجان قهوة؟

Substitute:

you(f)
something cold
they
he
glass of tea
we
she
glass of water
you (m)
juice
we
you (p)
milk
she

4. I am waiting for him. — ana mintaẓiru. — انا منتظره.

Substitute:

her
them
we
him
she
me
us

5. Given the cue sentence in the perfect tense, change it to the active participle form.

Example:

huwwa raaH. ⟶ huwwa raayiH. — هو راح. ⟵ هو رايح.

Continue:

ana astanneet.	انا استنيت.
širibna šaahi.	شربنا شاهي.
miin sa'al as-su'aal?	مين سال السؤال؟
huwwa ma gidir yiruuH.	هو ما قدر يروح.
jaabat sayyaaratha.	جابت سيارتها.
ana šilt Haajaat katiir.	انا شلت حاجات كثير.
mišiina.	مشينا.
al-walad 9adda š-šaari9.	الولد عدى الشارع.
huwwa waafag.	هو وافق.
9amal fi šarikat axuu.	عمل في شركة اخوه.
mita waṣalt?	متا وصلت؟
ma ṣaraf fuluus katiir.	ما صرف فلوس كثير.
simi9tak.	سمعتك.
saab al-kutub 9aṭ-ṭarabiiza.	ساب الكتب عالطربيزة.

6. I am sorry. | <u>ana mit'assif</u>. | انا متأسف

Substitute:

we
she
he
they
returning
going
I
she
sleeping
he
was sleeping
we
they
see ('are seeing')
he
do you (f) see?
agree?
you (p)
understand?

7. We have been waiting for them for a long time. | iHna mistanniinhum min zamaan. | احنا مستنينهم من زمان.

Substitute:

waiting for him
have seen him
have seen them
I
have seen her
have written it (f)
we
she
has written it (m)
has drunk it (m)
he
has opened it
has opened them
we
have opened it (m)

8. Why is he returning? | <u>huwwa</u> leeš <u>raaji9</u>? | هو ليش راجع؟

Substitute:

going
they
not able
she
you (m)
sleeping
you (f)
he
coming
they
she
leaving that (m)
you (m)
you (p)

returning
we
you (m)
he

Situations

1.
A. Would you like to drink coffee?
B. No, I have to go to my brother's house. He is waiting for me.
A. Are you returning soon?
B. After about half an hour, if God wills.

2.
A. Where do you live?
B. My house is at the end of this street, on the right.
A. My friends lived in that house, but I didn't see it.
B. Maybe you can see it from here.
A. No, I can't see anything.
B. Come over later.
A. OK, maybe I can.

3.
A. What are you carrying?
B. Only some old books. I just bought them yesterday. With your permission, may I leave them in that room?
A. I've given that room to Ahmad, but I'm sure it's OK.
B. When will he be back?
A. In half an hour or less. I'll tell him that the books are yours.
B. Thanks.

Cultural Notes

1. It is considered poor manners to neglect serving a guest something to drink, in a home or office, even during a short visit. You should always accept something, even if you only taste it.

2. Tea is preferred in glasses throughout the Arab world.

LESSON 23

Dialogue

A.	Where are you (m) going?	feen raayiH?	فين رايح ؟
	appointment	maw9ad	موعد
	minister	waziir	وزير
B.	I have an appointment with the Minister of Finance.	9indi maw9ad ma9a waziir al-maaliyya.	عندي موعد مع وزير المالية.
A.	At the Finance Ministry?	fi wizaarat al-maaliyya?	في وزارة المالية؟
	hotel	fundug	فندق
	sea	baHr	بحر
	red	aHmar	احمر
	because	li'ann	لأن
	official	mas'uul	مسؤول
	all	kull	كل
	staying	naazil	نازل
B.	No, at the Red Sea Hotel, because all the officials are staying there.	la', fi fundug al-baHr al-aHmar, li'ann al-mas'uuliin kullahum naazliin hinaak.	لاء، في فندق البحر الاحمر، لان المسؤولين كلهم نازلين هناك.
	who, which	alli	ألّي
	sitting	jaalis	جالس
	in the morning	fiṣ-ṣubuH	فى الصبح
A.	Those who were sitting in the office this morning?	humma alli kaanu jaalsiin fil-maktab fiṣ-ṣubuH?	هم الي كانوا جالسين فى المكتب في الصبح ؟
B.	Yes, the ones which you saw [them].	iiwa, humma n-naas alli inta šuftahum.	ايوه ، هم الناس الي انتَ شفتَهم.

Structure Sentences

1.	He arrived on time.	waṣal fil-maw9ad.	وصل في الموعد.
2.	He arrived in the evening.	waṣal fil-masa.	وصل في المَسا.
3.	He slept because he is tired.	naam li'annu ta9baan.	نام لأنه تعبان.
4.	[It is] you who are responsible.	inta alli mas'uul.	انتَ الي مسؤول.

5.	We all stayed in a big hotel.	kullana nazalina fi fundug kabiir.	كلنا نزلنا فى فندق كبير.
6.	Did he go upstairs or downstairs?	ṭili9 foog walla nazal taHat?	طلع فوق ولّا نزل تحت؟
7.	Who is the man who is standing there?	miin ar-rijjaal alli waagif hinaak?	مين الرجال الي واقف هناك ؟
8.	I want the suitcase which I bought yesterday.	abgha š-šanṭa alli aštareetaha ams.	ابغى الشنطة الي اشتريتها امس.
9.	Give me all the things which you took from me.	addiini kull al-Haajaat alli axadtahum min 9indi.	اديني كل الحاجات الي اخذتهم من عندي.
10.	He was sitting there.	kaan gaa9id hinaak.	كان قاعد هناك.

Grammatical Notes

1. /li'ann/ means 'because', and may be used alone or with pronoun suffixes:

li'aan al-mas'uuliin kullahum naazliin hinaak.	because all the officials are staying there
naam li'annu ta9baan.	He slept because he was tired.
laazim asta'zin li'anni at'axxart.	I must be leaving because I'm late.

2. /ṣubuH/ and /masa/ are the forms used ordinarily with reference to 'morning' and 'evening' (we saw these used for 'a.m.' and 'p.m.' in Lesson 12). /ṣabaaH/ and /masaa'/ are classical equivalents of these words, most often reserved for use in the expressions 'Good morning' and 'Good evening'.

3. /kull/, 'all', is used before a definite, plural noun. It may also be used with pronoun endings. (cf. Structure Sentences 5 and 9.)

kullahum	all of them
kullakum	all of you (p)
kullana	all of us
kull al-Haajaat	all the things
kull an-naas	all the people

4. /mas'uul/, literally, 'responsible', is used idiomatically for 'official' (as a noun).

5. /nazal, yinzal/, literally, 'to descend', is used idiomatically to mean 'staying' in a hotel or home.

6. /alli/, 'which, who, whom', is not declined. It is used to introduce a phrase or clause, as a relative pronoun. If the clause includes a verb which takes a direct or indirect object, an object pronoun is also used. (This sounds redundant in English):

humma alli kaanu jaalsiin	they who were sitting
humma alli inta šuftahum	they whom you saw [them]

aš-šanṭa alli aštareetaha ams	the suitcase which I bought [it] yesterday
al-Haajaat alli axadtahum	the things which I took [them]
ar-rijjaal alli addeetu fuluus	the man to whom I gave [him] money

/alli/ may also be used to mean 'he who', 'those who', 'whoever':

alli yiHubb yiji yigulli.	Whoever wants to come, tell me.

7. /fil-maw9ad/, 'on time' (literally, 'in the appointment'), is an idiom.

8. /foog/, 'above', and /taHat/, 'below', can also be used to mean 'upstairs' and 'downstairs'.

9. /ga9ad, yug9ud/ is another common word meaning 'to sit'.

Vocabulary Notes

maw9ad, mawaa9iid	appointment	موعد مواعيد
šanṭa, šunaṭ	suitcase, briefcase, purse	شنطة شنط
waziir, wuzara	minister (of government)	وزير وزرا
fundug, fanaadig	hotel	فندق فنادق
mas'uul, -a, -iin	responsible, ('official')	مسؤول - ين
nazal, yinzal	descend, ('stay')	نزل ينزل
ṭili9, yiṭla9	ascend	طلع يطلع
jalas, yijlis	sit	جلس يجلس
ga9ad, yug9ud	sit	قعد يقعد
wigif, yiwgaf	stand	وقف يوقف

Drills

1. I have an appointment in the Red Sea Hotel.	9indi maw9ad fi fundug al-baHr al-aHmar.	عندي موعد في فندق البحر الاحمر.

Substitute:

at the American Embassy
at the Ministry of Petroleum
with officials of the government
in the evening
at the airport
with the Minister of Communications
with my friends
at school
at the Ministry of Defense

2. You (m) must go downstairs.	laazim tinzal taHat.	لازم تنزل تحت.

Substitute:

go upstairs
sit here
stand beside the door
you (p)
bring your son too
come back in the evening

you (f)
see her soon
study English in school
go on time

3. Substitute the first or second half of the sentence, repeating the question and its answer:

Example: Why did he sleep? Because he's tired.

leeš huwwa naam? ⟶ li'annu ta9baan. ليش هو نام؟ ← لأنه تعبان.

Continue:

Why did he sleep?	Because he arrived late.
Why didn't he come?	Because he arrived late.
Why didn't she come?	Because she arrived late.
Why didn't she come?	Because she doesn't agree.
Why didn't you (m) go?	Because I don't agree.
Why didn't you (m) go?	Because I don't have much money.
Why didn't you (m) spend much?	Because I don't have much money.
Why didn't you (p) spend much?	Because we don't have much money.
Why didn't you (p) spend much?	Because we didn't like the things.
Why didn't he spend much?	Because he didn't like the things.

4. Who are they who were sitting there?	miin humma alli kaanu jaalsiin hinaak?	مين هم الي كانوا جالسين هناك؟

Substitute:

who were standing there
who were staying in the hotel
who were returning
who were coming upstairs
who were going home
who were coming here
who were carrying the suitcases
who were sleeping in the room
who were responsible

5. They are the people whom you saw.	humma n-naas alli inta šuftahum.	هم الناس الي انت شفتهم.

Substitute:

whom you know
whom I brought in my car
whom I asked about
whom I gave money to
whom I greeted
whom I took home

6. I want the suitcase which I bought yesterday.	abgha š-šanṭa alli aštareetaha ams.	ابغى الشنطة الي اشتريتها امس

Substitute:

which I saw yesterday
the table

the new chair
which he brought from the office
which my husband likes
the books
which you (m) are carrying
the coffee
which is in that cup
which you (m) can't drink

Situations

1.
A. Let's go see the man who arrived yesterday.
B. OK, in a couple hours.
A. Why can't you come now?
B. Because I have to sleep, I'm tired.
A. I'll come at 7:00.
B. Fine.

2.
A. Do you know Mr. Muhammad?
B. No, but I've heard about him.
A. He lives next to us.
B. I know that he is in the Ministry of Defense.
A. Yes, I'm not sure where exactly. In the minister's office, I think.

3.
A. Bring us coffee, please.
B. How many?
A. Four. And one tea with sugar.
B. Do you (f) want cream?
A. Of course. Then ('later') at 3:00 we have an appointment at the university. Can you take us in the car?
B. Yes. When will you (p) return?
A. After about an hour, if God wills.

LESSON 24

Dialogue

(In a front office)

A.	Please, is Mr. Mahmoud here?	min faḍlak, as-sayyid maHmuud mawjuud?	من فضلك، السيد محمود موجود ؟
	he went out	xaraj	خرج
B.	No, he's gone out.	la', xaraj.	لاء، خرج .
	again	taani	ثاني
A.	Will he be back again?	raH-yiji taani?	رَح يجي ثاني؟
B.	In a little while, have a seat.	ba9d šwayya, atfaḍḍal.	بعد شويه ، اتفضل .
	message	risaala	رسالة
A.	May I leave him a message?	mumkin asiblu risaala?	ممكن اسيبله رسالة؟
B.	Certainly.	atfaḍḍal.	اتفضل .
	project	mašruu9	مشروع
	number	ragam	رقم
	telephone	tilifoon	تليفون
A.	Tell him that Mr. Jones wants to talk to him about our project. Do you have my telephone number?	gullu innu mistar Jones yibgha yitkallamu 9an mašruu9ana. 9indak ragam tilifooni?	قلله انه مستر جونز يبغى يتكلمه عن مشروعنا . عندك رقم تليفوني؟
B.	No. What is the number?	la'. kam ar-ragam?	لاء . كم الرقم؟
A.	25875	xamsa wu 9išriin, tamanmiyya wu xamsa wu sab9iin.	خمسة وعشرين، ثمنمية وخمسة وسبعين .

Structure Sentences

1.	Is Mr. Mahmoud here?	as-sayyid maHmuud fii?	السيد محمود فيه ؟
2.	We'll be ('we are') home today.	al-yoom iHna fii.	اليوم احنا فيه .
3.	Can I get you coffee?	mumkin ajiblak gahwa?	ممكن اجيبلك قهوة؟
4.	Is this for you (m)?	haada lak?	هادا لك؟
5.	Yes, this letter is for me.	iiwa, haada l-jawaab liyya.	ايوه ،هادا الجواب لي .
6.	I owe you money.	lak fuluus 9indi.	لك فلوس عندي .
7.	I owe Ahmad ten riyals.	9alayya 9ašara riyaal li aHmad.	علي عشرة ريال لاحمد .

Grammatical Notes

1. /mawjuud/ (/mawjuuda/, /mawjuudiin/) may be used to mean 'present', 'in attendance'. Just as common is the use of /fii/ to mean 'present'. (cf. Structure Sentences 1 and 2.)

2. /taani/ may be used as an adverb to mean 'again'.

3. /ragam/, 'number', is the classical word; the borrowed word /nimra/ is often heard.

4. Telephone numbers are usually given in tens or hundreds, the first two and then the last three:

25875	xamsa wu 9išriin, tamanmiyya wu xamsa wu sab9iin
27416	sab9a wu 9išriin, arba9miyya wu sitta9š

If the number combinations are unusual, modifications may be made:

20005	9išriin alf wu xamsa
11002	iHda9š alf w itneen

If you use individual numbers, you will be understood.

5. The indirect object is usually suffixed to the verb. If there is no verb, the word /l-/, 'to, for', is used with a pronoun as an independent word.

lu	to him, for him	له
laha	to her, for her	لها
lahum	to them, for them	لهم
lak	to you (m), for you (m)	لكْ
liki	to you (f), for you (f)	لكِ
lakum	to you (p), for you (p)	لكم
liyya	to me, for me	ليّ
lana	to us, for us	لنا

hadool al-kutub lana iHna.	Those books are for <u>us</u>.
lak katiir mistanni hina?	Have you been waiting here long?
liyya hina tult saa9a.	I've been here for 20 minutes.

/l-/ can be used with money to mean 'is owed to'. Owing may be expressed with /9ind/ or /9ala/:

liyya xamsa riyaal.	I am owed five riyals. ('To me five riyals.')
liyya xamsa riyaal 9indak.	You owe me five riyals. ('To me five riyals with you.')
9aleena fuluus katiir.	We owe a lot of money. ('On us a lot of money.')

6. /risaala/, 'message', may also mean 'note' or 'letter'; it is the classical word. However, the word /jawaab/ (literally, 'answer') is usually used in this dialect to mean 'letter'.

Vocabulary Notes

mašruu9, mašaarii9	project	مشروع مشاريع
risaala, rasaayil	note, message	رسالة رسايل
jawaab, -aat	letter	جواب -ات
ragam, arqaam	number	رقم ارقام
nimra, nimar	number	نمرة نمر
tilifoon, -aat	telephone	تليفون -ات
Hisaab, -aat	account	حساب -ات
šughul, ašghaal	work	شغل اشغال
taşmiim, -aat	design	تصميم -ات
xuţţa, xuţaţ	plan	خطة خطط
ţalab, -aat	order	طلب -ات
muštarawaat	purchases	مشتروات
mubii9aat	sales	مبيعات
ittifaag, -aat	agreement	اتفاق -ات
xaraj, yuxruj	go out	خرج يخرج
daxal, yudxul	enter	دخل يدخل

Drills

1. May I leave him a message? — mumkin <u>asiblu risaala</u>? — ممكن اسيبله رسالة؟

Substitute:

bring you (m) coffee?
carry this suitcase for you?
make an appointment for you (p)?
write her a letter?
do anything for you (f)?
give them the money?
buy you (m) a glass of tea?

2. Is this for you (m)? — haada <u>lak</u>? — هادا لَك؟

Substitute:

for us
for you (p)
for me
for her
for you (f)
for them

3. I owe you money. — <u>lak</u> fuluus <u>9indi</u>. — لَك فلوس عندي.

Substitute:

she owes you
they owe you
they owe us
you (m) owe us
she owes us
she owes her
I owe her
I owe them

4. My telephone number is 25875.	ragam tilifooni xamsa wu 9išriin, wu tamanmiyya xamsa wu sab9iin.	رقم تليفوني خمسة وعشرين وثمنمية خمسة وسبعين.

Sbustitute:

63957
21020
29000
65338
62117
27504

5. He wants to talk about our project.	yibgha yitkallam 9an mašruu9ana.	يبغى يتكلم عن مشروعنا.

Substitute:

I
our account
our plan
our work
we
our agreement
our design
our order
our purchases
he
his project
his sales

6. When did he go out?	mita xaraj?	متا خرج؟

Substitute:

she
they
entered
you (f)
he
you (p)
went out
you (m)

Situations

1.
A. Where is Mr. Sharif?
B. He went out half an hour ago. He said he'll return soon.
A. May I wait?
B. Of course. Can I get you something?
A. Yes, either coffee or tea.

2.
A. I want to see the plan.
B. Which plan?
A. The design of the new building.
B. Mr. Jones took it and left.
A. Tell him that I was here. I'll leave you my telephone number.
B. Where will you be?
A. At the hotel, after 3:00.

3.
A. I owe you money. How much?
B. About 30 riyals, I'm not sure. I forgot.
A. Take 30 now, and I'll see the account again later.
B. OK, thanks. Good night.
A. Good night.

LESSON 25

Dialogue

(On the telephone)

A.	Hello. Who are you, sir?	aloo. miin Haḍratak?	آلو. مين حضرتك؟
B.	This is Mr. Jones. Is Mahmoud there?	ana mistar Jones. maHmuud fii?	انا مستر جونز. محمود فيه؟
	if you please	law samaHt	لو سمحت
	you (m) remain	xalliik	خليك
	line	xaṭṭ	خط
A.	Just a minute, please. Stay on the line.	dagiiga law samaHt. xalliik 9al-xaṭṭ.	دقيقة لو سمحت. خليك عالخط.
C.	Hello, this is Mahmoud. ('I am Mahmoud')	aloo. ana maHmuud.	آلو. انا محمود.
B.	Hello Mahmoud. How are you?	ahlan maHmuud. keef Haalak?	اهلا محمود. كيف حالك؟
	I tried	Haawalt	حاولت
	I call you	akallimak	اكلمك
	I found	lageet	لقيت
	busy	mašghuul	مشغول
C.	Fine, thanks. I tried to call you and found the line busy.	ṭayyib, al-Hamdu lillaah. ana Haawalt akallimak, wu lageet al-xaṭṭ mašghuul.	طيب، الحمد لله. انا حاولت اكلمك ولقيت الخط مشغول.
	director	mudiir	مدير
B.	Maybe the director was using the telephone.	yimkin al-mudiir kaan b-yista9mil at-tilifoon.	يمكن المدير كان بيستعمل التليفون.
C.	When can I see you in the office?	mita agdar ašuufak fil-maktab?	متا اقدر اشوفك في المكتب؟
B.	I'm free today in the afternoon.	ana faaḍi l-yoom ba9d aḍ-ḍuhur.	انا فاضي اليوم بعد الظهر

Structure Sentences

1.	We tried to arrive early.	Haawalna niwṣal badri.	حاولنا نوصل بدري.
2.	We were writing letters.	kunna b-niktub jawaabaat.	كنا بنكتب جوابات.
3.	I was waiting there.	kunt mistanni hinaak.	كنت مستني هناك.
4.	You can find pretty things at his place (shop).	mumkin tilaagi Haajaat Hilwa 9indu.	ممكن تلاقي حاجات حلوة عنده.

5. Someone called me on the telephone.	waaHid kallamni bit-tilifoon.	واحد كلمني بالتليفون.
6. Someone is talking.	aHad b-yitkallam.	احد بيتكلم.
7. Nobody answers.	maHad yirudd.	ماحد يرد.
8. Wrong number.	an-nimra ghalaṭ.	النمرة غلط.

Grammatical Notes

1. /Haawal, yiHaawil/, 'to try', is used as a helping verb with other verbs. This means 'try' in the sense of 'attempt'; /jarrab, yijarrib/ means 'try' in the sense of 'try out':

Haawalt akallimak.	I tried to call you.
jarrabt aš-šaahi.	I tried the tea.

2. /kallam, yikallim/, 'to talk to', is used with a direct object:

Haawalt akallimak.	I tried to talk to you (call you).
kallamni bit-tilifoon.	Call me on the telephone.

Note that /atkallam/, 'to speak', is used with /ma9a/ before the object:

laazim atkallam ma9a ṣaaHbi.	I must talk to my friend.

3. /laga, yilaagi/, 'to find', is slightly irregular in the perfect tense because it is missing a root consonant:

Perfect	Imperfect		
huwwa laga	yilaagi	يلاقي	لقى
hiyya lagat	tilaagi	تلاقي	لقت
humma lagu	yilaagu	يلاقوا	لقوا
inta lageet	tilaagi	تلاقي	لقيت
inti lageeti	tilaagi	تلاقي	لقيت
intu lageetu	tilaagu	تلاقوا	لقيتوا
ana lageet	alaagi	الاقي	نقيت
iHna lageena	nilaagi	نلاقي	لقينا

4. /kaan/ may be used with an imperfect verb to form the "past progressive" tense, i.e., 'was doing':

al-mudiir kaan yista9mil at-tilifoon.	The director was using the telephone.
hiyya kaanat tiktub.	She was writing.

5. /b-/ is prefixed to an imperfect verb when speaking of "continuous" or on-going action (it is optional):

huwwa b-yitkallam daHHiin.	He is talking now.
kaan b-yitkallam.	He was talking.
kaan b-yista9mil at-tilifoon.	He was using the telephone.
hiyya b-tiktub jawaab.	She is writing a letter.

This prefix is optionally used for habitual or recurring action (see page 110).

6. /aHad/ is the usual word for 'someone'; it has only one form. Sometimes you will hear /waaHid/ (/waHda/) used as well. (cf. Structure Sentences 5 and 6.)

Vocabulary Notes

mudiir, -iin*	director, manager, boss	مدير -ين
mudiir maktab	appointments secretary (for a high official)	مدير مكتب
musaa9id, -iin*	assistant	مساعد -ين
naayib, nuwwaab	deputy	نايب نواب
sikirteer, -iin*	secretary	سكرتير -ين
mušrif, -iin*	supervisor	مشرف -ين
muwaẓẓaf, -iin*	employee	موظف -ين
aHad	someone	احد
maHad	nobody	محد
xaṭṭ, xuṭuuṭ	line	خط خطوط
mašghuul, -iin	busy	مشغول - ين
xarbaan, -iin	out of order	خربان -ين

*(The above nouns referring to employment titles can be made feminine by adding /-a/, and the plural /-iin/ would change to /-aat/.)

Drills

1. Stay on the line. (to a man) — xalliik 9al-xaṭṭ. — خليك عالخط.

Substitute:

(to a woman)
(to a group)

2. I tried to call you (m). — Haawalt akallimak. — حاولت اكلمَك.

Substitute:

We tried to call you (m).
We tried to call them.
We tried to call all of you.
We tried to see all of you.
She tried to write to you (p).
She tried to write to us.
She tried to write to him.
She tried to call him on the telephone.
I tried to call him on the telephone.
I tried to answer him.
He tried to answer him.
They tried to answer him.

3. State the question, then answer it.

Example:

Did he talk to you (m)? → Yes, he talked to me.
huwwa kallamak? ⟶ iiwa, kallamni.

هو كلمَك؟ ← ايوه ،كلمني.

Continue:

Did she talk to you (m)?	Yes, she talked to me.
Did she talk to them?	Yes, she talked to them.
Did she talk to him?	No, she did not talk to him.
Did you (p) talk to him?	Yes, we talked to him.
Did you (f) talk to him?	No, I did not talk to him.
Did they talk to her?	No, they did not talk to her.
Did they talk to you (m)?	Yes, they talked to me.

4. Did you (m) call him? kallamtu? كلمته ؟

Repeat the question, and answer:

Yes, but I found the line busy.
Yes, but nobody answered.
Yes, but I waited a long time.
Yes, but he wasn't there. (/mawjuud/).
Yes, but he wasn't free.
Yes, but I talked to his assistant.
No, I forgot his number.
No, the telephone is out of order.

5. The director was using the telephone. al-mudiir kaan b-yista9mil at-tilifoon. المدير كان بيستعمل التليفون.

Substitute:

was coming in*
was going to the Ministry of Interior
was writing a letter
was talking to somebody
was going out
had to leave
was sitting outside
was buying expensive things

*Remember to use active participles where appropriate.

6. I must speak to the manager. laazim akallim al-mudiir. لازم اكلم المدير.

Substitute:

the employees
the supervisor
the secretary (f)
the deputy
the appointments secretary
the assistant
the minister's assistant

Situations

1.
A. Call him on the telephone.
B. I can't, the line is busy.
A. Try again.
B. Now nobody answers.

2.
A. I want to see the director.
B. I'm sorry, he's out.
A. Can I see his deputy?
B. Just a moment, I'll ask. No, he's not free now.
A. I'll leave him a message.
B. Go ahead.

3.
A. Where is the company president staying?
B. In the Red Sea Hotel.
A. Is it near here?
B. Not far. Take a taxi.
A. How much would it cost?
B. Only two riyals.

LESSON 26

Dialogue

(In an office)

A. Is Khalid here?	xaalid hina?	خالد هنا؟
B. Not yet.	lissa9.	لسع.
have him	xallii	خليه
as soon as	awwal-ma	اول ما
A. Have him call me as soon as he arrives.	xallii yikallimni awwal-ma yiwṣal.	خليه يكلمني اول ما يوصل.
very well; as you wish (literally 'ready')	Haaḍir	حاضر
service	xidma	خدمة
B. Very well, any service. Where will you be?	Haaḍir, ayy xidma. feen Ha-tikuun?	حاضر، اي خدمة. فين حتكون؟
until	ileen	الين
A. I'll be in the office until five o'clock. Then I'll go to the airport.	H-akuun fil-maktab ileen as-saa9a xamsa. ba9deen H-aruuH al-maṭaar.	حاكون في المكتب الين الساعة خمسة. بعدين حاروح المطار.
B. Why?	leeš?	ليش؟
traveling	misaafir	مسافر
airplane	ṭayyaara	طيارة
A. I'm going on the five o'clock plane.	ana misaafir 9ala ṭayyaarat as-saa9a xamsa, in šaa' aḷḷaah.	انا مسافر على طيارة الساعة خمسة ان شاء الله.
before	gabl-ma	قبلما
B. Maybe he will meet you here before you go.	yimkin huwwa yigaabilak hina gabl-ma timši.	يمكن هو يقابلك هنا قبلما تمشي.

Structure Sentences

1. When you (m) arrive, tell me.	lamman tiwṣal, gulli.	لمن توصل قللي.
2. He left without saying goodby to them.	miši biduun-ma yisallim 9aleehum.	مشي بدون ما يسلم عليهم.
3. I must see him before he leaves.	laazim ašuufu gabl-ma yimši.	لازم اشوفه قبلما يمشي.
4. We stood up after she entered.	wigifna ba9d-ma daxalat.	وقفنا بعدما دخلت.

5. Every time I travel I forget something at home.	kull-ma asaafir ansa Haaja fil-beet.	كلما اسافر انسى حاجة في البيت.
6. We went to France last year.	saafarna faraansa s-sana l-maaḍya.	سافرنا فرانسا السنة الماضيه.
7. They haven't come yet.	lissa9 ma joo.	لسع ما جوا.

Grammatical Notes

1. /xalla, yixalli/, 'to leave', 'to let', is used alone or as a helping verb. It has several translations in English, depending on context:

xallii.	Leave it [here].
xalliik 9al-xaṭṭ.	Stay on the line. ('Let you be on the line')
xalliik hina.	Stay here.
xalliiki 9indana.	Stay (f) at our house.
xalliihum jaalsiin.	Let them stay seated.
xalliiha talaata.	Let it be three (price).
xallii yimši.	Let him go. Have him go.
xalliihum yištaghilu.	Let them work. Make them work.

2. /awwal-ma/ and /gabl-ma/ are examples of a set of words which precede a verb and require /-ma/ before the verb (in this case, it is not a negative word):

awwal-ma yiwṣal	as soon as he arrives	اول ما بوصل
gabl-ma yimši	before he leaves	قبلما يمشي
ba9d-ma daxalat	after she entered	بعد ما د خلت
biduun-ma yisallim 9aleehum	without greeting them	بدون ما يسلم عليهم
kull-ma asaafir	whenever I travel	كلما اسافر
liHadd-ma yiji	until he comes	لحد ما يجي
ileen-ma yiji	until he returns	الينما يجي

Both /liHadd-ma/ and /ileen-ma/ mean 'until' and are used with verbs. They can be used with time expressions, in which case the suffix /-ma/ is dropped:

li-Hadd as-saa9a xamsa	until five o'clock
ileen as-saa9a xamsa	until five o'clock

3. Note that /liHadd-ma/ is an example of a word in which three consonants occur in a cluster. In a case where three or four consonants would occur together, a short vowel is inserted to break up the cluster. This is not written in the text, however, because it is not really part of the word; it merely facilitates pronounciation:

	(actual pronunciation)
liHadd-ma	liHadd^{i}-ma
šuft muHammad	šuft^{i} muHammad
nuṣṣ saa9a	nuṣṣ^{i} saa9a

4. /Haaḍir/, 'ready' is usually used as a response to an order.

5. /lamman/ is also used before verbs, and means 'when' as a subordinating conjunction (not a question):

lamman waṣalna	when we arrived
lamman šuftu	when I saw him

6. /lissa9/ may be used with a negative verb (see Structure Sentence 7) or alone, to mean 'not yet'. Remember that with any other predicate, it means 'still' (Lesson 12). In the case of /lissa9/, /ma/ is a negative word:

lissa9 ma raaH.	He hasn't gone yet.
lissa9 ma gaabaltu.	I haven't met him yet.

7. /saafar/, 'to travel', implies a long distance; otherwise, /raaH/ is used. /saafar/, like /raaH/, is used without a preposition:

saafarna faraansa.	We traveled to France.

Vocabulary Notes

ṭayyaara, -aat	airplane	طيارة -ات
xidma, xadamaat	service	خدمة خَدَمات
saafar, yisaafir	travel	سافر يسافر
xalla, yixalli (xalleet)	let, leave	خلى يخلي (خليت)

Drills

1. Have him call me. — xallii yikallimni. — خليه يكلمني.

Substitute:

have her
have them
see me
see us
have him
come to us
come to him
return to him
return to me
give me money
have her
buy me coffee

2. Let him go. — xallii yimši. — خليه يمشي.

Substitute:

travel
let her
let me
enter
let them
meet him
take the suitcases
let us
try
stand here a little while

3. Stay (m) here. xalliik hina. خليك هنا٠

Substitute:

at my house
there
on the line
standing
at the airport
waiting until I arrive
downstairs

4. I'm going to travel ('traveling') tomorrow. ana misaafir bukra. انا مسافر بكرة٠

Substitute:

we
were traveling last month
she
is traveling today
was traveling the day before yesterday
they
are traveling soon
are going overseas next week

5. When we arrive, tell me. lamman niwṣal, gulli. لمن نوصل قللي٠

Substitute:

before we arrive
as soon as we arrive
as soon as they arrive
after they arrive
after you (m) arrive
before you (m) arrive
before she arrives
when she arrives
when you (p) arrive
as soon as you (p) arrive
as soon as you (f) arrive
every time you (f) arrive

6. They still haven't come. lissa9 ma joo. لسع ما جوا٠

Substitute:

seen her
I
called her
called my sister
gone to my sister's house
we
met the bank president
you (m)
talked to me about the proposal
spent the money
she
drunk the tea
he
written the letters
gone upstairs

7. He sat here until I met him. — jalas hina liHadd-ma gaabaltu. — جلس هنا لحد ما قابلته ·

Substitute:

until I returned
until I brought him the books
until we sat beside him
until they stood up
until all of them went out
until the director came
until they closed the office

8. He went without seeing me. — raaH biduun-ma yišuufani. — راح بدون ما يشوفني·

Substitute:

without greeting me
without saying anything
without asking about my health
without closing the door
without knowing why
without buying anything
without meeting his assistant
without drinking the tea

Situations

1.
A. On which plane are you (m) traveling?
B. The four o'clock plane.
A. Good. It's still early.
B. The man hasn't brought my suitcases yet. Where could they be? (/feen yikuunu/)
A. Ask the clerk ('employee').
B. When he returns, I'll ask him.

2.
A. Excuse me, may I ask a question?
B. Of course, any service.
A. I don't know where my suitcases are.
B. After you entered the airport, where did you put them?
A. I gave them to a man who was standing beside me.
B. He took them to the airline company, I'm sure.

3.
A. Stay here until I return.
B. How long?
A. Not more than ten minutes.
B. I want to drink something.
A. You can buy coffee or tea over there.
B. Yes, of course. Thanks.

LESSON 27

Dialogue

A.	Do you speak Arabic?	titkallam 9arabi?	تتكلم عربي؟
	I study	azaakir	ازاكر
	every	kull	كل
B.	A little. I study an hour every day.	šwayya. azaakir 9arabi saa9a kull yoom.	شويه . ازاكر عربي ساعة كل يوم
	in order to	9ašaan	عشان
A.	I'm studying English in order to go to America.	ana adrus ingiliizi 9ašaan asaafir amriika.	انا ادرس انكليزي عشان اسافر أمريكا.
	we practice	nitmarran	نتمرن
	together	ma9a ba9ḍ	مع بعض
B.	We can practice together.	mumkin nitmarran ma9a ba9ḍ.	ممكن نتمرن مع بعض.
A.	Yes. You speak English with me and I speak Arabic with you.	iiwa. inta titkallam ingiliizi ma9aaya w ana atkallam 9arabi ma9aak.	ايوه . انت تتكلم انكليزي معايَ وانا أتكلم عربي معاك.
	late afternoon	il-9aṣur	العصر
B.	Can you come to my house late this afternoon?	tigdar tijiili fil-9aṣur?	تقدر تجيلي في العصر؟
A.	Of course.	ṭab9an.	طبعا.
	don't	laa	لا
B.	Don't forget.	laa tinsa.	لا تنسَ.

Structure Sentences

1.	We must study.	laazim nizaakir.	لازم نزاكر.
2.	I studied for six months.	darast sitta šuhuur.	درستْ ستة شهور.
3.	We saw each other yesterday.	šufna ba9ḍ ams.	شفنا بعض امس.
4.	Do you (m) agree with me?	inta muwaafig ma9aaya?	انتَ موافق معايَ؟
5.	You (m) must speak with him.	laazim titkallam ma9aa.	لازم تتكلم معاه .
6.	I have an appointment in the afternoon.	9indi maw9ad ba9d aḍ-ḍuhur.	عندي موعد بعد الظهر.

7. Come (m) in order to see them.	ta9aal 9ašaan tišuufahum.	تعال عشان تشوفهم.
8. He went because he has an appointment.	raaH 9ašaan 9indu maw9ad.	راح عشان عنده موعد.

Grammatical Notes

1. /zaakar/ refers to 'study' in the sense of a momentary activity, i.e., studying at a desk. /daras/ refers to 'study' in the sense of pursuing an academic subject.

2. /kull/ may be used with indefinite words in the singular, to mean 'each' or 'every':

kull yoom	every day
kull sana	every year
kull waaHid	every one, everyone

Remember that this contrasts with its use meaning 'all' (Lesson 23).

3. /9ašaan/ means 'in order to' when used with a verb.

adrus ingiliizi 9ašaan asaafir amriika.	I'm studying English in order to go to America.
ta9aal 9ašaan tišuufahum.	Come in order to see them.

It may also be used to mean 'because' (this is a borrowing from the Egyptian dialect; /li'ann/ is more common).

raaH 9ašaan 9indu maw9ad.

When used with a noun, /9ašaan/ means 'for' (Lesson 16).

4. /ba9ḍ/ is usually translated 'each other' in English; it refers to a reciprocal action. It may be used as a direct or indirect object:

nitmarran ma9a ba9ḍ.	We practice with each other.
šufna ba9ḍ.	We saw each other.
katabna li ba9ḍ.	We wrote to each other.

5. /ma9a/, when used with pronoun objects, has the base form /ma9aa-/:

ma9aa	with him	معاه
ma9aaha	with her	معاها
ma9aahum	with them	معاهم
ma9aak	with you (m)	معاك
ma9aaki	with you (f)	معاكِ
ma9aakum	with you (p)	معاكم
ma9aaya	with me	معايَ
ma9aana	with us	معانا

6. Times of the day are many in Saudi Arabia, because they may also refer to the five prayer times (these are starred):

al-fajr*	dawn	الفجر
aṣ-ṣubuH	morning	الصبح
aḍ-ḍuhur*	noon	الظهر
al-9aṣur*	late afternoon	العصر
al-maghrib*	sunset	المغرب
al-masa	evening	المسا
al-9iša*	evening	العشا
al-leel	night	الليل

The prayer-times are frequently used with /gabl/, 'before', and /ba9d/, 'after':

ba9d aḍ-ḍuhur	afternoon
gabl al-maghrib	before sunset (etc.)

7. The negative command in Arabic is formed by using the word /laa/ with the imperfect verb:

laa tiruuH.	Don't go (m).
laa tiruuHi.	Don't go (f).
laa tiruuHu.	Don't go (p).
laa tinsa.	Don't forget (m).
laa tikallimha.	Don't talk (m) to her.

8. /atmarran/, 'to practice', takes the preposition /9ala/ if followed by a noun:

laazim atmarran 9ala l-9arabi.	I must practice Arabic.

Vocabulary Notes

sawa*	together	سوا
zaakar, yizaakir	study	زاكر يزاكر
nisi, yinsa (nisiit)	forget	نسي ينسى (نسيت)
atmarran, yitmarran	practice	اتمرن يتمرن

*This alternates with /ma9a ba9ḍ/.

Drills

1. I study every day. __azaakir kull yoom__. ازاكر كل يوم.

Substitute:

I go
every year
every week
I meet him
I see them
every ten minutes
every time
I talk to her
every night
every month

2. Come (m) in order to see them. — ta9aal 9ašaan tišuufahum. — تعال عشان تشوفهم.

Substitute:

go (m)
in order to ask him
in order to bring money from the bank
in order to study
sit down (f)
in order to use the telephone
speak Arabic (p)
in order to practice with me
in order to understand the people

3. We saw each other yesterday. — šufna ba9ḍ ams. — شفنا بعض امس.

Substitute:

went with each other
agreed with each other
they
met each other
sat beside each other
you (p)
talked to each other
worked together
greeted each other
we
studied in the university together
liked each other
wrote to each other

4. You (m) must speak English with me. — laazim titkallam ingiliizi ma9aaya. — لازم تتكلم انكليزي معايَ.

Substitute:

with us
with him
with them
with her
with all of them
with the girls
with the Americans
with the secretary (f)

5. I have an appointment in the afternoon. — 9indi maw9ad ba9d aḍ-ḍuhur. — عندي موعد بعد الظهر.

Substitute:

after sunset
after dawn
before evening (prayer)
in the evening
at night
after mid-afternoon
in the morning
at noon

6. Don't forget (m). laa <u>tinsa</u>. لا تنسَ.

Substitute:

(to a man):
go
come back early
tell her
(to a woman):
try
let him come
leave your purse here
(to a group)
sit here
go upstairs
bring your children

7. Given the verb in the perfect tense (m, f, or p), change the sentence to a negative command.

Example: raaH badri. ⟶ laa tiruuH badri. راح بدري. ← لا تروح بدري.

Continue:

zaakar fil-maktab. زاكر في المكتب.
zaakarat fil-maktab. زاكرت في المكتب.
9amalat mawaa9iid katiir. عملت مواعيد كثير.
katabu fil-kitaab. كتبوا في الكتاب.
istannu. استنوا.
nazal fil-fundug. نزل في الفندق.
xallaahum yiju. خلاهم يجوا.

Situations

1.
A. Come with me.
B. I can't yet. I have to meet my boss.
A. OK, I'll wait an hour.
B. Don't go without me, please.

2.
A. Whom does he want to see?
B. The director of the company.
A. Have him leave him a note and come back later.
B. I already told him.

3.
A. Do you (p) know each other?
B. Yes, we met each other at school.
A. You are friends?
B. Yes, I've known Khalid for a long time.

LESSON 28

Dialogue

	professor	ustaaz	استاذ
A.	Are you a professor here?	inta ustaaz hina?	انتَ استاذ هنا؟
	student	ţaalib	طالب
	third (f)	taalta	ثالثة
B.	No, I'm a third-year student.	la', ana ţaalib fi sana taalta.	لا. انا طالب فى سنة ثالثة.
	college	kulliyya	كلية
	engineering	handasa	هندسة
	isn't that so?	muu kida?	مو كده ؟
A.	In the College of Engineering, aren't you?	fi kulliyyat al-handasa, muu kida?	فى كلية الهندسة، مو كده ؟
	yes	illa	الّا
	I was educated	at9allamt	اتعلمت
	Egypt	maşur	مصر
	first (adverb)	fil-awwal	في الاول
	I finished	kammalt	كملت
	high school	saanawi	ثانوي
B.	Yes. I was educated in Egypt first and finished high school there.	illa. at9allamt fi maşur fil-awwal wu kammalt saanawi hinaak.	الا. اتعلمت في مصر في الاول وكملت ثانوي هناك.
	at night	fil-leel	في الليل.
A.	Do you (p) study at night?	tidrusu fil-leel?	تدرسوا في الليل؟
	in the daytime	fin-nahaar	في النهار
B.	No, it's all in the daytime.	la', kullu fin-nahaar.	لا، كله في النهار.

Structure Sentences

1.	He is a junior high school teacher.	huwwa mudarris i9daadi.	هو مدرس اعدادي.
2.	She is in the first grade of elementary school.	hiyya fi sana uula ibtidaa'i.	هي في سنة اولى ابتدائي.

3.	My two children are in nursery school. (or: kindergarten).	awlaadi l-itneen fil-Haḍaana.	اولادي الاثنين في الحضانة.
4.	There are many students in the College of Education.	fii ṭalaba katiir fi kulliyyat at-tarbiya.	فيه طلبة كثير في كلية التربية.
5.	He is well educated.	huwwa mit9allim kwayyis.	هو متعلم كويس.
6.	You (m) must finish your education abroad.	laazim tikammil at-ta9liim barra.	لازم تكمل التعليم برا.
7.	This is the last time.	haadi aaxir marra.	هادي آخر مرة.
8.	Where did you learn English?	feen at9allamt ingiliizi?	فين اتعلمت انكليزي؟

Grammatical Notes

1. The ordinal numerals are:

Masculine		Feminine		
awwal	اول	uula	اولى	first
taani	ثاني	taanya	ثانية	second
taalit	ثالث	taalta	ثالثة	third
raabi9	رابع	raab9a	رابعة	fourth
xaamis	خامس	xaamsa	خامسة	fifth
saadis	سادس	saadsa	سادسة	sixth
saabi9	سابع	saab9a	سابعة	seventh
taamin	ثامن	taamna	ثامنة	eighth
taasi9	تاسع	taas9a	تاسعة	ninth
9aašir	عاشر	9aašra	عاشرة	tenth

Notice that from 'second' on, they follow a predictable vowel pattern.

If the ordinal numeral follows the noun, it must agree in gender:

al-beet al-awwal	the first house
al-marra t-taalta	the third time
marra taanya	a second time; another time

These numerals may also be used <u>before</u> the noun, in which case they remain masculine:

awwal šaari9*	the first street
raabi9 beet	the fourth house
raabi9 marra	the fourth time
raabi9 sana	the fourth year

*Note the difference between this phrase and /awwal aš-šaari9/, 'at the beginning of the street' (Lesson 15).

/aaxir/, 'last', is usually used before nouns:

aaxir beet	the last house
aaxir marra	the last time

Ordinal numerals have a special form only for the numbers 1-10; after this, the regular numeral form is used, always after the noun:

al-beet al-iHḍa9š	the eleventh house
al-marra l-xamasṭa9š	the fifteenth time

2. The "colleges" in Saudi universities are:

aadaab	Arts	آداب
9uluum	Sciences	علوم
ziraa9a	Agriculture	زراعة
tijaara	Commerce	تجارة
tarbiya	Education	تربية
handasa	Engineering	هندسة
ṣaydala	Pharmacy	صيدلة
ṭibb	Medicine	طب
iqtiṣaad	Economics	اقتصاد

3. There are several words which may be translated 'education' in English:

wizaarat al-ma9aarif	The Ministry of Education (literally, 'knowledge')
kulliyyat at-tarbiya	The College of Education (literally, 'upbringing')
ta9liim	education, learning

4. /muu kida/, 'isn't that so?' is used after any statement, to check its correctness. It is equivalent to English 'isn't it?', 'aren't you?', etc., or 'n'est-ce pas?' in French. There are several common variations of this phrase, among them:

miš kida? (borrowed from Egyptian)
muu ṣaHH?
muu ṣaHiiH?

5. /illa/ is an emphatic way of saying 'yes'. It is also used in response to a negative question, to emphasize the affirmative answer. Another way of saying 'yes' is /ee na9am/ (this is more common in the eastern part of the country).

6. The levels of education in Saudi Arabia are:

Haḍaana	nursery school; kindergarten	حضانة
ibtidaa'i	elementary	ابتدائي
i9daadi	intermediate (junior high)	اعدادي
saanawi	secondary (senior high)	ثانوي
jaam9a	university	جامعة
bakaluryoos	Bachelor's degree	بكلوريوس
majisteer	Master's degree	مجستير
dukturaa	Doctor's degree	دكتورا

When used with the word /madrasa/, 'school', the adjective is feminine:

madrasa ibtidaa'iyya	elementary school
madrasa i9daadiyya	intermediate school
madrasa saanawiyya	secondary school

7. To say 'both', 'all three', etc., the definite article is used with the numeral, after the noun:

awlaadi l-itneen	my two children; both of my children

awlaadi t-talaata	all three of my children
al-madaaris al-arba9a	all four schools

Vocabulary Notes

ustaaz, asaatiza	professor	استاذ اساتذة
mudarris, -iin (-aat)	teacher	مدرس -ين -ات
ţaalib, ţalaba (ţullaab)*	student	طالب،طلبة (طلاب)
at9allam, yit9allim	be educated, learn	اتعلم يتعلم
kammal, yikammil	finish	كمل يكمل
mit9allim, -a, -iin	educated	متعلم -ين

*This word has two plurals.

Drills

1. I am a third-year student. ana ţaalib fi sana taalta. انا طالب في سنة ثالثة.

Substitute:

first
second
third
fourth
fifth
sixth

2. This is the tenth house. haada l-beet al-9aašir. هادا البيت العاشر.

Substitute:

fourth
sixth
third
second
eighth
first
fifth
seventh
tenth
eleventh
twentieth

3. This is the fourth year. haadi raabi9 sana. هادي رابع سنة.

Substitute:

fifth
second
tenth
eleventh
sixth
eighth
third

4. In the College of Engineering, right? — fi kulliyyat al-handasa, muu kida? — فى كلية الهندسة، مو كده؟

Substitute:

Commerce
Agriculture
Education
Sciences
Medicine
Arts
Engineering
Pharmacy
Economics

5. I was educated in Egypt first. — at9allamt fi maṣur fil-awwal. — اتعلمت في مصر في الاول.

Substitute:

we
you (m)
she
they
you (f)
he
you (p)
I

6. I finished high school there. — kammalt saanawi hinaak. — كملت ثانوي هناك.

Substitute:

the university
my Bachelor's degree ('the Bachelor's degree')
intermediate school
elementary school
my Master's degree
my doctorate
secondary school

7. Both of my children are in school. — awlaadi l-itneen fil-madrasa. — اولادي الاثنين في المدرسة.

Substitute:

all four
all six
all three
all five
all seven
both

8. Given the phrase with a numeral and plural noun, change it to a singular noun with an ordinal numeral.

Example: talaata siniin ⟶ sana taalta — ثلاثة سنين ← سنة ثالثة

Continue:

talaata ayyaam — ثلاثة ايام
itneen muwaẓẓafiin — اثنين موظفين

xamsa madaaris	خمسة مدارس
9ašara rijaal	عشرة رجال
sitta ṭalaba	ستة طلبة
sab9a ṭayyaaraat	سبعة طيارات

Situations

1.
A. When will you (p) travel?
B. The plane leaves at night.
A. All of your children are going with you, aren't they?
B. Yes, all three of my children and my wife, too.
A. Is this the first time you (p) go together?
B. No, no...maybe the tenth time. We travel together often ('much').

2.
A. I finished my education ('the education') in Egypt before I returned here.
B. I heard that you are a professor in the university.
A. Yes, in the College of Commerce, Riyadh University.
B. Do you teach in the daytime only?
A. Daytime and nightime both.

3.
A. Is your brother a student now?
B. Yes, he's still in intermediate school. He'll finish next year, if God wills.
A. And then go to secondary school?
B. Yes, after the exams.

Cultural Notes

1. In Saudi Arabia (and in most of the Arab countries), the elementary level of education is six years, intermediate is three years, and secondary is three years. General examinations are given for one week at the end of each year, which must be passed with a certain percentage score for the student to continue to the next year. National (government-controlled) examinations are usually held at the end of each of the three levels.

LESSON 29

Dialogue

doctor	duktoor	دكتور
A. I'd like to introduce you to Dr. Said.	aHubb a9arrifak 9ala d-duktoor sa9iid.	احب اعرفك على الدكتور سعيد.
tidarris	you (m) teach	تدرّس
B. I'm honored. Where do you teach?	atšarraft. feen Haḍratak tidarris?	اتشرفت. فين حضرتك تدرس؟
department	gism	قسم
history	taariix	تاريخ
A. In the College of Arts, History Department.	fi kulliyyat al-aadaab, gism at-taariix.	في كلية الآداب، قسم التاريخ.
B. From where did you get your doctorate?	axadt ad-dukturaa min feen?	اخذت الدكتورا من فين؟
Beirut	beeruut	بيروت.
scholarship	minHa	منحة
A. From Beirut. I had a scholarship.	min beeruut. kaan 9indi minHa.	من بيروت. كان عندي منحة.
I visited	zurt	زرت
Lebanon	libnaan	لبنان
time, occasion	marra	مرة
B. Beirut! I've visited Lebanon twice.	beeruut! ana zurt libnaan marrateen.	بيروت! انا زرت لبنان مرتين.

Structure Sentences

1. This is the engineer Abdalla.	haada l-muhandis 9abdaḷḷa.	هادا المهندس عبد الله
2. Where is the emir's office?	feen maktab al-amiir?	فين مكتب الامير؟
3. I teach in the English department	adarris fi gism al-ingiliizi.	ادرس في قسم الانكليزي.
4. The government gives scholarships to Saudi students.	al-Hukuuma ti9ṭi minaH liṭ-ṭalaba s-su9uudiyiin.	الحكومة تعطي منح للطلبة السعوديين.
5. The airplane left late.	aṭ-ṭayyaara gaamat mit'axxira.	الطيارة قامت متأخرة.

Grammatical Notes

1. The most common personal titles in Saudi Arabia are:

al-muhandis	المهندس	engineer (this may refer to anyone with a degree in the sciences--architect, economist, etc.)
ad-duktoor	الدكتور	Doctor
al-ustaaz	الاستاذ	Professor (this is also used as a title of respect)
al-waziir	الوزير	Minister
aš-šeex	الشيخ	Sheikh
as-safiir	السفير	Ambassador
al-amiir, -a	الامير، ـة	Emir, Prince; Princess
al-malik, -a	الملك، ـة	King; Queen
al-axx	الاخ	brother (this is used in referring to a close friend)
al-uxt	الاخت	sister (this is used for a friend or as a title of respect)

Note that the titles are used with the definite article before the name:

haada l-axx maHmuud.	This is (my friend) Mahmoud.
haada d-duktoor sa9iid.	This is Dr. Said.

2. "Colleges" in universitites are sub-divided into departments according to subject, for example:

taariix	history	تاريخ
jughraafya	geography	جغرافيا
riyaaḍa	mathematics	رياضيات
kiimya	chemistry	كيميا
9uluum siyaasiyya	political science	علوم سياسية
diraasaat aš-šarq al-awsaṭ	Middle Eastern studies	دراسات الشرق الاوسط

3. /a9ṭa, yi9ṭi/, 'to give', is a classicized word which is used almost as frequently as /adda, yiddi/. It is more common in formal situations. It is usually used with direct objects, although /l-/, 'to', is sometimes heard.

Perfect	Imperfect		
huwwa a9ṭa	yi9ṭi	يعطي	اعطى
hiyya a9ṭat	ti9ṭi	تعطي	اعطت
humma a9ṭu	yi9ṭu	يعطوا	اعطوا
inta a9ṭeet	ti9ṭi	تعطي	اعطيت
inti a9ṭeeti	ti9ṭi	تعطي	اعطيتِ
intu a9ṭeetu	ti9ṭu	تعطوا	اعطيتوا
ana a9ṭeet	a9ṭi	اعطي	اعطيت
iHna a9ṭeena	ni9ṭi	نعطي	اعطينا

4. The verb /kaan, yikuun/ can be used with modal words to express past and future tense:

9indi minHa.	I have a scholarship.
kaan 9indi minHa.	I had a scholarship.
raH-yikuun 9indi minHa.	I will have a scholarship.
laazim yiruuH.	He must go.
kaan laazim yiruuH.	He had to go. He should have gone.

mumkin niji ba9deen.	We can come later.
kaan mumkin niji ba9deen.	We could have come later.

Vocabulary Notes

minHa, minaH	scholarship	منحة منح
9aaṣima, 9awaaṣim	capital	عاصمة عواصم
marra, -aat	time, occasion	مرة -ات
gism, agsaam	department	قسم اقسام
a9ṭa, yi9ṭi	give	اعطى يعطي
darras, yidarris	teach	درّس يدرّس
zaar, yizuur (zurt)	visit	زار يزور (زرت)
gaam, yiguum (gumt)	stand up, get up, ascend	قام يقوم (قمت)
muhandis, -iin	engineer	مهندس -ين
duktoor, dakaatra	doctor	دكتور دكاترة
šeex, šuyuux	sheikh	شيخ شيوخ
safiir, sufara	ambassador	سفير سفرا
amiir, umara	prince	امير امرا
amiira, -aat	princess	اميرة -ات
malik, muluuk	king	ملك ملوك
malika, -aat	queen	ملكة -ات

	Arab State	Nationality Adjective		
Saudi Arabia	as-su9uudiyya	su9uudi	سعودي	السعودية
Yemen	al-yaman	yamaani	يماني	اليمن
The Emirates	al-imaaraat	---		الإمارات
Oman	9umaan	9umaani	عماني	عُمان
Qatar	qaṭar	qaṭari	قطري	قطر
Bahrein	al-baHreen	baHreeni	بحريني	البحرين
Kuwait	al-kuweet	kuweeti	كويتي	الكويت
Lebanon	libnaan	libnaani	لبناني	لبنان
Syria	suuriya	suuri	سوري	سوريا
Jordon	al-urdun	urduni	اردني	الاردن
Iraq	al-9iraaq	9iraaqi	عراقي	العراق
Morocco	al-maghrib	maghribi	مغربي	المغرب
Algeria	al-jazaayir	jazaayiri	جزايري	الجزاير
Tunisia	tuunis	tuunisi	تونسي	تونس
Libya	liibya	liibi	ليبي	ليبيا
Egypt	maṣur	maṣri	مصري	مصر
Sudan	as-suudaan	suudaani	سوداني	السودان
Palestine	falasṭiin	falasṭiini	فلسطيني	فلسطين

	Capital City	
Riyadh	ar-riyaaḍ	الرياض
Sanaa	ṣan9a	صنعا
Abu Dhabi	abuu ẓabi	ابو ظبي
Muscat	masqaṭ	مسقط
Doha	ad-dooHa	الدوحة
Manama	al-manaama	المنامة
Kuwait City	al-kuweet	الكويت
Beirut	beeruut	بيروت
Damascus	dimišq	دمشق
Amman	9ammaan	عمان
Baghdad	baghdaad	بغداد
Rabat	ar-rabaaṭ	الرباط
Algiers	al-jazaayir	الجزاير

Tunis	tuunis	تونس
Tripoli	ṭarablus	طرابلس
Cairo	al-qaahira	القاهرة
Khartoum	al-xarṭuum	الخرطوم
Jerusalem	al-guds	القدس

Drills

1. I'd like to introduce you to Dr. Said. — aHubb a9arrifak 9ala d-duktoor sa9iid. — احب اعرفك على الدكتور سعيد.

Substitute:

the prince
"brother" Ahmad
the minister
Professor Abdalla
"engineer" Mahmoud
the ambassador
the king
the princess
"sister" Miryam
the queen
Dr. Said
Sheikh Muhammad

2. I teach in the History Department. — adarris fi gism at-taariix. — ادرّس في قسم التاريخ.

Substitute:

the Mathematics Department
the Chemistry Department
the Political Science Department
the Geography Department
the Middle East Studies Department

3. Beirut! I've visited Lebanon twice. — beeruut! ana zurt libnaan marrateen. — بيروت! انا زرت لبنان مرتين.

Substitute:

Amman - Jordan
Sanaa - Yemen
Baghdad - Iraq
Abu Dhabi - The Emirates
Damascus - Syria
Cairo - Egypt
Tunis - Tunisia
Tripoli - Libya
Muscat - Oman
Manama - Bahrein
Algiers - Algeria
Khartoum - Sudan
Doha - Qatar
Kuwait City - Kuwait
Rabat - Morocco
Riyadh - Saudi Arabia
Beirut - Lebanon

4. Where is the Emir's office? — feen maktab al-amiir? — فين مكتب الامير؟

Substitute:

the king
the Minister of Finance
the Minister of Education
the Minister of Defense
the ambassador
the professor
the engineer
the doctor
the teacher
the manager
Mr. Smith
the supervisor

5. She will get up now. (i.e., in order to leave) — Ha-tiguum daHHiin. — حتقوم دحين.

Substitute:

will leave
he
visit his father
I
drive the car
stand up
we
visit our family
learn the new lesson
she
get up

6. I visited him yesterday. — zurtu ams. — زرته امس.

Substitute:

I visited them
she visited them
she saw them
we
drove the car twice
got up at 4:30
saw all of them
he
drove to the house

7. He gave me money. — a9ṭaani fuluus. — اعطاني فلوس.

Substitute:

she gave me
the letter
they gave him
they gave us
the order
I gave you (m)
I gave the manager

the note
we gave somebody
the scholarship

(Repeat the drill, changing it to future tense)

8. Given the name of the country, use a sentence with the nationality adjective.

Example: huwwa min as-suudaan.→ huwwa suudaani. هو من السودان. ← هو سوداني.

Continue:

huwwa min al-yaman.	هو من اليمن.
gaṭar.	قطر
libnaan	لبنان
al-9iraaq	العراق
tuunis	تونس
al-maghrib	المغرب
al-kuweet	الكويت
suuriya	سوريا
al-baHreen	البحرين
liibya	ليبيا
maṣur	مصر
9umaan	عمان
al-urdun	الاردن
as-su9uudiyya	السعودية
falasṭiin	فلسطين
al-jazaayir	الجزاير
as-suudaan	السودان

Situations

1.
A. I'm leaving for Egypt tomorrow.
B. Really, why?
A. I have a scholarship to study history at Cairo University.
B. Congratulations! Will you stay long? ('much')
A. Until I finish my Master's degree, if God wills.
B. When you return, will you teach in the university?
A. Yes, I'll be a professor.

2.
A. Yesterday I met the sheikh.
B. What did you (p) discuss?
A. We discussed education and health. ('the education and the health')
B. Good, I want to visit him soon, too.
A. He asked me to visit him next month at the Emir's house. (/9ind al-amiir/)
B. Maybe you and the ambassador can both go.

3.
A. There are many Eguptian teachers and professors in Saudi Arabia, aren't there?
B. Oh yes, in elementary, intermediate, and secondary schools, and in the university, too.
A. And in girls' education?
B. In girls' education [even] more! Women teachers are Egyptian and Palestinian.
A. But Saudi women are now studying education.
B. Yes, in the Girls' College here there is a Department of Education.

LESSON 30

Review last nine dialogues.

Supplementary Drills

1. I don't know what he bought. — ma adri eeš ištara. — ما ادري ايش اشترى.

Substitute:

what he saw
where the glass is
if he agrees or not ('is agreeing or no')
why they are in a hurry
where the driver is
[whether] he wants coffee or tea
when he met the minister
the telephone number
who is the manager's assistant
how many employees are in the company
why nobody answers
who she went with
what time the plane left ('ascended')
how old his daughter is
where he was educated
how many colleges are in the university
what the capital of Iraq is
which department he teaches in
the prince's name

2. When will you (m) go to the doctor? — mita Ha-tiruuH lid-duktoor? — متا حتروح للدكتور؟

Substitute:

have ('drink') tea at my house?
be able to return?
speak to the driver?
finish your education?
tell me about the agreement?
be free?
will someone tell him?
will we go together?
will we see each other?
will your son enter kindergarten?
will you (m) visit me?

3. In Saudi Arabia there are many cars. — fis-su9uudiyya fii sayyaaraat katiir. — في السعودية فيه سيارات كثير.

Substitute:

buildings
offices
companies
foreigners
Americans
embassies
airplanes
streets
ministers

princes
projects
plans
employees
teachers
professors
students
universities
colleges
doctors
schools
families
cities
airports
Egyptians
Arabs
banks

Narratives

1. I live in the big house near the post office. I work as the manager of an American company which has been in Saudi Arabia three years. Every day I drive my car to the office about 8:30. My wife is a teacher and we have two children, a boy and a girl. We like Arabia and [have] traveled to Yemen, Lebanon, and also Jordan. Next year we will go to Egypt, we hope. The children are in the American school, where one (m) is in the fifth grade and one (f) is in the second grade. They speak a little Arabic because they study it in school two hours every week. I met their teacher last week, and she said that they are studying well and learning quickly. We are all happy here and have many friends, both Arab and American.

2. When I entered the university at first I studied history. Later I studied political science for the M.A., and then I worked for the government. I like to travel, especially in the Middle East, and I want to learn Arabic in order to talk to the people whom I meet.

3. Please come to my house soon; my wife wants to meet your wife, and bring the children, of course. There are many things we could talk about; I want to learn about Saudi Arabia--the people, the history, the geography, the commerce. Call me on the telephone after 9:00 a.m.--you know my office phone, don't you? And I'll give you my home telephone number too. Sorry, do you have a piece of paper and a pen? Thanks. If God wills, we'll hear from you (p) soon.

4. Excuse me, what time is it? Oh, I'm late and I have an appointment at the ministry! Can I find a taxi here? Across from that big building? Thanks.

5. Take me to the Ministry of Defense, please. I'm in a hurry, but drive carefully. Where are you from? Sudan, really? How long have you been here in Arabia? Ten years! That's a long time! Are you happy here? Thank God. Yes, I speak Arabic because I studied it for ten months. I like to speak Arabic; I meet nice people. Turn left here--here is fine. How much? Take it (/atfaḍḍal/). Goodby.

LESSON 31

Dialogue

(At the airport)

	ticket	tazkira	تذكرة
	passport	jawaaz as-safar	جواز السفر
A.	Ticket and passport, please.	at-tazkira wu jawaaz as-safar min faḍlak.	التذكرة وجواز السفر، من فضلك.
B.	Right here.	atfaḍḍal.	اتفضل
	visa	ta'šiira	تأشيرة
	entry	duxuul	دخول
A.	Give them to me. Do you have an entry visa?	addiinihumma. 9indak ta'šiirat duxuul?	ادينيهم. عندك تأشيرة دخول؟
B.	Yes.	iiwa.	ايوه.
A.	How many bags?	kam šanṭa?	كم شنطة؟
	red (p)	Humur	حمر
B.	Those three red suitcases.	at-talaata šunaṭ al-Humur hadool.	الثلاثة شنط الحمر هدول.
	weight	wazn	وزن
	excess	ziyaada	زيادة
	tax	ḍariiba	ضريبة
A.	You must pay 25 riyals for excess weight, plus the airport tax.	laazim tidfa9 xamsa wu 9išriin riyaal wazn ziyaada, zaayid ḍariibat al-maṭaar.	لازم تدفع خمسة وعشرين ريال وزن زيادة، زايد ضريبة المطار.

Structure Sentences

1.	Where is passport control?	feen al-jawaazaat?	فين الجوازات؟
2.	You must will out this card.	laazim timalli haada l-kart.	لازم تملي هادا الكرت.
3.	Where is the waiting room (lobby)?	feen ghurfat al-intiẓaar?	فين غرفة الانتظار؟
4.	Where is the rest room?	feen al-Hammaam?	فين الحمام؟
5.	I showed it (m) to her?	warreetahahuwwa.	وريتهاهو.
6.	I like the blue car.	aHubb as-sayyaara z-zarga.	احب السيارة الزرقا.

7. I made a reservation. 9amalt Hajz. عملت حجز.

8. Is this your luggage? haada 9afšak? هارا عفشك؟

Grammatical Notes

1. /jawaaz as-safar/, 'the passport', literally means 'the travel permit'. /jawaaz safar/ means 'a passport' (formed by making the second noun indefinite). The borrowed word /basboor, basboorṭaat/ is also used.

2. Some verbs take both a direct object and an indirect object. If these are both pronouns, they may both be suffixed to the verb.

(1) The indirect object is expressed before the direct object.

(2) The indirect object may be expressed as if it were direct, i.e., without /l-/.

(3) Only /huwwa/, /hiyya/, and /humma/ are used as the second object in these constructions.

addiinihuwwa.*	Give it to me.	('Give [to] me it (m).')
addiilihuwwa.*	Give it to me.	('Give to me it (m).')
addiiluhuwwa.	Give it to him.	('Give to him it (m).')
warreetahahuwwa.	I showed it (m) to her.	('I showed [to] her it (m).')
jaablihumma.	He brought them to me.	('He brought to me them.')
laazim tijiiblahahiyya.	You must bring it (f) to her.	

*Both are correct, although the first form is more used.

With other pronouns, this construction is avoided by expressing one of the objects with a noun.

3. While /šanṭa, šunaṭ/ refers to briefcases or suitcases, the word /9afš/ is usually used to refer to 'luggage' as a whole.

4. Colors must agree with the noun in gender and number. Most colors follow a predictable vowel pattern; some names are of foreign origin and do not change:

Masculine		Feminine		Plural		
aHmar	احمر	Hamra	حمرا	Humur	حمر	red
azrag	ازرق	zarga	زرقا	zurg	زرق	blue
axḍar	اخضر	xaḍra	خضرا	xuḍur	خضر	green
aṣfar	اصفر	ṣafra	صفرا	ṣufur	صفر	yellow
aswad	اسود	sooda	سودا	suud	سود	black
abyaḍ	ابيض	beeḍa	بيضا	beeḍ	بيض	white
banafsaji	بنفسجي					purple
burtukaani	برتكاني					orange
bunni	بني					brown
rumaadi	رمادي					gray

Examples:

at-talaata šunaṭ al-Humur (or: at-talaata šunaṭ al-Hamra)	the three red suitcases
al-waraga l-beeḍa	the white piece of paper
al-beet al-abyaḍ	the white house
al-kitaab al-aṣfar	the yellow book
as-sayyaara l-rumaadi	the gray car
9ajabni l-axḍar.	I liked the green [one].

Vocabulary Notes

jawaaz, -aat (safar)	passport	جواز سفر -ات
tazkira, tazaakir	ticket	تذكرة - تذاكر
ta'šiira, -aat	visa	تأشيرة -ات
ḍariiba, ḍaraayib	tax	ضريبة ضرايب
kart, kuruut	card	كرت كروت
malla, yimalli (malleet)	fill	ملى يملي (مليت)
warra, yiwarri (warreet)	show	ورّى يورّي (وريت)

Drills

1. Give them [to] me.   addiinihumma.   اد ينيهمّ.

Continue:

to him
to her
to us
Give it (m)
to me
to him
Give it (f)
to them
to me

2. Can you show it (m) to me?   mumkin tiwarriinihuwwa?   ممكن تورينيهوّ ؟

Continue:

to us
to them
give it (m)
to her
pay it (m)
to him
to me
but it (f)
for them
for us
sell them
for him
for her
bring it (m)
for me
for him
fill it (m) out
for them
for us

3. Those three red suitcases.   at-talaata šunaṭ al-Humur hadool.   الثلاثة شنط الحمر هدول.

Continue:

blue
yellow
gray
black
white
purple
green
brown
red

4. I like the blue car. aHubb as-sayyaara <u>z-zarga</u>. احب السيارة الزرقا.

Continue:

green
black
red
yellow
orange
gray
brown
white

5. Express the sentence in Arabic, first with a direct object and indirect object, then substitute the object pronouns.

Example: Give the book to Ahmad. ⟶ Give it to him.

addi l-kitaab l-aHmad. ⟶ addiiluhuwwa. ادّ الكتاب لاحمد. ← اديلوهُوّ.

Continue:

Give the suitcase to Miriam.
Fill out the card for the official ('employee').
Make the reservation for him.
Read the lesson to the students.
Bring the coffee to the lady.
Take the books to the professor.
Carry the suitcase for the girl.
Do the homework for me.
Leave [behind] the message for him.
Sell the car for me.

Situations

1.
A. Where do I take my ticket?
B. [Over] there, at the airline office (/maktab aṭ-ṭayaraan/).
A. Can I leave my suitcase here?
B. Are these all yours?
A. No, only the black ones.
B. Leave them for me. I'll carry them.

2.
A. Have you seen my friend (m)?
B. Yes, he's waiting for you in the waiting room.
A. Can you show it to me?
B. Of course. Go straight, then turn right.
A. Is there a restroom there?
B. Yes, of course.

3.
A. What are you (f) going to buy?
B. Maybe I'll buy this red purse. Do you (m) like it?
A. Yes, but I like the white one better. It's bigger.
B. But more expensive too. See the green one? Can you (m) get it for me?
A. Here (/atfaḍḍali/). This is the prettiest [one]. Buy it.

LESSON 32

Dialogue

(At a gasoline station)

A. Fill it (f) up.	malliiha.	مليها.
regular, ordinary	9aadi	عادي
excellent	mumtaaz	ممتاز
B. Regular or super?	9aadi walla mumtaaz?	عادي ولّا ممتاز؟
clean (m)	naḍḍif	نظيف
glass	guzaaz	قزاز
oil	zeet	زيت
A. Regular. Clean the glass and check ('see') the oil too, please.	9aadi. naḍḍif al-guzaaz wu šuuf az-zeet kamaan, min faḍlak.	عادي. نظف القزاز وشوف الزيت كمان من فضلك.
forbidden	mamnuu9	ممنوع
exit	xuruuj	خروج
B. OK. Sorry, no exit ('exiting is forbidden') from here.	ṭayyib. aasif, mamnuu9 al-xuruuj min hina.	طيب. آسف، ممنوع الخروج من هنا.
I take out	axarrij	اخرّج
A. From where can I take the car out?	min feen axarrij as-sayyaara?	من فين اخرّج السيارة؟
entrance	madxal	مدخل
B. From the entrance.	min al-madxal.	من المدخل.

Structure Sentences

1. I must find a gas station.	laazim alaagi maHaṭṭat banziin.	لازم الاقي محطة بنزين
2. No entry.	mamnuu9 ad-duxuul.	ممنوع الدخول.
3. No standing.	mamnuu9 al-wuguuf.	ممنوع الوقوف.
4. The car is very clean.	as-sayyaara marra naḍiifa.	السيارة مرة نظيفة.
5. Where is the bus station?	feen mawgif al-utubiis?	فين موقف الاتوبيس؟

Grammatical Notes

1. /naḍḍaf/, 'to clean', and /daxxal/, 'to bring', are examples of "causative" verbs in Arabic. These verbs can be recognized by the doubled consonants in the middle, and always follow the pattern:

Perfect	Imperfect
$C_1aC_2C_2aC_3$	$yiC_1aC_2C_2iC_3$
naḍḍaf	yinaḍḍif
daxxal	yidaxxil

The meaning of these verbs is 'to cause to do' or 'to cause to be'. /naḍḍaf/ is related to /naḍiif/, 'to clean', and literally means 'to cause to be clean'. /daxxal/ is related to /daxal/, 'to enter', and literally means 'to cause to enter'.

The following causative verbs are related to words introduced so far:

Verb		Related to:	
daxxal	bring in	daxal	دخّل
waṣṣal	take to a destination	waṣal	وصّل
fahham	explain, help to understand	fihim	فهّم
šayyal	load	šaal	شيّل
xarraj	expel	xaraj	خرّج
waggaf	stop, make stop	wigif	وقّف
nazzal	take down	nazal	نزّل
ṭalla9	carry up	ṭili9	طلّع
xallaṣ	finish	xalaṣ	خلّص
9arraf	inform	9irif	عرّف
rajja9	return (something)	riji9	رجّع
naḍḍaf	clean	naḍiif	نظّف
darras	teach	daras	درّس

2. /aasif/ (/aasfa, aasfiin/) is another way to say 'sorry'. It is used as often as /mit'assif/.

3. /xuruuj/ is an example of a "verbal noun". Verbal nouns are formed from the verb, and are usually translated into English as a gerund, i.e., a verb form ending in "-ing" which is used as a noun.

mamnuu9 al-xuruuj.	Departure is forbidden. Going out is forbidden.

Many verbal nouns follow a predictable vowel pattern, but there are variations:

duxuul	entry	دخول
xuruuj	exit, departure	خروج
wuguuf	standing	وقوف
juluus	sitting	جلوس
wuṣuul	arriving, arrival	وصول
kalaam	speaking	كلام
kitaaba	writing	كتابة
šurb	drinking	شرب
noom	sleeping	نوم

4. /madxal/ is an example of a "noun of place". Nouns of place are formed by using /ma-/ as a prefix to a verbal root. The pattern is usually:

$maC_1C_2aC_3$ plural: $maC_1aaC_2iC_3$

A noun of place may be literally translated as 'a place of doing'.

Not all verbs have nouns of place. Some of the more common ones are:

Noun of Place		Related to:	
madxal, madaaxil	entrance	daxal	مدخل مداخل
mawgif, mawaagif	stop, stand (bus, taxi)	wigif	موقف مواقف
maktab, makaatib	office	katab	مكتب مكاتب
maktaba, -aat	library, bookstore	katab	مكتبة -ات
madrasa, madaaris	school	daras	مدرسة مدارس
manzil, manaazil	house*	nazal	منزل منازل
majlis, majaalis	"majlis" (the king's public session)	jalas	مجلس مجالس
masjid, masaajid	mosque	sajad ('bow down')	مسجد مساجد
maṭaar, -aat	airport	ṭayyaara	مطار -ات
maHaṭṭa, -aat	station	Haṭṭ	محطة -ات
makaan, amaakin	place	kaan	مكان اماكن

*/manzil/ is more classicized than /beet/.

Vocabulary Notes

mumtaaz, -a, -iin	excellent	ممتاز -ين
9aadi, -iyya, -yiin	regular, ordinary	عادي -يين
naḍiif, -a, nuḍaaf	clean	نظيف، نظاف
mamnuu9, -a, -iin	forbidden, prevented	ممنوع -ين
utubiis, -aat	bus	اتوبيس -ات

Drills

1. Given a word, form the causative verb related to it.

Example: naḍiif ⟶ naḍḍaf — نظيف ← نظّف،

Continue:

waṣal — وصل
nazal — نزل
xaraj — خرج
xalaṣ — خلص
daxal — دخل
šaal — شال
wigif — وقف
daras — درس
9irif — عرف

2. You (m) must clean the glasses. — laazim tinaḍḍif al-guzaaz. — لازم تنظف القزاز.

Substitute:

you (f)
you (p)
we
finish early
he
I
the employees
she

explain it to him (use /fahham/)
I
his sister
the teachers
teach well
he
they
take in the suitcases
he
the men
we
take her there (use /waṣṣal/)
I
Ahmad

3. Clean (m) the glass. naḍḍif al-guzaaz. نظّف القزاز.

Substitute:

clean (f)
clean (p)
take (m) upstairs
the luggage
take out (f)
take out (m)
have him carry
have her carry
take down (m)
take down (p)
the books
clean (m)
the station
the glass

4. Given the verb, form the verbal noun:

xaraj خرج
daxal دخل
jalas جلس
katab كتب
atkallam اتكلم
wasal وصل
naam نام
širib شرب
wigif وقف

5. No exit here. mamnuu9 al-xuruuj hina. ممنوع الخروج هنا.

Substitute:

no entry
no standing
no talking
no drinking
no sitting
no sleeping
no writing

6. Given a word, form the noun of place related to it:

daras درس
katab (two nouns) كتب
ṭayyaara طيارة

wigif — وقف
daxal — دخل
nazal — نزل
kaan — كان
jalas — جلس

7. He went to the airport. raaH al-maṭaar. راح المطار.

Substitute:

the house
the library
the entrance of the building
the new office
many places
his son's school
the bus station
the gas station
the bus stop
the airport

8. Where is the bus stop? feen mawgif al-utubiis? فين موقف الاتوبيس؟

Substitute:

the entrance of the station
the airline office
the university library
the passport office (/jawaazaat/)
the rest room
the blue card
the waiting room
the visa department
the ticket office
the bus stop

Situations

1.
A. Fill it up, please.
B. OK. Super or regular?
A. Super. How much?
B. Eight riyals. [Shall] I clean the glass?
A. Please. And check the oil, too.
B. Any service.

2.
A. Where is the bus stop?
B. At the beginning of the next street.
A. When does the bus come?
B. Every half hour. Perhaps I can take you in my car. Where are you going?
A. To the university library. I'm a student in the Commerce Department.
B. Pleased to meet you.

3.
A. Sorry, no sitting here.
B. Why [not]?
A. This is the entrance of the lobby. Go ahead inside.
B. Thanks. Is there a rest room here?
A. Turn right at the desk, then straight ahead.
B. Thanks very much.

LESSON 33

Dialogue

	souk (bazaar market)	suug	سوق
	I pay	adfa9	ادفع
	bill	Hisaab	حساب
	shop	dukkaan	دكان
	fabric	gumaaš	قماش
A.	I want to go to the souk. I have to pay a bill at the fabric shop.	abgha aruuH as-suug. laazim adfa9 Hisaab fi dukkaan al-gumaaš.	ابغى اروح السوق. لازم ادفع حساب في دكان القماش.
	I look for	adawwir (9ala)	ادور (على)
	radio	raadyu	راديو
B.	I'll go with you, in order to look for a radio.	H-aruuH ma9aak 9ašaan adawwir 9ala raadyu.	حاروح معاك عشان ادور على راديو.
	middle	wasaṭ	وسط
	radios	rawaadi	روادي
	televisions	tilifizyoonaat	تلفزيونات
	recorders	musajjilaat	مسجلات
A.	I know a good shop in the middle of the souk. They sell radios, televisions, and recorders.	a9rif dukkaan kwayyis fi wasaṭ as-suug. yibii9u rawaadi wu tilifizyoonaat wu musajjilaat.	اعرف دكان كويس فى وسط السوق. يبيعوا روادي و تلفزيونات ومسجلات.
	I hope	9asa	عسى
	everywhere	kull makaan	كل مكان
B.	I hope there will be one. I've looked everywhere.	9asa yikuun fii waaHid. ana dawwart fi kull makaan.	عسى يكون فيه واحد. انا دورت في كل مكان.
	our Lord	rabbana	ربنا
	he gives success	yiwaffig	يوفق
A.	Good luck. ('May our Lord give you success')	rabbana yiwaffig.	ربنا يوفق.
B.	Thanks. ('If God wills')	in šaa' aḷḷaah.	ان شاء الله.

Structure Sentences

1.	There were many people there.	kaan fii naas katiir hinaak.	كان فيه ناس كثير هناك.
2.	There wasn't time.	ma kaan fii wagt.	ما كان فيه وقت.
3.	I ordered a radio from him.	ṭalabt raadyu min 9indu.	طلبت راديو من عنده.
4.	I asked for help from him.	ṭalabt minnu musaa9ada.	طلبت منه مساعدة.
5.	The account is balanced.	al-Hisaab maẓbuuṭ.	الحساب مظبوط.
6.	This is the best store.	haada aHsan maHall.	هادا احسن محل.
7.	His father is a merchant in the old souk.	abuu taajir fis-suug al-gadiima.	ابوه تاجر في السوق القديمة.

Grammatical Notes

1. Foreign words like /tilifoon/ and /tilifizyoon/ usually take the /-aat/ plural. When in doubt, guess this plural first.

2. /9asa/ may be translated 'I hope', 'it is hoped', 'possibly'. It may be used with a verb or with a pronoun suffix:

9asaa	it is hoped that he	عسى
9asaaha	it is hoped that she	عساها
9asaahum	it is hoped that they	عساهم
9asaak	it is hoped that you (m)	عساكْ
9asaaki	it is hoped that you (f)	عساكِ
9asaakum	it is hoped that you (p)	عساكم
9asaani	it is hoped that I	عساني
9asaana	it is hoped that we	عسانا

9asa yikuun fii waaHid.	I hope there will be one.
9asaahum yiktubuulana.	I hope they write to us.

3. /fii/ and /ma fii/, 'there is (not)', 'there are (not)', may be used with /kaan/:

kaan fii naas katiir hinaak.	There were many people there.
9asa yikuun fii waaHid.	I hope there will be one.
ma kaan fii wagt.	There wasn't time.
ma Ha-yikuun fii wagt.	There will not be time.

4. /ṭalab/ may mean 'to order' (in the sense of 'to place an order') or 'to ask for, request' (cf. Structure Sentences 3 and 4). Note the difference between /ṭalab/, 'to ask for (a thing)' and /sa'al/, 'to ask (information, a question)'.

5. /dukkaan/ generally refers to a small shop, while /maHall/is used for a larger store. However, the terms are often used interchangeably.

Vocabulary Notes

dafa9, yidfa9	pay	دفع يدفع
dawwar, yidawwir (9ala)	look for	دور يدور (على)
ţalab, yuţlub	ask for, request, order	طلب يطلب
raadyu, rawaadi	radio	راديو روادي
tilifizyoon, -aat	television	تلفزيون -ات
musajjil, -aat	recorder	مسجل -ات
wagt, awgaat	time	وقت اوقات
taajir, tujjaar	merchant	تاجر تجار
suug, aswaag*	souk, market	سوق اسواق
dukkaan, dakaakiin	shop	دكان دكاكين
maHall, -aat	store	محل -ات
maẓbuuţ, -a, -iin	accurate, correct	مظبوط -ين

*This word is feminine.

Drills

1. I want to go to the souk. — abgha aruuH as-suug. — ابغى اروح السوق.

Substitute:

the store
the shop
the gas station
the elementary school
the radio store ('radios store')
the souk

2. I have to pay a bill at the fabric shop. — laazim adfa9 Hisaab fi dukkaan al-gumaaš. — لازم ادفع حساب في دكان القماش.

Substitute:

humma — هم
iHna — احنا
hiyya — هي
huwwa — هو
inta — انتَ
ana — انا
inti — انتِ

3. I know a good shop in the middle of the souk. — a9rif dukkaan kwayyis fi wasaţ as-suug. — اعرف دكان كويس في وسط السوق.

Substitute:

in the beginning of the souk
at the end of the souk
in the old souk
in the new souk
in the middle of the souk

4. I hope there will be one. — 9asa yikuun fii waaHid. — عسى يكون فيه واحد.

Substitute:

there will be many

there will be time
we will arrive early
he will buy a television
we will finish the work soon
I can order a car

5. I've looked everywhere. ana dawwart fi kull makaan. انا دورت في كل مكان.

Substitute:

we
she
in every store
they
you (f)
in every bookstore
he
I

Situations

1.
A. Excuse me, do you sell recorders?
B. Yes, of course. Our recorders are the best and the cheapest.
A. I don't have much time. Can you show me a small one?
B. This one is Japanese, lightweight and excellent.
A. I like it. How much?
B. Only 300 riyals. (After the purchase): Congratulations.
A. Thanks.

2.
A. How much is our account now?
B. You owe me 15 riyals.
A. Here you are.
B. Thank you. Now the account is balanced. Do you want anything else?
A. No, thanks. Some other time, if God wills.

3.
A. Did you visit your sister in Riyadh?
B. No, there wasn't time. I was there only one day.
A. Why did you go?
B. One of my friends opened a small shop and he asked me to help ('asked from me help').
A. Where is the shop?
B. In the middle of the souk. He sells fabrics, for both men and women.
A. Good luck [to him].
B. Thanks.

Cultural Notes

1. The "souk" is the old marketplace found in virtually every city and town in the Middle East. It usually consists of many small shops arranged along narrow lanes, all of which display a wide variety of goods. Sometimes large souks have "quarters" where merchants specialize in one type of merchandise. It is a crowded, busy area, the scene of bargaining and socializing, and a favorite place for bargain-hunters.

Sometimes the word /suug/ is used to mean 'downtown'. The sentence 'I'm going to the souk' may just mean 'I'm going shopping'.

LESSON 34

Dialogue

	weather	jaww	جو
	hot	Harr	حر
A.	The weather here is very hot!	al-jaww hina marra Harr!	الجو هنا مرة حر!
	you (m) get used to	tit9awwid (9ala)	تتعود (على)
B.	Yes, but you (m) get used to it.	iiwa, laakin tit9awwid 9alee.	ايوه لاكن تتعود عليه.
	like, similar to	zayy	زي
	south	januub	جنوب
	west	gharb	غرب
	United States	al-wilaayaat al-muttaHida	الولايات المتحدة
A.	It's like the southwest United States.	zayy januub gharb al-wilaayaat al-muttaHida.	زي جنوب غرب الولايات المتحدة.
	I heard	simi9t	سمعت
	like that	kida	كده
	cold	bard	برد
B.	Yes, I [have] heard that. Not all of America is cold.	iiwa, simi9t kida. amriika mahi kullaha barda.	ايوه سمعت كده. امريكا مهي كلها بردة.
	of course not	ṭab9an la'	طبعا لاء
	north	šamaal	شمال
	the world	ad-dunya	الدنيا
	winter	šita	شتا
A.	Of course not. Only in the north is it cold in the winter. ('the world is cold')	ṭab9an la'. bass fiš-šamaal ad-dunya bard fiš-šita.	طبعا لاء. بس في الشمال الدنيا برد في الشتا.
	I read	giriit	قريت
B.	I [have] read about America's weather.	giriit 9an jaww amriika.	قريت عن جو امريكا.

Structure Sentences

1.	The weather here is cold.	al-jaww hina bard.	الجو هنا برد.
2.	Today is windy. ('north [wind]')	al-yoom šamaal.	اليوم شمال.

3.	I'm cold.	ana bardaan.	انا بردان.
4.	I'm hot.	ana Harraan.	انا حران.
5.	The coffee is hot.	al-gahwa Harra.	القهوة حرة.
6.	I hope you're better soon. ('your safety')	salaamatak.	سلامتك.
7.	Spring and fall are the best seasons.	ar-rabii9 wu l-xariif aHsan fuṣuul.	الربيع والخريف احسن فصول.
8.	I believe so.	a9taqid kida.	اعتقد كده.

Grammatical Notes

1. Terms for weather are:

al-jaww Harr.	The weather is hot.
al-jaww bard.	The weather is cold.
al-jaww mu9tadil.	The weather is moderate.

Also used is the word /ad-dunya/, 'the world', which is used as an idiom to mean 'It's hot', etc. This means, however, the weather only temporarily (today), whereas /al-jaww/ refers to a more permanent type of weather.

ad-dunya Harr.	It's hot.
ad-dunya bard.	It's cold.
ad-dunya šams.	It's sunny ('sun').

Note that /dunya/ takes a masculine adjective.

2. Adjectives which describe a temporary state often have the suffix /-aan/. They always take the /-a/ suffix for feminine and /-iin/ for plural. Among the most frequent are:

Harraan	hot	حران
bardaan	cold	بردان
ta9baan	tired	تعبان
jii9aan	hungry	جيعان
9aṭšaan	thirsty	عطشان
ghalṭaan	wrong	غلطان
xarbaan	out of order	خربان

Note that, for example, /Harraan/, /bardaan/, and /ghalṭaan/ are used to describe a person's state, not /Harr/, /bard/, and /ghalaṭ/, which are used for inanimate nouns.

3. The four directions are:

šamaal	north	شمال
januub	south	جنوب
šarg	east	شرق
gharb	west	غرب

When two directions are combined, they are placed in a noun construct:

januub gharb al-wilaayaat al-muttaHida	the southwest United States
ana min šamaal šarg wilaayat New York	I am from northeast New York State.

4. Since most Saudis are not very familiar with American place names, it is clearer to identify places as 'the state of Ohio', 'the state of New York', 'the city of Chicago', etc.:

ana min wilaayat New York.	I am from the state of New York.
ana min madiinat Boston.	I am from the city of Boston.

5. The four seasons are:

aṣ-ṣeef	summer	الصيف
aš-šita	winter	الشتا
ar-rabii9	spring	الربيع
al-xariif	fall	الخريف

aṣ-ṣeef al-maaḍi	last summer
aṣ-ṣeef al-jayy	next summer
(etc.)	

In Saudi Arabia, one rarely refers to spring and fall.

6. /simi9t kida/, 'I've heard that', and /giriit kida/'I've read that', are idioms. /kida/ may be used in this way with other types of verbs to mean 'I thought so', 'I hoped so', 'I feared that', etc.

simi9t kida.	I've heard that.
giriit kida.	I've read that.
a9taqid kida.	I believe so.

7. /simi9/ is used with /9an/ to express 'to hear about':

simi9t 9annu.	I've heard about him.
simi9t 9an al-mašruu9.	I've heard about the project.

8. The expression /ta9baan šwayya/, literally, 'a little tired', is often used as a euphemism to mean 'sick'. (The word is /mariiḍ/, but this usually means it is quite serious.)

9. When someone mentions illness, the appropriate statement is:

salaamatak	your (m) safety
salaamatu	his safety
salaamatha	her safety
(etc.)	

The response is:

aḷḷaah yisallimak	[May] God make you (m) safe.
aḷḷaah yisallimik	[May] God make you (f) safe.
aḷḷaah yisallimkum	[May] God make you (p) safe.

<u>Vocabulary Notes</u>

at9awwad, yit9awwid (9ala)	get used to, become accustomed to	اتعود يتعود (على)
simi9, yisma9	hear	سمع يسمع
giri, yigra (giriit)	read	قري يقرى (قريت)
a9taqad, ya9taqid	believe	اعتقد يعتقد

faṣl, fuṣuul	season, class	فصل فصول
wilaaya, -aat	state (of the U.S.A.)	ولاية -ات

Drills

1. The weather is hot.	al-jaww Harr.	الجو حر.

Substitute:

cold
moderate
sunny
very hot
like winter
bad
pleasant

2. You [will] get used to it.	tit9awwid 9alee.	تتعود عليه.

Substitute:

he
we
she
they
you (f)
you (p)
the children
the foreigners

3. It's like the southwest United States.	zayy januub gharb al-wilaayaat al-muttaHida.	زي جنوب غرب الولايات المتحدة.

Substitute:

north
east
south
northeast
west
southwest

4. In the north the weather is cold in winter.	fiš-šamaal ad-dunya bard fiš-šita.	في الشمال الدنيا برد في الشتا.

Substitute:

in the fall
in the spring
in the west
warm
in the summer
in the fall
in the east
cold
pleasant
in the winter
in the north
cold

5. I've read about it. giriit 9annu. قريت عنه ٠

Substitute:

we
she
will read
he
you (m)
must read
they
you (p)
did not read
you (f)
I
they

6. I'm cold. ana bardaan. انا بردان٠

Substitute:

wrong
tired
we
hot
hungry
thirsty
sick
he
a little hungry
very hungry
they
cold
wrong
thirsty
hot

Situations

1.
A. Do you know that summer is very hot in Saudi Arabia?
B. Yes, I've read that (/kida/). But I like the heat (/al-Harr/). And you?
A. No, but I got used to it.
B. Which season is best here?
A. The winter, that is (/ya9ni/), December, January, and February.

2.
A. Where are you going?
B. To visit a Saudi family which I met in America. Would you like to come?
A. Certainly. This will be the first time [that] I visit a Saudi home.
B. They have heard about you, and they want to meet you.

3.
A. The account is not correct.
B. I'm sorry, I'm wrong. I forgot that you paid last week.
A. Never mind. How is your health? Better, if God wills?
B. A little, but I'm still tired.
A. Really? "Hope you're feeling better soon".
B. "Thanks".

LESSON 35

Dialogue

	rain	maṭar	مطر
A.	Is there rain in Jidda?	fii maṭar fi jidda?	فيه مطر في جدة؟
	mountains	jibaal	جبال
B.	Never. But there is rain in Taif, in the mountains.	muu katiir. laakin fii maṭar fiṭ-ṭaayif, fil-jibaal.	مو كثير. لاكن فيه مطر في الطايف، في الجبال.
A.	Mountains?	al-jibaal?	الجبال؟
	desert	ṣaHra	صحرا
	seacoasts	šawaaṭi'	شواطئ
B.	Of course. Saudi Arabia is not all desert[s] and seacoasts.	ṭab9an. as-su9uudiyya mahi kullaha ṣaHra wu šawaaṭi'.	طبعا. السعودية مهي كلها صحرا وشواطئ.
	always	dayman	دايمن
	they think	yiẓunnu	يظنوا
	composed of	9ibaara 9an	عبارة عن
	sand	raml	رمل
	oases	waaHaat	واحات
	palmtrees	naxil	نخل
A.	Foreigners always think that it is composed of desert, sand, oases, and palmtrees.	al-ajaanib dayman yiẓunnu annaha 9ibaara 9an ṣaHra wu raml wu waaHaat wu naxil.	الاجانب دايمن يظنوا انها عبارة عن صحرا ورمل وواحات ونخل.
	rivers	anhaar	انهار
	areas, regions	manaaṭig	مناطق
	agricultural	ziraa9iyya	زراعية
B.	That's true, but there are also rivers and agricultural areas.	haada ṣaHiiH, laakin fii kamaan anhaar wu manaaṭig ziraa9iyya.	هادا صحيح لاكن فيه كمان انهار ومناطق زراعية.

Structure Sentences

1.	We go to Taif usually in the summer.	niruuH aṭ-ṭaayif 9aadatan fiṣ-ṣeef.	نروح الطايف عادة في الصيف.
2.	There is never [any] snow.	ma fii talj abadan.	ما فيه ثلج ابدا.
3.	He never went. (He has never gone.)	ma raaH abadan.	ما راح ابدا.
4.	I have never met the prince.	ma gaabalt al-amiir abadan.	ما قابلت الامير ابدا.

5.	The trees are green.	aš-šajar axḍar.	الشجر اخضر.
6.	The flowers are pretty.	al-ward Hilu.	الورد حلو.
7.	I want to buy three flowers.	abgha aštari talaata wuruud.	ابغى اشتري ثلاثة ورود.

Grammatical Notes

1. /abadan/ is used with a negative verb (cf. Structure Sentences 2 and 3).

2. Arabic has, in addition to singular, dual, and plural nouns, a special "collective plural" for some nouns. Most collective plurals are formed by omitting the /-a/ feminine ending of a singular noun:

warda	a flower	وردة
ward	flowers	ورد
šajara	a tree	شجرة
šajar	trees	شجر
naxla	a palmtree	نخلة
naxil	palmtrees	نخل
leemuuna	a lemon	ليمونة
leemuun	lemons	ليمون

The collective plural is always <u>masculine</u> <u>singular</u>:

al-ward Hilu.	The flowers are pretty.
aš-šajar axḍar.	The trees are green.
an-naxil kabiir wu Hilu.	The palmtrees are big and pretty.
al-leemuun raxiiṣ.	The lemons are cheap.

When the noun is "counted" with a numeral, it takes its regular plural:

abgha aštari talaata wuruud.	I want to buy three flowers.
fii arba9a naxlaat kubaar wara beeti.	There are four big palmtrees behind my house.

The collective plural is used when referring to a group of things in general, whereas the "counted" plural is used with numerals. Collective plurals are also used when buying something by weight, e.g., "a kilo of lemons" (/kiilu leemuun/). They are especially common for all types of foods which are measured by weight or volume, and more will be introduced in Lesson 37.

Vocabulary Notes

jabal, jibaal	mountain	جبل جبال
nahar, anhaar	river	نهر انهار
šaaṭi', šawaaṭi'	seacoast	شاطئ شواطئ
ṣaHra, ṣaHaari	desert	صحرا صحاري
manṭiga, manaaṭig	area, region	منطقة مناطق
šajara, ašjaar	tree	شجرة اشجار
naxla, -aat	palmtree	نخلة -ات
warda, wuruud	flower	وردة ورود
waaHa, -aat	oasis	واحة -ات
ẓann, yiẓunn (ẓanneet)	think	ظن يظن (ظنيت)

Drills

1. Is there rain in Jidda?   fii maṭar fi jidda?   فيه مطر في جدة؟

Substitute:

in Riyadh
snow
in Saudi Arabia
in the mountains
sun
at the seacoast
rain
cold
in the city

2. It ('she') is composed of desert.   hiyya 9ibaara 9an ṣaHra.   هي عبارة عن صحرا٠

Substitute:

sand
palmtrees
seacoasts
oases
mountains
many trees
cities
rivers
agricultural areas
desert

3. We usually go in the summer.   niruuH 9aadatan fiṣ-ṣeef.   نروح عادة في الصيف٠

Substitute:

in the winter
in the fall
every year
in the spring
always
early in the year
twice
in the middle of the summer
in April

4. He never went.   ma raaH abadan.   ما راح ابدا٠

Substitute:

traveled
bought a television
met the prince
drove
cleaned the car
taught Arabic
finished his education
visited me
said that (/kida/)

5. Given the singular noun, change it to collective plural and then counted plural:

naxla	نخلة
šajara	شجرة
warda	وردة
leemuuna	ليمونة

6. The trees are green. <u>aš-šajar axḍar</u>. الشجر اخضر.

Substitute:

palmtrees
pretty
flowers
red
yellow
big
trees
expensive
lemons
cheap
green
small
palmtrees
numerous ('many')
tall

<u>Situations</u>

1.
A. How is the weather in Yemen?
B. It is always very cold in the winter because Yemen consists of many mountains. There is rain and snow, too.
A. Really? I thought it was ('is') a desert.
B. Not at all! (/abadan/) There are rivers and trees and many large agricultural areas in the west. The desert is in the middle and in the east.
A. I would like to visit Sanaa.
B. I hope you can.

2.
A. Are you going to the beach this Friday?
B. I think we'll go to the desert. The children like the sand. My wife will prepare (/tisawwi/) food for us.
A. Excellent. There is an oasis near here.
B. Like the oases in the Eastern Region?
A. Bigger and prettier. There is a river and flowers.
B. Good. I'll tell my wife.

LESSON 36

Dialogue

(At the tailor)

	I need ('needing')	miHtaaj	محتاج
	suit	badla	بدلة
	cotton	guṭun	قطن
A.	I need a new cotton suit.	ana miHtaaj li badla guṭun jadiida.	انا محتاج لبدلة قطن جديدة.
B.	Welcome. Any service.	ahlan wu sahlan. ayy xidma.	اهلا وسهلا. اي خدمة.
	jacket	jakitta	جكتة
	(pair of) trousers	banṭaloon	بنطلون
A.	I want a jacket and two trousers.	abgha jakitta wu banṭalooneen.	ابغى جكتة و بنطلونين.
	size	magaas	مقاس
B.	Let me take your measurements.	xalliini aaxud magaasak.	خليني آخذ مقاسك.
	sleeves	akmaam	اكمام
	narrow	ḍayyig	ضيق
A.	I want the jacket longer than that. And the sleeves narrow.	abgha al-jakitta aṭwal min kida. wu l-akmaam ḍayyiga.	ابغى الجكتة اطول من كده. والاكمام ضيقة.
	you (m) measure	tigiis	تقيس
B.	Fine. Come for a fitting ('to "measure" it') next week.	ṭayyib. ta9aal 9ašaan tigiisaha l-usbuu9 al-jayy.	طيب. تعال عشان تقيسها الاسبوع الجي.

Structure Sentences

1.	She is a seamstress.	hiyya xayyaaṭa.	هي خياطة.
2.	He is sewing the vest now.	huwwa 9ammaal yixayyiṭ as-sideeri daHHiin.	هو عمال يخيط السديري دحين.
3.	Leave the pants wide at the bottom.	siib al-banṭaloon waasi9 min taHat.	سيب البنطلون واسع من تحت.
4.	This shirt is [too] tight.	haada l-gamiiṣ ḍayyig.	هادا القميص ضيق.
5.	I want to buy a leather belt.	abgha aštari Hizaam jild.	ابغى اشتري حزام جلد.

6. I don't need anything else.	mana miHtaaj šayy taani.	منا محتاج شي ثاني.
7. I have to measure it.	laazim agiisu.	لازم اقيسه.

Grammatical Notes

1. 'To need' is expressed with the active participle /miHtaaj/, 'needing', sometimes used with the preposition /l-/ (/li-/):

ana miHtaaj li badla guṭun jadiida.	I need a new cotton suit.
hiyya miHtaaja musaa9ada.	She needs help.
ana kunt miHtaajlu.	I needed him.
iHna miHtaajiinlu.	We need him.

2. Adjectives of "quality" which describe the material of which something consists are used in the masculine singular form only:

badla guṭun	a cotton suit
šanta jild	a leather purse
Hizaam jild	a leather belt
fustaan ṣuuf	a wool dress
fasaatiin ṣuuf	wool dresses

Note that these nouns are not in a construct state.

3. In English we say "a pair of pants", "a pair of shoes", etc., making the noun plural. In Arabic, it is expressed as singular:

abgha banṭaloon jadiid.	I want a new [pair of] pant[s].
aštareet jazma sooda.	I bought black shoe[s].
aštareet jizam katiir.	I bought many [pairs of] shoes.
feen jazmati?	Where are my shoes?

4. /9ammaal/ is also used before verbs to indicate an on-going action. It is not conjugated:

huwwa 9ammaal yixayyiṭ.	He is sewing.
hiyya 9ammaal titkallam.	She is talking.

Vocabulary Notes

waasi9, -iin*	wide	واسع -ين
ḍayyig, -iin*	narrow	ضيق -ين
sahl, -iin*	easy	سهل -ين
ṣa9b, -iin*	difficult, hard	صعب -ين
miHtaaj, -iin	needing, in need of	محتاج -ين
gaas, yigiis (gist)	measure, try on	قاس يقيس (قست)
xayyaṭ, yixayyiṭ	sew	خيط يخيط

magaas, -aat	size	مقاس -ات
xayyaaṭ, -a, -iin	tailor, seamstress	خياط -ين
badla, bidal	suit	بدلة بدل
jakitta, -aat	jacket	جكتة -ات
banṭaloon, -aat	trousers	بنطلون -ات،
gamiiṣ, gumṣaan	shirt	قميص قمصان
karafiṭṭa, -aat	necktie	كرفتة -ات
fustaan, fasaatiin	dress	فستان فساتين
bluuza, -aat	blouse	بلوزة -ات
kumm, akmaam	sleeve	كم اكمام
jazma, jizam	shoes	جزمة جزم

*Since these words refer to inanimate nouns, the plural usually heard is /-a/.

Drills

1. I need a new cotton suit. — ana miHtaaj li <u>badla guṭun jadiida</u>. — انا محتاج لبدلة قطن جديدة.

Substitute:

wool suit
wool jacket
lightweight jacket
lightweight [pair of] trousers
pair of shoes
shirt
cotton shirts
leather belt

2. I want a jacket. — abgha <u>jakitta</u>. — ابغى جكتة.

Substitute:

two trousers
two shirts
a long dress
a blue necktie
a leather suitcase
a smaller size

3. I want the jacket longer than that. — abgha <u>al-jakitta aṭwal</u> min kida. — ابغى الجكتة اطول من كده.

Substitute:

shorter
heavier
wider
the belt
cheaper
prettier
the blouse
smaller

4. He is sewing the vest now. — <u>huwwa</u> 9ammaal <u>yixayyiṭ</u> <u>as-sideeri</u> daHHiin. — هو عمال يخيط السديري دحين.

Substitute:

the dress
she
is finishing
is cleaning
the shoes
the suitcase
I
the belt
the trousers

5. Leave the pants wide at the bottom. siib al-banṭaloon waasi9 min taHat. سيب البنطلون واسع من تحت.

Substitute:

narrow
at the top (/min foog/)
sleeve
at the bottom
wide
dress
short

Situations

1.
A. Can you (f) make ('sew') me a dress?
B. Yes, which material?
A. I need a cotton dress because the weather is [so] hot now.
B. That will be easy. Let me take your (f) measurements.
A. Can you make it quickly?
B. If God wills, in two days ('after two days').

2.
A. I heard that prices are good in that store.
B. Yes, especially ties and shirts.
A. Let's go ask.
B. OK, I can put the car here.
A. "No standing" here. Try that place.
B. No, that's [too] hard.
A. Wait for me. I'll go in and ask and come back quickly.

3.
A. I'm thirsty. [Shall] we go and drink something?
B. OK. The weather is sunny, especially in the afternoon.
A. It's always like this (/kida/) in the summer. But in the mountains it's moderate. We must visit Taif.
B. I agree. I have wanted ('want') to see Taif since last year.

LESSON 37

Dialogue

(An invitation to dinner)

	meat	laHam	لحم
A.	Welcome. Go ahead [and have some of] the meat.	ahlan wu sahlan. atfaḍḍal al-laHam.	اهلا وسهلا · اتفضل اللحم·
	delicious	ṭi9im	طِعِم
	rice	ruzz	رز
B.	Thank you. It's delicious. And the rice, too.	šukran. huwwa ṭi9im. w ar-ruzz kamaan.	شكرا· هو طعم· والرز كمان·
	strength	9aafiya	عافية
	you (m) honored	šarraft	شرفت
A.	To your strength. You have honored us.	bil-9aafiya. šarraftana.	بالعافية· شرفتنا·
	table (of food)	sufra	سفرة
	eternal	daayma	دايمة
B.	I am honored. That's enough, thanks be to God. [May your] table always be thus.	šukran, kifaaya, al-Hamdu lillaah. sufra daayma.*	شكرا، كفاية الحمد لله · سفرة دايمة·
	presence	wujuud	وجود
A.	Due to your presence.	b-wujuudakum.	بوجودكم·

*Also commonly said to the host is /9aamir/, 'filled'.

Structure Sentences

1.	The food was placed on the table.	al-akl anHaṭṭ 9as-sufra.	الاكل انحط عالسفرة·
2.	The money was spent.	al-fuluus anṣarafat.	الفلوس انصرفت·
3.	The money must be spent.	al-fuluus laazim tinṣarif.	الفلوس لازم تنصرف·
4.	May your hands be blessed (literally, 'made safe').	tislam iideekum.	تسلم ايديكم·
5.	Don't trouble yourself.	laa tita99ib nafsak.	لا تتعّب نفسَك·
6.	Not at all--it's no trouble.	abadan--ma fii ta9b.	ابدا · ما فيه تعب·
7.	The food is excellent.	al-akl mumtaaz.	الاكل ممتاز·
8.	Eat [some] grapes.	kul 9inab.	كل عنب·

9.	I bought a lemon.	aštareet Habba leemuun.	اشتريت حبة ليمون.
10.	He talked to himself.	kallam nafsu.	كلم نفسه .

Grammatical Notes

1. The passive verb in Saudi Arabic can be expressed in several ways. The most frequent is the use of the prefix /an-/ or /at-/ with the perfect tense, which becomes infixed (in the middle of the word) in the imperfect tense. It is a regular pattern:

anṣaraf, yinṣarif	be spent
anfataH, yinfatiH	be opened
ankatab, yinkatib	be written

Other types of verbs:

anHaṭṭ, yinHaṭṭ	be put, placed
anšaaf, yinšaaf	be seen
atšarraf, yitšarrif	be honored

You cannot predict which prefix will be used with each verb, so you should learn each passive verb separately. However, the /an-/ prefix is much more common.

Quite rare is a passive expressed with an active-form verb, but it occurs sometimes in classicized expressions (it is also a rare pattern in Classical Arabic):

tislam iideekum.	May your hands be blessed.

The passive verb is conjugated for all persons, and is of course derived from transitive verbs (which take an object). Not all verbs can be made passive; it is a matter of style that some expressions are simply always said in the active voice, for example:

jaabu.	It was brought. ('He brought it'.)

(/anjaab/ is grammatically correct but sounds unnatural in style.)

Some of the most common passive verbs are:

ankatab, yinkatib	be written	انكتب ينكتب
anfataH, yinfatiH	be opened	انفتح ينفتح
angafal, yingafil	be closed	انقفل ينقفل
anṣaraf, yinṣarif	be spent	انصرف ينصرف
an9amal, yin9amil	be done	انعمل ينعمل
anšaaf, yinšaaf	be seen	انشاف ينشاف
anšaal, yinšaal	be carried	انشال ينشال
ansaab, yinsaab	be left behind	انساب ينساب
anHaṭṭ, yinHaṭṭ	be put, placed	انحط ينحط
atšarraf, yitšarrif	be honored	اتشرف يتشرف
at9arraf, yit9arrif	be introduced	اتعرف يتعرف
at9awwad, yit9awwid	be accustomed	اتعود يتعود
at9allam, yit9allim	be educated	اتعلم يتعلم

2. /sufra/ refers to a dining table, or more precisely, the top of it or the place where food is spread out. /ṭarabiiza/ refers to any table.

3. /iideen/, 'hands' (literally, 'two hands') becomes /iidee-/ before pronoun endings. There is an alternative way to say 'hands' (discussed in Lesson 44), but this form is used for this expression.

tislam iideekum.	May your (p) hands be blessed.
tislam iideek.	May your (m) hands be blessed.
tislam iideeki.	May your (f) hands be blessed.

This expression is used to compliment the quality of something which has been produced by someone's hands. You will hear it used most often referring to food.

4. The expression presented in Structure Sentence 5 is very commonly said by a guest to his host. Structure Sentence 6 is the conventional response.

5. The word /Habba/ means 'one' or 'a piece'. It is used referring to items of food.

Habba leemuun	one lemon
Habba Halaawa	a piece of candy
Habba tuffaaH	an apple

6. To express 'self' as the reflexive object ('I hurt myself', etc.), /nafs-/ is used with pronoun endings:

nafsu	himself	نفسه
nafsaha	herself	نفسها
nafsahum	themselves	نفسهم
nafsak	yourself (m)	نفسَك
nafsik	yourself (f)	نفسِك
nafsakum	yourselves	نفسكم
nafsi	myself	نفسي
nafsana	ourselves	نفسنا

laa tita99ib nafsak.	Don't trouble ('tire') yourself (m).
laa tita99ibi nafsik.	Don't trouble yourself (f).
laa tita99ibu nafsakum.	Don't trouble yourselves.
kallam nafsu.	He talked to himself
kallamat nafsaha.	She talked to herself.

Vocabulary Notes

(Words given as collective plurals)

Meats (laHam, luHuum) لحم لحوم

dajaaj, -aat	chicken	دجاج -ات
xaruuf, xirfaan	lamb	خروف خرفان
samak, asmaak	fish	سمك اسماك
laHam bagar	beef ('cow meat')	لحم بقر

Vegetables (xuḍaar) خضار

baṣal	onions	بصل
baṭaaṭis	potatoes	بطاطس
ṭamaaṭim	tomatoes	طماطم
bazaaliya	peas	بزاليا
faaṣuuliyya xadṛa	green beans	فاصوليا خضرا
xiyaar	cucumbers	خيار
xaṣṣ	lettuce	خس

Fruits (faakha, fawaakih) فاكهة فواكه

9inab	grapes	عنب
burtukaan	oranges	برتكان
tuffaaH	apples	تفاح
balaH	red dates	بلح
tamur	dried dates	تمر
mooz	bananas	موز

Other

xubz	bread	خبز
zibda	butter	زبدة
ruzz	rice	رز
beeḍ	eggs	بيض
ṣaḷaṭa	salad	صلطة
milH	salt	ملح
filfil	pepper	فلفل
šarraf, yišarrif	honor	شرف يشرف
at9arraf, yit9arrif (9ala)	to be introduced to, become acquainted with	اتعرف يتعرف (على)
ta99ab, yita99ib	tire, bother	تعّب يتعّب
akal, yaakul	eat	اكل ياكل
ṭi9im, -a, -iin*	delicious	طعم -ين

*The plural form /ṭi9miin/ may refer to people, for example, children, and mean 'lovely'.

Drills

1. Go ahead [and have some] meat. — atfaḍḍal al-laHam. — اتفضل اللحم.

Substitute:

the chicken
the fish
the salad
the dates
the potatoes
the lamb
the butter

2. You (m) have honored us. — šarraftana.* — شرفتنا.

you (f)
you (p)

*This expression is usually used with 'us'.

3. Given the verb in the active voice, change it to passive (perfect and imperfect).

Example: katab ⟶ ankatab, yinkatib — كتب ← انكتب ينكتب

Continue:

ġafal	قفل
šaaf	شاف
Haṭṭ	حط
saab	ساب
9arraf	عرّف
9allam	علّم
ṣaraf	صرف
9amal	عمل
šarraf	شرّف
9awwad	عوّد
fataH	فتح
šaal	شال

4. The food was placed on the table. — al-akl anHaṭṭ 9as-sufra. — الاكل انحط عالسفرة.

Substitute:

the rice
the water
the salad
the tea
the salt
the coffee
the sugar
the fruit

5. The money must be spent. — al-fuluus laazim tinṣarif. — الفلوس لازم تنصرف.

Substitute:

be removed (use /šaal/)
the food
be put [down]
the books
be opened
be carried
the boy
be educated
be introduced to the man
I
become accustomed to the weather

6. He talked to himself. — kallam nafsu. — كلم نفسه.

Substitute:

she
I
we
saw
they
you (m)
heard
you (f)
he
the children
cleaned
tired

Situations

1.
A. Welcome! Sit down and eat with us.
B. Thanks. I'm a little hungry.
A. Have more rice ('rice also'). You have honored us.
B. I'm honored. The food is delicious. Bless your (p) hands.
A. Thanks. Due to your presence. Welcome.
B. I hope you (p) honor me in my home soon.
A. Have [some] again.
B. No, thanks. Thanks be to God, I've eaten enough.

2.
A. I'm going to the souk.
B. To buy food?
A. Yes, [some] vegetables and fruits. What would you like?
B. Buy bananas, also onions and potatoes. And bread, of course. But don't tire yourself.
A. I'll be back ('return') soon, if God wills.
B. Goodby.
A. Goodby.

Cultural Notes

1. An Arab host repeats phrases of welcome to his guest frequently, and presses food on him. Many polite expressions are exchanged. Since the host will continue to insist that you eat more and more, take small amounts of food at the beginning; you will probably be expected to eat three courses. Go hungry; eating a lot is one way to express appreciation for the food, and helps the host display his generosity and hospitality.

Before eating, Saudis often say the phrase /bism illaah ar-raHmaan ar-raHiim/, 'In the name of God, the Merciful, and Compassionate'. After the meal it is customary to say /al-Hamdu lillaah/ (or /al-Hamdu lillaah wu šukran/). The dialogue presented in this lesson reflects the routine expressions used between the host and guests during a typical meal.

LESSON 38

Dialogue

(In a restaurant)

	requests	ṭalabaat	طلبات
A.	May I help you? (literally, 'What are your requests?')	eeš ṭalabaatakum?*	ايش طلباتكم؟
	menu	lista	لستة
	lunch	ghada	غدا
B.	A menu, please. I'd like to order lunch.	al-lista, min faḍlak. aHubb aṭlub ghada.	اللستة من فضلك. احب اطلب غدا.
	fresh	ṭaaza	طازة
A.	Today we have fresh fish.	al-yoom 9indana samak ṭaaza.	اليوم عندنا سمك طازة.
B.	OK. And bring techina and salad, and a Pepsi.	ṭayyib. wu jiib ṭaHiina wu ṣalaṭa wu bibsi-kuula.	طيب. وجيب طحينة وصلطة وبيبسي كولا.
	dessert (literally, 'something sweet')	šayy Hilu	شي حلو
A.	Right away. Would you like dessert?	Haaḍir. tibgha šayy Hilu?	حاضر. تبغى شي حلو؟
	check ('account')	Hisaab	حساب
	the change ('the rest')	al-baagi	الباقي
B.	Baklawa, and then bring the check. Keep the change.	baglaawa, wu ba9deen jiib al-Hisaab. xalli l-baagi lak.	بقلاوة، وبعدين جيب الحساب. خلّ الباقي لك.

*An alternative opening statement is /ayy xidma lakum?/, 'Any service for you?'.

Structure Sentences

1.	I'd like to order dinner.	aHubb aṭlub 9aša.	احب اطلب عشا.
2.	What time is breakfast?	as-saa9a kam al-faṭuur?	الساعة كم الفطور؟
3.	The tip is 15%.	al-xidma xamasṭa9š fil-miyya.**	الخدمة خمستعش في المية.
4.	He is a good writer.	huwwa ṣufraji ṭayyib.	هو صفرجي طيب.
5.	I ate in the same restaurant.	akalt fi nafs al-maṭ9am.	اكلت في نفس المطعم.
6.	We arrived at the same time.	waṣalna fi nafs al-wagt.	وصلنا في نفس الوقت.

7. Let's go to his house ('to him') some time.	xalliina niruHlu marra.	خلينا نروحله مرة.
8. We ate stuffed peppers and shish kabob.	akalna filfil maHši wu kabaab.	اكلنا فلفل محشي وكباب.

**Another common word for 'tip' is /baxšiiš/.

Grammatical Notes

1. /ţaaza/, 'fresh', is not declined for gender or number.

2. To express 'per cent', use /fil-miyya/:

xamasţa9š fil-miyya	15%
xamsa wu 9išriin fil-miyya	25%
miyya fil-miyya	100%

3. /al-baagi/ literally means 'the rest', 'the remaining'. The word for 'change' (money) is /fakka/.

4. Some of the more common Saudi dishes are:

maHši (bidinjaan, kuusa, filfil)	stuffed (eggplant, squash, peppers) (etc.)	محشي (بدنجان، كوسا، فلفل)
kabaab	shish kabob	كباب
kufta	ground spiced meat	كفتة
şayaaḑiyya	fish, onions, and rice	صياضية
mašwi (dajaaj, xaruuf)	grilled (chicken, lamb)	مشوي (دجاج، خروف)
ţaHiina	sesame dip	طحينة
ruzz 9adas	rice with lentils	رز عدس
saliig	rice cooked with milk and meat	سليق
baglaawa	baklava (syrup-covered pastry)	بقلاوة

5. /nafs/ may be used with a definite noun to mean 'same':

nafs al-maţ9am	the same restaurant
fi nafs al-wagt	at the same time

6. /marra/, 'occasion', may be used alone to mean 'some time':

xalliina niruHlu marra.	Let's go to his place some time.

Vocabulary Notes

lista, lisat	menu	لستة لست
şufraji, -yiin	waiter	صفرجي -يين
maţ9am, maţaa9im	restaurant	مطعم مطاعم

Drills

1. I'd like to order lunch.	aHubb aţlub ghada.	احب اطلب غدا.

Substitute:

dinner
we
breakfast
they
lunch
I

2. Today we have fresh fish.	al-yoom 9indana <u>samak ţaaza</u>.	اليوم عندنا سمك طازة.

Substitute:

shish kabob
stuffed peppers
chicken and rice
grilled lamb

3. The tip is 15%.	al-xidma <u>xamasţa9š</u> fil-miyya.	الخدمة خمستعش في المية.

Substitute:

50%
25%
10%
5%

4. I ate in the same restaurant.	akalt <u>fi nafs al-maţ9am</u>.	اكلت في نفس المطعم.

Substitute:

at the same time
in the same house
with the same man
in the same room
the same food yesterday

5. Let's go to his place some time.	<u>niruHlu</u> marra.	نروحله مرة.

Substitute:

let's visit him
let's eat there
let's try to go
let's travel together
let's clean the car
let's talk to the director
let's send them a letter
let's practice

Situations

1.
A. A menu, please. We'd like to order dinner.
B. Right away. We have Arab food here.
A. Do you have grilled chicken?
B. Of course. We have grilled lamb for the same price.
A. (to his wife): What would you like?
C. Lamb. And stuffed squash. And bread and butter.

A. I, too. How much is the tip?
C. Between ten and fifteen per cent. 15% is better.
A. (to the waiter) Keep the change.

2.
A. Did your family go to the seashore last Friday?
B. Yes, we all went in the same car. We have a cabin (/kabiina/) there.
A. I heard that there is a restaurant there.
B. Yes, they have French food.
A. I'll try to go with you (p) the next time. Don't forget to tell me.
B. Welcome, any time. The children send their greetings ('greet you').

3.
A. What time is lunch?
B. Lunch in the hotel restaurant is from 12:00 to 3:00.
A. Are the waiters good?
B. Yes, the service (/xidma/) is excellent.
A. Let's go there some time.
B. OK, maybe tomorrow.

LESSON 39

Dialogue

(At a fruit stand)

	kilo	kiilu	كيلو
A.	I want to buy a kilo of oranges.	abgha aštari kiilu burtukaan.	ابغى اشتري كيلو برتكان.
B.	[They are] three riyals a kilo.	al-kiilu b-talaata riyaal.	الكيلو بثلاثة ريال.
A.	Not cheaper than that?	muu arxaṣ min kida?	مو ارخص من كده ؟
	not	la'	لأ
B.	Of course not, madam.	ṭab9an la' ya sitt.*	طبعا لأ يا ست.
A.	Do you have change for ('of') fifty riyals?	9indak fakkat xamsiin riyaal?	عندك فكة خمسين ريال ؟
	sorrow	asaf	اسف
	you (f) change	tiṣrufi	تصرفي
	moneychanger	ṣarraaf	صراف
B.	No, unfortunately. ('with sorrow'). You can change your money at the moneychanger's.	la', ma9a l-asaf. mumkin tiṣrufi fuluusik 9ind aṣ-ṣarraaf.	لأ مع الاسف. ممكن تصرفي فلوسك عند الصراف.

*Also commonly heard is /ya madaam/.

Structure Sentences

1.	I'll take two and one-half meters.	aaxud mitreen wu nuṣṣ.	آخذ مترين ونص.
2.	Give me two kilos.	addiini itneen kiilu.	اديني اثنين كيلو.
3.	Its weight is three pounds.	waznu talaata arṭaal.	وزنه ثلاثة ارطال.
4.	What is the width of this fabric?	kam 9arḍ haada l-gumaaš?	كم عرض هادا القماش؟
5.	Why not?	leeš la'?	ليش لأ ؟
6.	I want to change the appointment.	abgha aghayyir al-maw9ad.	ابغى اغير الموعد.
7.	Give me a dozen pens.	addiini dastat aglaam.	اديني دستة اقلام.

Grammatical Notes

1. Some nouns of measurement are used only in the singular:

addiini itneen kiilu.	Give me two kilos.
addiini talaata kiilu.	Give me three kilos.

addiini kiilu wu rub9.	Give me one and one-quarter kilos.
addiini 9ašara ghraam.	Give me ten grams.

Nouns of measurement which do not change form are:

kiilu	kilo	كيلو
ghraam	gram	غرام
litir	liter	لتر
ṣanti	centimeter	صنتي
buuṣa	inch	بوصة

Some nouns of measurement are declined for dual and plural:

aaxud mitreen wu nuṣṣ.	I'll take two and one-half meters.
aaxud talaata amṭaar.	I'll take three meters.
waznu talaata arṭaal.	Its weight is three pounds.

These nouns are:

mitir, amṭaar	meter	متر امتار
raṭl, arṭaal	pound	رطل ارطال
yarda, -aat	yard	يردة -ات
gadam, agdaam	foot	قدم اقدام
dasta, -aat	dozen	دستة -ات

2. /ṭab9an la'/, 'of course not', is an example of using /la'/ to mean 'not'. (We have already seen /walla la'?/, 'or not?'). Other structures like this are:

leeš la'?	Why not?
aẓuun la'.	I think not; I don't think so.
huwwa raaH w ana la'.	He went and I didn't.

3. /ghayyar/, 'to change', is used in the sense of changing an appointment, your clothes, an idea, etc. For money, you use /ṣaraf, yiṣruf/, or also /fakk, yifukk/, literally, 'to take apart':

fakkeet fuluusi.	I changed my money.

4. /ṣarraaf/ is an example of a noun which describes employment. Such nouns may be formed from verb root consonants, with the vowel pattern: $C_1aC_2C_2aC_3$. Some common nouns formed on this pattern are:

Noun		Related Word		
ṣarraaf	'money changer'	ṣaraf	'spend'	صراف
sawwaag	'driver'	saag	'drive'	سواق
xayyaaṭ	'tailor'	xayyaṭ	'sew'	خياط
ṭabbaax	'cook'	ṭabax	'cook'	طباخ
najjaar	'carpenter'	najar	'hew, carve'	نجار
xabbaaz	'baker'	xubz	'bread'	خباز
xaddaam	'servant'	xidma	'service'	خدام
Hammaal	'porter'	Hamal	'carry'	حمال
jazzaar	'butcher'	jazar	'slaughter'	جزار
baggaal	'grocer'	(none in common use)		بقال
jarraaH	'surgeon'	jaraH	'wound'	جراح
fallaaH	'peasant'	falaH	'cultivate'	فلاح

Vocabulary Notes

ghayyar, yighayyir	change	غير يغير
fakk, yifukk (fakkeet)	change (money); take apart	فك يفك (فكيت)
wazn, awzaan	weight	وزن اوزان
ṭuul	height, length	طول
9arḍ	width	عرض

Drills

1. I want to buy a kilo of oranges.	abgha aštari kiilu burtukaan.	ابغى اشتري كيلو برتكان.

Substitute:

one-half kilo
two kilos
five kilos
one dozen
two dozen

2. Not cheaper than that?	muu arxaṣ min kida?	مو ارخص من كده ؟

Substitute:

better
bigger
smaller
prettier
older
newer
more beautiful

3. Do you have change for fifty riyals?	9indak fakkat xamsiin riyaal?	عندَك فكة خمسين ريال؟

Substitute:

50 dollars
35 dollars
you (p)
100 riyals
500 riyals
he
10 dollars

4. You (f) can change your money at the moneychanger's.	mumkin tiṣrufi fuluusik 9ind aṣ-ṣarraaf.	ممكن تصرفي فلوسِك عند الصرافه .

Substitute:

you (m)
they
she
at the bank
you (p)
I
in the store
we
he
at the moneychanger's

5. I'll take two and one-half meters. aaxud mitreen wu nuṣṣ. آخذ مترين ونص.

Substitute:

3 meters
1 meter
1/2 meter
1 meter and 10 centimeters
25 centimeters
1 yard
1 1/4 yards
6 inches
2 feet
3 feet
1 liter
4 1/2 liters

6. Ask the questions and then answer it.

Example: What is its weight? Its weight is three pounds.

kam waznu? ⟶ waznu talaata arṭaal. كم وزنه ؟ ← وزنه ثلاثة ارطال.

Continue:

What is its width?	2 1/2 meters.
What is its length?	1 yard and 5 inches.
What is its weight?	About 150 pounds.
What is its length?	3 1/4 feet.
What is its width?	40 centimeters.
What is its weight?	15 kilos and 200 grams.

7. He works as a driver. huwwa yištaghil sawwaag. هو يشتغل سواق.

Substitute:

cook
servant
porter
tailor
carpenter
butcher

Situations

1.
A. I want to change my appointment with the minister.
B. OK, when would you like to come?
A. Give me an appointment the day after tomorrow.
B. Unfortunately he will be in Riyadh. Can you come Thursday?
A. I don't think so. I'll call you ('talk to you on the telephone').
B. Goodby.

2.
A. Let's go to the grocery store (/9ind al-baggaal/).
B. OK, I'll come with you.
\- - -

A. We want to buy two kilos of onions.
B. Anything else?
A. Do you have eggs?
B. Yes, how many dozen?
A. Two dozen are enough. Don't you have eggs bigger than that?
B. Yes, here. Just for you ('your sake').
A. Do you have change for 50 riyals?
B. Yes, ma'am. Any service.

3.
A. Please have some more [food]. (/atfaḍḍal kamaan/).
B. Thanks. Everything is delicious. A little rice, please.
A. No, you must eat more than that!
B. I can't, really (/waḷḷah/). OK, a little meat, too. You're an excellent cook!
A. We're honored by your presence.
B. May your hands be blessed.
A. Thank you. Come again. (/atfaḍḍal taani/).
B. If God wills.

LESSON 40

Review last nine dialogues.

Supplementary Drills

1. I want to go to the desert. — ana abgha aruuH aṣ-ṣaHra. — ابغى اروح الصحرا.

Substitute:

buy [some] material in the souk
finish my work early
find a bus stop near here
keep my car clean
pay my bill ('account')
ask him for help ('request from him help')
get accustomed to the heat
travel to Jordan
measure the rest
buy a ticket
exchange ('change') this jacket
buy a cotton jacket
get acquainted with him
eat at the new Italian restaurant
find a good carpenter

2. I heard that this restaurant is good. — simi9t innu haada l-maṭ9am ṭayyib. — سمعت انه هادا المطعم طيب.

Substitute:

you (m) haven't paid the doctor's bill
his brother is a surgeon
the Eastern Region is very wide
he wants to buy a recorder
the test is hard
the food was delicious
the weather is moderate in Taif
she bought a meter of fabric
you have a new houseboy ('servant')
they changed the size
they are living in the south
the flowers are yellow in the desert
he explained the lesson to his younger brother (use /fahham/)
there are many peasants in the south

3. Answer the questions:

kam dafa9t lit-tilifizyoon Haggak? — كم دفعت للتلفزيون حقك؟
tiHubb al-jaww hina? — تحب الجو هنا؟
b-kam litir al-banziin? — بكم لتر البنزين؟
ruHt as-suug al-usbuu9 al-maaḍi? — رحت السوق الاسبوع الماضي؟
9indak jawaaz safar su9uudi? — عندك جواز سفر سعودي؟
eeš akalt fil-fatuur? — ايش اكلت في الفطور؟
kam magaas jazmatak? — كم مقاس جزمتك؟
tiHubb taakul fawaakih? — تحب تاكل فواكه ؟

4. Respond to the statements and questions:

laazim asta'zin.	لازم استأذن.
waHaštani.	وحشتني.
as-salaamu 9aleekum.	السلام عليكم.
ṣabaaH al-xeer.	صباح الخير.
tiṣbaH 9ala xeer.	تصبح على خير.
šukran.	شكرا.
ma9a s-salaama.	مع السلامة.
šloonak?	شلونك؟
ismaHli.	اسمحلي.
aHubb a9arrifak 9ala s-sayyid šariif.	احب أعرفك على السيد شريف.
rabbana yiwaffig.	ربنا يوفق.
šarraftana.	شرفتنا.
ahlan wu sahlan.	اهلا وسهلا.
atfaḍḍal.	اتفضل.
tislam iideek.	تسلم ايديك.
marHaba.	مرحبا.
9an iznak.	عن اذنك.
salaamatak.	سلامتك.
mabruuk.	مبروك.
ana aasif.	انا آسف.
keef Haalak?	كيف حالك؟
huwwa yisallim 9aleek.	هو يسلم عليك.

Narratives

1. I went to the souk today and bought two shirts--a blue one and a white one. They are lightweight cotton because [the] summer is coming and the weather is already hot. I also bought a blue blouse for my wife and a beautiful purse for my daughter. I talked to a friend who told me that the prices are high ('expensive') here, more than in Lebanon. But everything is available (/mawjuud/) in the souk.

2. You're a little tired? To your safety! If God wills you will be well tomorrow. Do you want [any] help in anything? Your friends asked about you this morning. Go ahead home--you need sleep. Telephone me later.

3. I want a kilo of sugar and a dozen eggs. Do you have fresh fruits? Where are these dates from? I heard that the best dates are in September. OK, give me only half a pound.

LESSON 41

Dialogue

	I rent	asta'jir	استأجر
	apartment	šagga	شقة
A.	I want to rent an apartment.	abgha asta'jir šagga.	ابغى استأجر شقة.
	if	iza	اذا
	rent	iijaar	ايجار
B.	I don't have any empty apartments now, but if you want a house, I heard that there is one for rent.	ma 9indi šugag faaḍya daHHiin, laakin iza tiHubb beet, ana simi9t innu fii waaHid lil-iijaar.	ما عندي شقق فاضية دحين، لاكن اذا تحب بيت انا سمعت انه فيه واحد للايجار.
A.	How much is the rent?	kam al-iijaar?	كم الايجار؟
	bedrooms	ghuraf noom	غرف نوم
B.	It's expensive--about 3,000 riyals per month. [There are] in it three bedrooms.	huwwa ghaali--Hawaali talaata alaaf riyaal fiš-šahar. fii talaata ghuraf noom.	هو غالي. حوالي ثلاثة الاف ريال في الشهر. فيه ثلاثة غرف نوم.
	at the expense of	9ala Hisaab	على حساب
A.	OK, let's see it. My rent is at company expense. What's the address?	ṭayyib, xalliina nišuufu. iijaari 9ala Hisaab aš-šarika. eeš al-9inwaan?	طيب خلينا نشوفه. ايجاري على حساب الشركة. ايش العنوان؟
	hospital	mustašfa	مستشفى
B.	I'm not sure. It's near the new hospital.	ana mana mit'akkid. gariib min al-mustašfa l-jadiid.	انا منا متأكد. قريب من المستشفى الجديد.

Structure Sentences

1.	My rent is at government expense.	iijaari 9ala Hisaab al-Hukuuma.	ايجاري على حساب الحكومة.
2.	My address is on this card.	9inwaani 9ala haada l-kart.	عنواني على هادا الكرت.
3.	I want a two-bedroom apartment.	abgha šagga b-ghurfateen noom.	ابغى شقة بغرفتين نوم.
4.	The kitchen is [too] small.	al-maṭbax ṣaghiir.	المطبخ صغير.
5.	Is there air-conditioning?	fii takyiif?	فيه تكييف؟

Grammatical Notes

1. /iza/, 'if', is used when speaking of the conditional present, past, or future:

iza tiHubb	if you like; if you would like
iza raaHu	if they went
iza niruuH bukra	if we go tomorrow

The word /law/, 'if', is used when speaking of the conditional which is "contrary to fact":

law raaHu	if they had gone (but they did not)
law kunt malik	if I were king

Using the conditional in Arabic is not difficult. Conditional structures may vary from the above rules, depending on the speaker (there is considerable variation in its use among the dialects of Arabic). For your own production, stay with the above rule and you will be correct. But you may also hear /iza/ used with the perfect verb even when referring to present or future:

iza Habbeet tiruuH	if you want to go
iza ruHna bukra	if we go tomorrow

Some speakers also use /law/ in this way:

law Habbeet tiruuH	if you want to go
law ruHna bukra	if we go tomorrow

2. Often used with the conditional are some "compounded" verb tenses, for example:

law ruHt, kunt waşalt daHHiin.	If I had gone, I would have arrived [by] now.
law 9irift, kunt gultalak.	If I had known, I would have told you.

For this tense, a form of /kaan/ is used with the perfect verb. It is also used as the "past perfect":

kaan raaH.	He had gone.
kaan giidu raaH.	He had already gone.
as-saa9a talaata, kunt kammalt ad-dars.	At three o'clock, I had finished the lesson.

The future form, /Ha-yikuun/, may be used with the perfect verb to form the "future perfect":

H-akuun ruHt.	I will have gone.
Ha-nikuun waşalna.	We will have arrived.
as-saa9a talaata H-akuun kammalt ad-dars.	At three o'clock, I will have finished the lesson.

4. Areas in a house are:

şaala	entrance area	صالة
ghurfat al-juluus	living room	غرفة الجلوس
şaloon	guests' receiving room	صالون
ghurfat as-sufra	dining room	غرفة السفرة
ghurfat an-noom	bedroom	غرفة النوم
maţbax	kitchen	مطبخ

Hammaam	bathroom	حمام
siib, asyaab	hall	سيب اسياب
dulaab, dawaaliib	closet	دولاب دواليب
balakoona, -aat	balcony	بلكونة -ات
garaaj	garage	كراج
jineena, janaayin	garden	جنينة جناين

Vocabulary Notes

asta'jar, yista'jir	rent	استأجر يستأجر
mustašfa, -yaat*	hospital	مستشفى -يات
šagga, šugag	apartment	شقة شقق

*This word is masculine.

Drills

1. I want to rent an apartment.	abgha asta'jir šagga.	ابغى استأجر شقة.

Substitute:

a room
a house
a big house
a three-bedroom apartment
a house near the embassy
a house on Mecca Road
a small apartment

2. If you (m) want a house...	iza tiHubb beet...	اذا تحب بيت...

Substitute:

another apartment
you (m) find
we find
we need
a bigger house
a prettier house
they need
they buy
I buy
I want
you (f) want
you (m) want

3. My rent is at company expense.	iijaari 9ala Hisaab aš-šarika.	ايجاري على حساب الشركة.

Substitute:

government expense
my expense
my ticket
their expense
company expense
our room
our gasoline
my car's gasoline
government expense
my rent

4. The kitchen is small. al-maṭbax ṣaghiir. المطبخ صغير.

Substitute:

the closets
the living room
the children's bedroom
the dining room
large
the balcony
the kitchen
the bathroom

5. Is there airconditioning? fii takyiif? فيه تكييف؟

Substitute:

a big garage
enough closets
a school nearby
a hospital nearby
a balcony
a place for my books
an address
airconditioning

Situations

1.
A. Will you rent a house here?
B. If my family arrives next month, I'll rent one. If they don't come, I'll wait.
A. Rent ('the rent') is expensive here.
B. Yes, many foreigners have come in the last two years, and there aren't any apartments or houses free.

2.
A. I need an apartment with (/b-/) airconditioning.
B. How many bedrooms?
A. Two are enough. And my wife wants a large kitchen and a balcony.
B. I know a new building. I forgot the address, but it is the tallest one, right behind the hospital.
A. Good. If I had known, I would have asked before this.

LESSON 42

Dialogue

	window	šubbaak	شباك
A.	Put the chair [over] there, next to the window.	Huṭṭ al-kursi hinaak, jamb aš-šubbaak.	حط الكرسي هناك، جنب الشباك.
	sofa	kanaba	كنبه
B.	And the sofa?	w al-kanaba?	والكنبه ؟
	wall	jadur	جدر
A.	The sofa and tables by that wall.	al-kanaba w aṭ-ṭarabiizaat jamb haada l-jadur.	الكنبه والطربيزات جنب هادا الجدر.
B.	I was going to put them by the door.	kunt H-aHuṭṭahum jamb al-baab.	كنت حاحطهم جنب الباب.
	idea	fikra	فكرة
	I prefer	afaḍḍil	افضل
A.	That's a good idea, but I prefer that they be here.	haadi fikra ṭayyiba, laakin afaḍḍil innahum yikuunu hina.	هادي فكرة طيبة لاكن افضل انهم يكونوا هنا.
	mood, opinion	keef	كيف
	box, trunk	ṣanduug	صندوق
	ma'am ('my lady')	sitti	ستي
B.	As you (f) wish, ma'am. And this box?	9ala keefik ya sitti. wu haada ṣ-ṣanduug?	على كيفك يا ستي. وهادا الصندوق ؟
	dog	kalb	كلب
	garden	Hooš*	حوش
A.	That's the dog's box. Back in the garden.	haada ṣanduug al-kalb. wara fil-Hooš.	هادا صندوق الكلب. ورا في الحوش.

*This word alternates with /jineena/.

Structure Sentences

1.	She was going to ask him.	kaanat Ha-tis'alu.	كانت حتسأله .
2.	That's a bad idea.	haadi fikra baṭṭaala.	هادي فكرة بطالة.
3.	That's quite a good ('not bad') idea.	haadi fikra mahi baṭṭaala.	هادي فكرة مهي بطالة.
4.	We prefer to leave after the evening [prayer].	nifaḍḍil nimši ba9d al-9iša.	نفضل نمشي بعد العشا.

5. This is the cat's food. haada akl al-bissa. هادا اكل البسة.

6. I have an idea. 9indi fikra. عندي فكرة.

Grammatical Notes

1. To express 'was going to', 'was planning to', use the perfect of /kaan/ with a future verb:

kunt H-aruuH.	I was going to go.
kaanat Ha-tis'alu.	She was going to ask him.

2. /faḍḍal, yifaḍḍil/ may be used as a helping verb with other verbs (cf. Structure Sentence 4).

3. This is a summary of all the verb tenses introduced:

Summary of Tenses

(Lesson 4)	Perfect	Suffixes: -Ø -at -u -t -ti -tu -t -na
(Lesson 5)	Imperfect	Prefixes: y- t- y- -u t- t- -i t- -u a- n-
(Lesson 14)	Future	Use /Ha-/ or /raH-/ + imperfect.
(Lesson 15)	Affirmative Command	Use second-person imperfect form, minus the /t-/ prefix.
(Lesson 22)	Habitual	Use imperfect, or /b-/ + imperfect.
(Lesson 22)	Present Perfect	Use a form of /giid-/, or the active participle.
(Lesson 25)	Present Progressive (continuous)	Use /b-/ + imperfect.
(Lesson 25)	Past Progressive	Use /kaan/ + imperfect, or /kaan/ + /b-/ + imperfect.
(Lesson 27)	Negative Command	Use /laa/ + imperfect.
(Lesson 36)	Ongoing Action	Use /9ammaal/ + imperfect.

(Lesson 41)	Past Perfect Future Perfect	Use /kaan/ + perfect. Use/Ha-yikuun/ + perfect.
(Lesson 42)	"Was Going to" (intention)	Use /kaan/ + future.

Vocabulary Notes

kanaba, -aat	sofa	كنبه -ات
sariir, surur	bed	سرير سرر
sujjaada, sajaajiid	carpet, rug	سجادة سجاجيد
šubbaak, šabaabiik	window	شباك شبابيك
jadur, judraan	wall	جدر جدران
ṣanduug, ṣanaadiig	box, trunk	صندوق صناديق
tallaaja, -aat	refrigerator	ثلاجة -ات
sitaara, sataayir	curtain, drapery	ستارة ستاير
fikra, afkaar	idea	فكرة افكار
kalb, -a, kilaab	dog	كلب كلاب
bissa, bisas	cat	بسة بسس
baṭṭaal, -a, -iin	bad	بطال -ين
faḍḍal, yifaḍḍil	prefer	فضل يفضل

Drills

1. Put the chair next to the window. — Huṭṭ al-kursi jamb aš-šubbaak. — حط الكرسي جنب الشباك.

Substitute:

the sofa
the table
next to the wall
the bed
the rug
next to the door
the refrigerator
next to the window
the chair

2. I was going to put them by the door. — kunt H-aHuṭṭahum jamb al-baab. — كنت حاحطهم جنب الباب.

Substitute:

[over] there
to bring them
to bring it (m)
she was
we were
in the car
take it (f)
put it (f)
I was
by the door

3. She was going to ask him. — kaanat Ha-tis'alu. — كانت حتسأله ·

Substitute:

asked
will ask
had asked
will have asked
wanted to ask
must ask
was going to ask

4. That's a good idea. <u>haadi fikra ṭayyiba</u>. هادي فكرة طيبة.

Substitute:

bad
wrong
not bad
accurate
plan
project
good
bad
situation
difficult
good
idea

5. I prefer that they be here. <u>afaḍḍil innahum yikuunu hina</u>. افضل انهم يكونوا هنا.

Substitute:

he
we
they
preferred
you (m)
it (m)
someplace else (/fi makaan taani/)
I
in another room
in the kitchen
here

6. That's the dog's box. <u>haada ṣanduug al-kalb</u>. هادا صندوق الكلب.

Substitute:

food
the cat's
room
bed
box
the dog's

Situations

1.
A. I prefer a large house because I have three children, a dog, and a cat.
B. You brought a dog and cat with you to the Kingdom?
A. Of course. They're very important. They have been with us for a long time.
B. If I had a dog or a cat, I would have left it in America.

2.
A. Clean (f) the walls and then the refrigerator.
B. And the rug?
A. No, the rug later. The kitchen is more important now.
B. When are the people coming?
A. They're coming tonight. Don't forget to clean the windows in the living room.
B. As you (f) wish.

3.
A. I want to buy something sweet for dinner.
B. Baklawa is good--foreigners like it.
A. Good idea. But I prefer ice cream (/ays kriim/).
B. Shall I buy it now?*
A. Yes, buy about a kilo.
B. OK, I have enough change.

*When you hear a foreign word, if it ends in /a-/, treat it as feminine; if not, as masculine. In this case, /ays kriim/ would be masculine.

Culture Notes

1. Saudis may own pets but most do not. They are often surprised by the affection lavished upon pets by foreigners. When Saudis visit an American's home, they usually do not appreciate having pets around. It is not considered appropriate for a dog to live inside the house.

LESSON 43

Dialogue

(At the post office)

	I send	arsil	ارسل
	air (adjective)	jawwi	جوي
	registered	musajjal	مسجل
A.	I want to mail ('send') a letter to America, airmail and registered.	abgha arsil jawaab li-amriika, bariid jawwi wu musajjal.	ابغى ارسل جواب لأمريكا، بريد جوي ومسجل.
	stamps	ṭawaabi9	طوابع
B.	Its weight is heavy. Four riyals for stamps.	waznu tagiil. arba9a riyaal liṭ-ṭawaabi9.	وزنه ثقيل. اربعة ريال للطوابع.
	I translate	atarjim	اترجم
A.	I want to translate this address.	abgha atarjim haada l-9inwaan.	ابغى اترجم هادا العنوان.
	I help (with)	asaa9id (fi)	اساعد (في)
	translation	tarjama	ترجمة
B.	I'll help you with the translation.	ana asaa9idak fit-tarjama.	انا اساعدك في الترجمة.
	I just	duubi	دوبي
	I sent	arsalt	ارسلت
	package	ṭard	طرد
A.	I just sent a package. When will it arrive?	ana duubi arsalt ṭard. mita yiwṣal?	انا دوبي ارسلت طرد. متا يوصل؟
	probability	iHtimaal	احتمال
B.	Probably ('the probability') in two weeks.	iHtimaal ba9d usbuu9een.	احتمال بعد اسبوعين.

Structure Sentences

1.	I want to send a letter regular mail.	abgha arsil jawaab bariid 9aadi.	ابغى ارسل جواب بريد عادي.
2.	Put the stamp on the envelope.	Huṭṭ aṭ-ṭaaba9 9ala ẓ-ẓarf.	حط الطابع على الظرف.
3.	This is an official letter.	haada jawaab rasmi.	هادا جواب رسمي.
4.	This is diplomatic mail.	haada bariid diblumaasi.	هادا بريد دبلوماسي.

5. I need an interpreter.	ana miHtaaj li-mutarjim.	انا محتاج لمترجم.
6. He just arrived.	huwwa duubu waṣal.	هو دوبه وصل.

Grammatical Notes

1. The word /duub-/ is used before another verb to mean 'just', in the sense of recently completing an action. It is conjugated for person:

duubu	he just	دوبه
duubaha	she just	دوبها
duubahum	they just	دوبهم
duubak	you (m) just	دوبك
duubik	you (f) just	دوبك
duubakum	you (p) just	دوبكم
duubi	I just	دوبي
duubana	we just	دوبنا

duubi arsalt ṭard.	I just sent a package.
duubu waṣal.	He just arrived.

An alternative word in common use for 'just' is /taww-/. It is also used with pronoun endings: /tawwu/, /tawwaha/, /tawwi/, etc.

Vocabulary Notes

ṭaaba9, ṭawaabi9	stamp	طابع طوابع
ṭard, ṭuruud	package	طرد طرود
ẓarf, ẓuruuf	envelope	ظرف ظروف
mutarjim, -a, -iin	interpreter	مترجم -ين
tarjam, yitarjim	interpret	ترجم يترجم
saa9ad, yisaa9id (fi)	help	ساعد يساعد (في)
arsal, yirsil	send	ارسل يرسل

Drills

1. I want to mail a letter to America, airmail.	abgha arsil jawaab li-amriika, <u>bariid jawwi</u>.	ابغى ارسل جواب لامريكا بريد جوي.

Substitute:

registered
regular mail
quickly
in this envelope
diplomatic mail
official mail
at government expense

2. I want to translate this address.	<u>abgha atarjim haada l-9inwaan</u>.	ابغى اترجم هادا العنوان.

Substitute:

this letter
this note
she
this book

the lesson
he
this address
his name

3. I'll help you with the translation. — ana asaa9idak fi t-tarjama. — انا اساعدَك في الترجمة.

Substitute:

the work
the writing
the lesson
the address
the food
the project
the translation

4. I just sent a package. — ana duubi arsalt ṭard. — انا دوبي ارسلت طرد.

Substitute:

he
you (m)
we
you (p)
she
they
I

5. He just arrived. — huwwa duubu waṣal. — هو دوبه وصل.

Substitute:

she
went
wrote to him
they
spent the money
we
I
requested a taxi
she
he
arrived

Situations

1.
A. Where is my interpreter?
B. He just went home.
A. Unbelievable! I told him that I need him tonight.
B. Never mind, I'll help you with the interpreting.

2.
A. Did you write to the director?
B. Yes, I sent the letter this morning from the post office. Airmail and registered.
A. I hope it arrives quickly.
B. I asked the employee and he said there is a probability that it will be on a plane today.

3.
A. Let's translate this together.
B. OK, if I can find my pen and notebook.
A. On the table beside the green chair.
B. Can you bring them for me?
A. The letter concerns (/9an/) our plan for the new building.
B. I'm sure it's important.

LESSON 44

Dialogue

	to you (m), for you (m)	bak	بَك
A.	What's wrong with you?	eeš bak?	ايش بك؟
	head	raas	راس
	it (f) hurts	tuja9	توجع
B.	I'm a little "tired". My head hurts (me).	ana ta9baan šwayya. raasi tuja9ni.	انا تعبان شويه · راسي توجعني·
A.	I hope you're better soon.	salaamatak.	سلامتك·
B.	Thank you. I wanted to go to the university but I won't be able to.	aḷḷaah yisallimak. kunt abgha aruuH al-jaam9a laakin ma H-agdar.	الله يسلمك· كنت ابغى اروح الجامعة لاكن ما حاقدر·
	you (m) rest	tistariiH	تستريح
A.	Never mind. You (m) have to rest.	ma9aleeš. laazim tistariiH.	معليش· لازم تستريح·
B.	Can you do me a favor?	mumkin ti9milli xidma?	ممكن تعملي خدمة؟
	gladly	ibšer	ابشر
A.	Gladly, what? ('say')	ibšer. guul.	ابشر· قول·
	medicine	dawa	دوا
	pharmacy	ṣaydaliyya	صيدلية
B.	Buy me this medicine at the pharmacy.	ištiriili haada d-dawa min aṣ-ṣaydaliyya.	اشتريلي هادا الدوا من الصيدلية·

Structure Sentences

1.	What's wrong with you (f)?	eeš bik?	ايش بِك؟
2.	My back hurts (me).	ḍahri yuja9ni.	ظهري يوجعني·
3.	My stomach hurts.	baṭni tuja9ni.	بطني توجعني·
4.	He should have come before this; he had to come before this.	kaan laazim yiji gabl kida.	كان لازم يجي قبل كده·
5.	I rested yesterday.	astaraHt ams.	استرحت امس·
6.	Other than that, we were happy.	gheer kida, kunna mabsuuṭiin.	غير كده· كنا مبسوطين·

Grammatical Notes

1. /eeš bak?/ is used to mean 'What's [wrong] with you?' and is conjugated:

eeš bak?	What's wrong with you (m)?
eeš bik?	What's wrong with you (f)?
eeš bakum?	What's wrong with you (p)?
eeš buh?	What's wrong with him?
eeš baha?	What's wrong with her?
eeš bahum?	What's wrong with them?

A variation of this is /eeš fiik/, /eeš fiiki/, etc.

2. Parts of the body may be grammatically masculine or feminine. Generally, two-member parts are feminine, and one-member parts are masculine (although this varies):

raas (m. or f.)	head	راس
ḍahr (m)	back	ظهر
baṭn (f)	stomach	بطن
iid, yadeen* (f)	hand	ايد يدين
diraa9, diraa9een (f)	arm	ذراع ذراعين
rijl, rujuul (f)	foot	رجل رجول
saag, saageen (f)	leg	ساق ساقين
9een, 9uyuun (f)	eye	عين عيون

*Note that some "plural" forms are in fact dual. Also note that /yadeen/ alternates with /iideen/, introduced in Lesson 37.

yadeenu	his hands
yadeenaha	her hands
yadeenahum	their hands
yadeenak	your (m) hands
yadeenik	your (f) hands
yadeenakum	your (p) hands
yadeeni	my hands
yadeena	our hands
rujuulu	his feet
rujuulaha	her feet
rujuuli	my feet
(etc.)	
9uyuunu	his eyes
9uyuunaha	her eyes
9uyuuni	my eyes
(etc.)	

3. /kaan/ in the perfect tense can be combined with some verbs in the imperfect tense. With verbs, it is conjugated for person:

kunt abgha aruuH.	I wanted to go.
kaanat tibgha tiji.	She wanted to come.

With modal words like /laazim/ and /mumkin/, /kaan/ may or may not be conjugated (it varies with different speakers). (See also Lesson 29).

kaan laazim aji.	I had to come; I should have come.
kunt laazim aji.	I had to come; I should have come.
kaan mumkin aji.	I was able to come.
kunt mumkin aji.	I was able to come.

4. /ibšer/, 'gladly', 'certainly', is used when responding to a request for a favor.

5. /kida/, 'like that', may be used idiomatically:

gabl kida	before that	قبل كده
ba9d kida	after that	بعد كده
ma9a kida	in spite of that, nevertheless	مع كده
gheer kida	other than that	غير كده
zayy kida	like that	زي كده

Vocabulary Notes

waja9, yuja9	hurt	وجع يوجع
astaraaH, yistariiH	rest	استراح يستريح
dawa, adwiya*	medicine	دوا ادوية

*This word is masculine.

Drills

1. What's wrong with you (m)? eeš __bak__? ايش بَك؟

Substitute:

you (f)
them
her
you (p)
him
you (m)

2. My head hurts (me). __raasi__ tuja9ni. راسي توجعني.

Substitute:

my back
my leg
my foot
my stomach
my arm
my eyes
my hand
my head

3. I wanted to go to the university. __kunt abgha aruuH al-jaam9a__. كنت ابغى اروح الجامعة.

Substitute:

I had to go
I had to return

to the airport
I could have returned ('it was possible that I return')
he could have returned
he could have visited
he wanted to visit
he wanted to see
the university
I wanted to see
I wanted to go

4. He should have come before this. — kaan laazim yiji gabl kida. — كان لازم يجي قبل كده.

Substitute:

he could have come
he could have left
after that
he wanted to leave
I
she
she had to leave
she had to finish
before that
we
he
he had to come

5. Other than that, we were happy. — gheer kida, kunna mabsuuṭiin. — غير كده كنا مبسوطين.

Substitute:

before that
after that
nevertheless
other than that

Situations

1.
A. Hello. What's wrong with you (m)?
B. I don't know. I'm a little tired.
A. Maybe you need a rest.
B. Yes, I'll try. My back hurts.
A. "I hope you're better soon."
B. "Thanks."

2.
A. I'm sorry, I'm wrong.
B. Never mind. It's not important.
A. I should have asked the boss first.
B. Next time.
A. Nevertheless, nobody is angry.

3.
A. How are you today?
B. My head still hurts. Other than that, I'm much better.
A. Thank God. All your friends send their greetings.
B. "Thanks." Can you do me a favor?
A. Gladly.
B. Give me the medicine which I left on the table.

LESSON 45

Dialogue

	during	xilaal	خلال
	vacation	9uṭla	عطلة
	Eid (Moslem holiday)	9iid	عيد
A.	What did you (p) do during the Eid vacation?	eeš sawweetu xilaal 9uṭlat al-9iid?	ايش سويتوا خلال عطلة العيد؟
	guests	ḍuyuuf	ضيوف
	Europe	urubba	اروبا
B.	We had guests from Europe.	kaan 9indana ḍuyuuf min urubba.	كان عندنا ضيوف من اروبا.
	party	Hafla	حفلة
A.	Can you (p) honor us at a party tomorrow night?	mumkin tišarrifuuna fi Hafla bukra fil-leel?	ممكن تشرفونا في حفلة بكرة في الليل؟
B.	I think so.	aẓunn kida.	اظن كده.
	well ('in goodness')	b-xeer	بخير
A.	Have a good holiday. ('May you (p) be well every year')	kull 9aam w intu b-xeer.	كل عام وانتو بخير.
B.	You too. ('And you (p) are of the same group')	w intu min ahlu.	وانتو من اهله.

Structure Sentences

1.	Christmas vacation begins next week.	9uṭlat 9iid al-miilaad tibda' al-usbuu9 al-jayy.	عطلة عيد الميلاد تبدأ الاسبوع الجي.
2.	Our family will travel on National Day.	9eelatna Ha-tisaafir fil-9iid al-waṭani.	عيلتنا حتسافر في العيد الوطني.
3.	We have guests from Africa.	9indana ḍuyuuf min afriqya.	عندنا ضيوف من افريقيا.
4.	Can you (m) honor us at a reception ('reception party')?	mumkin tišarrifna fi Haflat istigbaal?	ممكن تشرفنا في حفلة استقبال؟
5.	I want to invite you to a party.	abgha a9zimak 9ala Hafla.	ابغى اعزمك على حفلة.
6.	I have a meeting tonight.	9indi ijtimaa9 al-leela.	عندي اجتماع الليلة.

Grammatical Notes

1. Some holidays are:

(Moslem)	al-9iid al-kabiir (9iid al-aḍHa)	Big Eid (Feast of Sacrifice)	العيد الكبير (عيد الأضحى)
	al-9iid aṣ-ṣaghiir (9iid al-fiṭir)	Little Eid (Feast of Breaking the Fast)	العيد الصغير (عيد الفطر)
	mawlid an-nabi	The Prophet's Birthday	مولد النبي
(Christian and American)	9iid al-miilaad	Christmas	عيد الميلاد
	9iid al-giyaama	Easter	عيد القيامة
	9iid aš-šukr	Thanksgiving	عيد الشكر
	9iid al-istiqlaal	Independence Day	عيد الاستقلال
(Other)	al-9iid al-waṭani	National Day	العيد الوطني

2. The continents are:

urubba	Europe	اوربا
aasya	Asia	اسيا
afriqya	Africa	افريقيا
amriika š-samaaliyya	North America	امريكا الشمالية
amriika l-januubiyya	South America	امريكا الجنوبية

3. On the occasion of any annual holiday or commemoration (religious, national, one's birthday), the following expression is used:

kull 9aam w intu b-xeer.	May you (p) be well every year.
(inta)	(you (m))
(inti)	(you (f))

The response is:

w intu min ahlu.	And you (p) are of the same group.
(inta)	(you (m))
(inti)	(you (f))

Vocabulary Notes

9uṭla, 9uṭal	vacation	عطلة عطل
9iid, a9yaad	holiday, Eid	عيد اعياد
ḍeef, ḍuyuuf	guest	ضيف ضيوف
Hafla, Hafalaat	party	حفلة -ات
istigbaal, -aat	reception	استقبال -ات
ijtimaa9, -aat	meeting	اجتماع -ات
bada', yibda'	begin	بدأ يبدأ
9azam, yi9zim (9ala)	invite	عزم يعزم (على)

Drills

1. What did you (p) do during the Eid vacation?	eeš sawweetu xilaal 9uṭlat al-9iid?	ايش سويتوا خلال عطلة العيد؟

Substitute:

during Christmas vacation
during the summer vacation
on National Day
on Independence Day
on your (m) birthday
on the Prophet's birthday
on Easter
on Thanksgiving
during the Eid vacation

2. We had guests from Europe. — kaan 9indana ḍuyuuf min urubba. — كان عندنا ضيوف من اوربا.

Substitute:

Africa
North America
Asia
South America
Europe

3. (a man to a man)
kull 9aam w inta b-xeer.→ w inta min ahlu. — كل عام وانتَ بخير. ← وانتَ من اهله.

Repeat the exchange, between the following groups of persons:

(a man to a woman)
(a man to a group)
(a woman to a group)
(a woman to a woman)
(a group to a woman)
(a group to a man)
(a man to a man)

4. Christmas vacation begins next week. — 9uṭlat 9iid al-miilaad tibda' al-usbuu9 al-jayy. — عطلة عيد الميلاد تبدأ الاسبوع الجي.

Substitute:

(the) summer vacation
my work
the university
we
they
(the) school
the project
Thanksgiving vacation

5. I have a meeting tonight. — 9indi ijtimaa9 al-leela. — عندي اجتماع الليلة.

Substitute:

a party
a reception
the ambassador's reception
an official party
an official meeting
a diplomatic reception
three parties
a meeting

6. I want to invite you (m) to a party. <u>abgha a9zimak</u> 9ala Hafla. ابغى اعزمَك، على حفلة.

Substitute:

we want
she wants
to invite them
to invite him
he wants
to invite me
to invite us
they want
to invite you (f)
to invite you (m)
I want

Situations

1.
A. Can you (p) honor us at a reception?
B. Gladly. Where?
A. At our house, the day after tomorrow about eight o'clock.
B. May I bring guests with me?
A. Of course, welcome.
B. I'll tell them.
A. Goodby.
B. Goodby.

2.
A. Today is my birthday.
B. "Happy Birthday". (use annual greeting)
A. "Thank you".
B. How old are you?
A. 30. My wife invites you to a party tonight.
B. What time does it start?
A. After dinner.

3.
A. Where will you go during your vacation?
B. I and my family are traveling ('will travel') to Africa.
A. I hope you like Africa.
B. We have many friends who invited us.
A. People from the State Department?
B. Yes, all of them.

LESSON 46

Dialogue

	democracy, democratic	dimuqraaṭiyya	ديموقراطية
	two parties (political)	Hizbeen	حزبين
	republican	jumhuuri	جمهوري
A.	The American government is a democracy. We have two political parties, the Democratic and the Republican.	Hukuumat amriika dimuqraaṭiyya. 9indana Hizbeen, ad-dimuqraaṭi w al-jumhuuri.	حكومة امريكا ديموقراطية. عندنا حزبين، الديموقراطي والجمهوري.
	monarchy	malakiyya	ملكية
	similarly	kazaalik	كذلك
B.	Here in Saudi Arabia, the government is a monarchy. It's the same ('similarly') in Jordon.	hina fis-su9uudiyya, al-Hukuuma malakiyya. kazaalik fil-urdun.	هنا في السعودية الحكومة ملكية. كذلك الاردن.
	republic	jumhuuriyya	جمهورية
A.	But Egypt is a republic.	laakin maṣur jumhuuriyya.	لاكن مصر جمهورية.
	system	niẓaam	نظام
	socialist	ištiraaki	اشتراكي
B.	Yes, it has ('in it') a socialist system.	iiwa, fiiha niẓaam ištiraaki.	ايوه، فيها نظام اشتراكي.
	politics	as-siyaasa	السياسة
A.	Do you like to talk about politics?	tiHubb titkallam 9an as-siyaasa?	تحب تتكلم عن السياسة؟
	newspapers	jaraayid	جرايد
	magazines	majallaat	مجلات
	international ('wordly')	9aalami	عالمي
B.	Yes, very much. I read the international newspapers and magazines everyday.	illa, katiir. agra l-jaraayid wal-majallaat al-9aalamiyya kull yoom.	الا كثير. اقرا الجرايد والمجلات العالمية كل يوم.

Structure Sentences

1.	Communism is important in Russia.	aš-šuyuu9iyya muhimma fi ruusya.	الشيوعية مهمة في روسيا.
2.	The Arab governments are against Zionism.	al-Hukuumaat al-9arabiyya ḍidd aṣ-ṣahyuuniyya.	الحكومات العربية ضد الصهيونية.

3. He is a Zionist from Israel.	huwwa ṣahyuuni min isra'iil.	هو صهيوني من اسرائيل.
4. My country is a republic.	baladi jumhuuriyya.	بلدي جمهورية.
5. This article is from a Saudi newspaper.	haadi l-magaala min jariida su9uudiyya.	هادي المقالة من جريدة سعودية.
6. Do you have the new "Time" magazine?	9indak majallat "Time" al-jadiida?	عندَك مجلة تايم الجديدة؟

Grammatical Notes

1. Certain types of "abstract" nouns are formed with the suffix /-iyya/ added to a word stem. Some common ones relating to politics are:

dimuqraaṭiyya	democracy	ديموقراطية
malakiyya	monarchy	ملكية
ištiraakiyya	socialism	اشتراكية
šuyuu9iyya	communism	شيوعية
qawmiyya	nationalism	قومية
jumhuuriyya	republic	جمهورية
ṣahyuuniyya	Zionism	صهيونية

The adjective derived from this type of noun has the endings /-i/, (/-iyya/, /-yiin/):

dimuqraaṭi	democratic
jumhuuri	republican
ištiraaki	socialist
siyaasi	political
(etc.)	

2. Abstract nouns (of any type) are almost always used with the definite article /al-/ in Arabic, but this is not translated into English:

tiHubb titkallam 9an as-siyaasa?	Do you like to talk about politics?
aš-šuyuu9iyya muhimma fi-ruusya.	Communism is important in Russia.
al-Hukuumaat al-9arabiyya ḍidd aṣ-ṣahyuuniyya.	The Arab governments are against Zionism.

Statements which generalize about an idea usually have the definite article /al-/ with the noun, which is not the case in English.

In past lessons:

mamnuu9 al-xuruuj.	Exiting is forbidden.
..li'ann aṣ-ṣeef jayy	..because summer is coming
al-iijaar ghaali hina.	Rent is expensive here.
al-fuluus muhimma.	Money is important.
atkallamna 9an at-ta9liim waṣ-ṣiHHa.	We discussed education and health.
wu fi ta9liim al-banaat?	And in girls' education?

Other examples:

al-kiimya ṣa9ba.	Chemistry is difficult.
al-banziin raxiiṣ.	Gasoline is cheap.
aṣ-ṣiHHa muhimma.	Health is important.
al-akl as-su9uudi ṭi9im.	Saudi food is delicious.

Vocabulary Notes

Hizb, aHzaab	(political) party	حزب احزاب
niẓaam, nuẓum	system	نظام نظم
jariida, jaraayid	newspaper	جريدة جرايد
majalla, -aat	magazine	مجلة -ات
siyaasa, -aat	policy; politics	سياسة -ات
balad, bilaad (buldaan)*	country	بلد بلاد (بلدان)

*/balad/ or /bilaad/ may mean 'country'. At the same time, /bilaad/ and /buldaan/ may be the plural, 'countries'.

dimuqraaṭi, -yiin	democratic	ديموقراطي -يين
jumhuuri, -yiin	republican	جمهوري -يين
siyaasi, -yiin	political	سياسي -يين
malaki, -yiin	monarchist	ملكي -يين
ištiraaki, -yiin	socialist	اشتراكي -يين
šuyuu9i, -iin	communist	شيوعي -يين
9aalami, -yiin	international	عالمي -يين
ṣahyuuni, -yiin	Zionist	صهيوني -يين
isra'iili, -yiin	Israeli	اسرائيلي -يين

Drills

1. The American government is a democracy. — al-Hukuuma l-amrikiyya dimuqraaṭiyya. — الحكومة الامريكية ديموقراطية.

Substitute:

German
French
Italian
my
monarchy
Saudi
English
Jordanian
the government of my country
socialist
Egyptian
Sudanese
this government
communist
Russian

2. Egypt has a socialist system. — maṣur fiiha niẓaam ištiraaki. — مصر فيها نظام اشتراكي.

Substitute:

the United States (democratic)
Russia (communist)
Saudi Arabia (monarchist)
Libya (nationalist)
Israel (Zionist)

Lebanon (democratic)
Japan (democratic)
Egypt (socialist)

3.	Do you like to talk about politics?	tiHubb titkallam 9an as-siyaasa?	تحب تتكلم عن السياسة؟

Substitute:

she
about the government
about Zionism
they
about their country
about socialism and communism
he
about political parties
about the Democratic party
about the Republican party
about Israel's politics
you (f)
about the newspapers
about Arab politics
about political systems

4.	I read the international newspapers.	agra al-jaraayid al-9aalamiyya.	اقرا الجرايد العالمية.

Substitute:

American
magazines
international
German
Arab
newspapers
Saudi

5.	The Arab governments are against Zionism.	al-Hukuumaat al-9arabiyya ḍidd aṣ-ṣahyuuniyya.	الحكومات العربية ضد الصهيونية.

Substitute:

Israel
this policy
this idea
I
all of us
this plan
these plans
these policies
Russia's policy
your (p) policy

6.	He is a Zionist from Israel.	huwwa ṣahyuuni min isra'iil.	هو صهيوني من اسرائيل.

Substitute:

Europe
communist
socialist

Italy
America
Democrat
Republican

Situations

1.
A. What is the political system in the Arab countries?
B. There are many systems--monarchist socialist, and democratic.
A. And communist?
B. No, there is no communism.

2.
A. Have you seen today's paper?
B. Yes, I read the article about Zionism and Arab nationalism.
A. I know the man who wrote it.
B. I think he writes for a Saudi newspaper and an international newspaper as well (/kazaalik/), right?
A. Yes, and he writes the best political articles.

3.
A. There is a reception at the embassy tonight. Are you going?
B. Maybe, I'm not sure. I have guests.
A. Have them come with you.
B. I'll try. Why is there a party?
A. It's National Day.
B. Oh, yes, I forgot.

LESSON 47

Dialogue

	Ramadan	ramaḑaan	رمضان
A.	Tomorrow Ramadan begins.	bukra yibda' šahar ramaḑaan.	بكرة يبدأ شهر رمضان.
	they fast	yişuumu	يصوموا
	all ('the length of')	ţuul	طول
	even	Hatta	حتى
B.	Yes, all the Moslems will fast all month. They don't eat and don't drink and don't even smoke cigarettes.	iiwa, kull al-musḷimiin Ha-yişuumu ţuul aš-šahar. ma yaaklu wala yišrabu wu Hatta ma yišrabu sajaayir.	ايوه ،كل المسلمين حيصوموا طول الشهر. ما ياكلوا ولا يشربوا وحتى ما يشربوا سجاير.
	pillars, tenets	arkaan	اركان
	religion	diin	دين
	Islamic	islaami	اسلامي
A.	I know that there are five "pillars" in the Islamic religion.	a9rif innu fii xamsa arkaan fid-diin al-islaami.	اعرف انه فيه خمسة اركان في الدين الاسلامي.
	declaration of faith	aš-šihaada	الشهادة
	prayer	as-şalaa	الصلا
	alms	az-zakaa	الزكا
	fasting	aş-şoom	الصوم
	pilgrimage (to Mecca)	al-Hajj	الحج
B.	Yes, the five pillars are: the declaration of faith prayer, almsgiving, fasting, and the pilgrimage.	al-arkaan al-xamsa humma: aš-šihaada, aş-şalaa, az-zakaa, aş-şoom, wal-Hajj.	الاركان الخمسة هم: الشهادة، الصلا، الزكا، الصوم، والحج.

Structure Sentences

1.	I have to pray the sunset [prayer].	laazim aşalli l-maghrib.*	لازم اصلي المغرب.
2.	Alms are two and one-half per cent.	az-zakaa itneen wu nuşş fil-miyya.	الزكات اثنين ونص في المية.
3.	The declaration of faith is: [There is] no god but God and Muhammad is the Messenger of God.	aš-šihaada hiyya: laa ilaaha illa ḷḷaah wu muHammad rasuul aḷḷaah.	الشهادة هي: لا اله الا الله ومحمد رسول الله.

*the full expressions would be /şalaat al-maghrib/, 'the evening prayer'.

4. I didn't even see my family.	Hatta ma šuft ahli.	حتى ما شفت اهلي.
5. Even he knows.	Hatta huwwa yi9rif.	حتى هو يعرف.

Grammatical Notes

1. The Islamic months are:

muHarram	محرم
ṣafar	صفر
rabii9 al-awwal	ربيع الاول
rabii9 at-taani	ربيع الثاني
jumaad al-awwal	جماد الاول
jumaad at-taani	جماد الثاني
rajab	رجب
ša9baan	شعبان
ramaḍaan	رمضان
šawwaal	شوال
zu l-gi9da	ذو القعدة
zu l-Hijja	ذو الحجة

They are calculated according to a lunar system, which means that the Islamic year is eleven days shorter than the Western year. The calendar begins with the year 1 corresponding to 622 A.D., the date on which the Prophet Muhammad emigrated from Mecca to Medina. This emigration is called /al-Hijra/ in Arabic, and thus an Islamic date is referred to as /Hijri/, often abbreviated in English as A.H., while a date in the Western calendar is called /miilaadi/(referring to the birth of Jesus). Each lunar month begins with the new moon.

ana mawluud 9aam 1367 Hijri fi šahar ša9baan.
I was born in 1367 A.H. in the month of Shaban.

ana mawluud 9aam 1949 miilaadi fi šahar maaris.
I was born in 1949 A.D. in the month of March.

2. Note the use of /ṭuul an-nahaar/, 'all day long' (literally, 'the length of the daytime'), as opposed to /kull yoom/, 'every day'. /ṭuul/ may be used with other time words:

ṭuul aš-šahar	all month
ṭuul as-sana	all year
ṭuul al-usbuu9	all week

3. /širib/, 'to drink', is used idiomatically to mean 'to smoke':

ma yišrabu sajaayir.	They don't smoke cigarettes.

The verb /daxxan, yidaxxin/ is also commonly used to mean 'smoke'; its verbal noun is /tadxiin/:

ma adaxxin.	I don't smoke.
ma ašrab sajaayir.	I don't smoke.
mamnuu9 at-tadxiin.	No smoking.

4. /Hatta/ is used with an affirmative verb to mean 'even', and with a negative verb to mean 'not even':

Hatta huwwa yi9rif.	Even he knows.
Hatta dafa9t al-fuluus.	I even paid the money.

Hatta ma yišrabu sajaayir.	They don't even smoke cigarettes.
Hatta ma šuft ahli.	I didn't even see my family.
Hatta ma Ha-niHaawil.	We're not even going to try.

5. Major religions are:

al-islaam	Islam	الاسلام
al-masiiHiyya	Christianity	المسيحية
al-yahuudiyya	Judaism	اليهودية
al-buudiyya	Buddhism	البودية
al-hinduusiyya	Hinduism	الهندوسية

A follower of each religion is referred to as:

muslim, -a, -iin	Moslem	مسلم -ين
masiiHi, -iyya, -yiin	Christian	مسيحي -يين
yahuudi, -iyya, -yiin*	Jew	يهودي -يين (يهود)
buudi, -iyya, -yiin	Buddhist	بودي -يين
hinduusi, -iyya, -yiin	Hindu	هندوسي -يين

*/yahuud/ is another plural; it is more classical.

A follower of a religion other than the first three, or an atheist or a pagan, may be referred to as /kaafir/ (-a, -iin), 'unbeliever'.

Vocabulary Notes

diin, adyaan	religion	دين اديان
rukn, arkaan	pillar, support	ركن اركان
ṣaam, yiṣuum (ṣumt)	fast	صام يصوم (صمت)
ṣalla, yiṣalli (ṣalleet)	pray	صلى يصلي (صليت)
daxxan, yidaxxin	smoke	دخن يدخن

Drills

1. They don't even smoke cigarettes. — Hatta ma yišrabu sajaayir. — حتى ما يشربوا سجاير.

Substitute:

šaahi
moyya
sajaayir
yidaxxin
yištari
akl
yaakul
šayy

2. Even he knows. — Hatta huwwa yi9rif. — حتى هو يعرف.

Substitute:

I
they
went
she
came with us

doesn't know
you (f)
must return
you (p)
were going to forget
I
he
knows

3. I have to pray the sunset [prayer]. — laazim aṣalli l-maghrib. (or: /ṣalaat al-maghrib/) — لازم اصلي المغرب.

Substitute:

he
we
the evening prayer
the dawn prayer
they
the Moslems
all year
the afternoon prayer
the noon prayer
the people
the merchants
I
the Friday prayer
the sunset prayer

4. Tomorrow Ramadan begins. — bukra yibda' šahar ramaḍaan. — بكرة يبدأ شهر رمضان.

Substitute:

muHarram — محرم
ṣafar — صفر
rabii9 al-awwal — ربيع الاول
rabii9 at-taani — ربيع الثاني
jumaad al-awwal — جماد الاول
jumaad at-taani — جماد الثاني
rajab — رجب
ša9baan — شعبان
ramaḍaan — رمضان
šawwaal — شوال
zu l-gi9da — ذو القعدة
zu l-Hijja — ذو الحجة

5. Complete the sentence:

[One] of the five pillars in the Islamic religion [is]:

min al-arkaan al-xamsa fid-diin al-islaami: — من الاركان الخمسة في الدين الاسلامي:

the declaration of faith
prayer
alms [giving]
fasting
pilgrimage

Situations

1.
A. What are you studying now in your history book?
B. We're studying religions of the world.
A. You mean (/ya9ni/) Islam and Christianity?
B. Yes, and Judaism, Buddhism, and Hinduism as well (/kazaalik/).
A. Do you like the book?
B. Very much. It's the best book I've read about history.

2.
A. Why are the shops closed?
B. For the evening prayer. They will open again in a little while.
A. Shall we wait here?
B. Let's stand here ten minutes because I haven't even bought the things [which] I want.
A. Do the shops close like this (/kida/) every day?
B. Yes, and of course they are closed all day on Friday.

LESSON 48

Dialogue

	built	mabni	مبني
	exporting	taṣdiir	تصدير
	oil	nafṭ	نفط
A.	The economy of the Kingdom is built on the exporting of oil.	iqtiṣaad al-mamlaka mabni 9ala taṣdiir an-nafṭ.	اقتصاد المملكة مبني على تصدير النفط.
	we export	niṣaddir	نصدر
	we import	nistawrid	نستورد
	majority	mu9ẓam	معظم
	needs, necessities	Haajaat	حاجات
B.	Yes, we export oil and important most of our needs from abroad.	iiwa, niṣaddir al-baṭrool wu nistawrid mu9ẓam Haajaatana min barra.	ايوه ،نصدر البطرول ونستورد معظم حاجاتنا من برا.
	for example	masalan	مثلا
A.	What, for example?	eeš masalan?	ايش مثلا ؟
	types	anwaa9	انواع
	equipment ('equipments')	aǰhiza	اجهزة
B.	For example, cars and food and many types of equipment.	masalan sayyaaraat w akl w anwaa9 ajhiza katiir.	مثلا سيارات واكل وانواع اجهزة كثير.
	goods	biḍaa9a	بضاعة
	imported (f)	mistawrida	مستوردة
	world	9aalam	عالم
A.	I saw goods imported from all the countries of the world.	ana šuft biḍaa9a mistawrida min kull buldaan al-9aalam.	انا شفت بضاعة مستوردة من كل بلدان العالم.
	especially	xuṣuuṣan	خصوصا
B.	Especially Europe and Japan.	xuṣuuṣan urubba w al-yabaan.	خصوصا اروبا واليابان.

Structure Sentences

1.	The Kingdom produces 7 million barrels of oil every day.	al-mamlaka tintij sab9a malyoon barmiil nafṭ kull yoom.	المملكة تنتج سبعة مليون برميل نفط كل يوم.

2. There are many oil companies in Saudi Arabia and in the Arabian Gulf.	fii šarikaat baṭrool katiir fis-su9uudiyya wu fil-xaliij al-9arabi.	فيه شركات بطرول كثير في السعودية وفي الخليج العربي.
3. The oil embargo happened after the Ramadan War in 1972.	man9 al-baṭrool ṣaar ba9d Harb ramaḍaan sanat itneen wu sab9iin.	منع البطرول صار بعد حرب رمضان سنة اثنين وسبعين.
4. Most of the oil wells are in the Eastern Region.	mu9ẓam aabaar az-zeet fil-manṭiga š-šargiyya.	معظم آبار الزيت في المنطقة الشرقية.

Grammatical Notes

1. Three terms are used for 'oil': /nafṭ/ is the classical word and is often used when referring to unrefined oil. /zeet/ is the more colloquial word, and means everything from cooking oil to industrial oil. /baṭrool/ is a newly-borrowed word, and usually refers to petroleum or refined oil.

2. /mu9ẓam/, 'most', 'a majority of', is used with a plural noun in a construct state:

mu9ẓam Haajaatana	most of our needs
mu9ẓam an-naas muslimiin.	The majority of the people are Moslems.

Vocabulary Notes

mabni, -iyya, -yiin	built	مبني -يين
taṣdiir	exporting	تصدير
istiiraad	importing	استيراد
Haaja, -aat	need, necessity	حاجة -ات
jihaaz, ajhiza	equipment	جهاز اجهزة
barmiil, baraamiil	barrell	برميل براميل
Harb, Huruub*	war	حرب حروب
biir, aabaar	well	بير آبار
nuu9, anwaa9	type	نوع انواع
ṣaddar, yiṣaddir	export	صدر يصدر
astawrad, yistawrid	import	استورد يستورد
antaj, yintij	produce	انتج ينتج
ṣaar, yiṣiir	happen	صار يصير

*This word is feminine.

Drills

1. We export oil and import most of our needs.	niṣaddir al-baṭrool wu nistawrid mu9ẓam Haajaatana.	نصدر البطرول ونستورد معظم حاجاتنا.

Continue, substituting the following pairs of words:

cars - food
books - international newspapers
food - equipment
coffee - medicine
sugar - airplanes
fabrics - shoes
meat - fruit
oil - most of our needs

2. The Kingdom produces 7 million barrels of oil every day. — al-mamlaka tintij sab9a malyoon barmiil nafṭ kull yoom. — المملكة تنتج سبعة مليون برميل نفط كل يوم.

Substitute:

the Gulf
America
produces much equipment
airplanes
France
many kinds of goods
buys
Japan
oil from the Middle East
fabrics
produces
cars
the Kingdom
7 million barrels of oil every day

3. Answer the question:

When did you visit the Kingdom? — mita zurt al-mamlaka? — متا زرت المملكة؟

after the oil embargo
before the Ramadan War
in 1972
after Ramadan
during Hajj month
after the big Eid
during the winter vacation

4. Most of the oil wells are in the Eastern Region. — mu9ẓam aabaar az-zeet fil-manṭiga š-šargiyya. — معظم آبار الزيت في المنطقة الشرقية.

Substitute:

companies
in the Hijaz
people
cities
the Najd
the bedouins
the ministers
the foreigners
the Eastern Region
the oil companies
the oil wells

Situations

1.
A. We want to invite you to a meeting next week at the Ministry of Petroleum.
B. OK, let me talk to the director.
A. Is he back from the Eastern Region?
B. He returned last night from visiting ('a visit to') the oil wells there.

2.
A. I read an article in a magazine about the oil embargo of ('in the year of') 1972.

B. Yes, the oil embargo occurred after the war.
A. Which countries in the Middle East export oil?
B. The Kingdom of Saudi Arabia, the Arabian Gulf, Iraq and Iran (/iiraan/) export most of the oil. The economy of the Kingdom is built on oil.

3.
A. Do you (p) like to talk about international politics?
B. Oh, of course. Especially politics and economics of the Middle East.
A. The Middle East has become very important to ('in') the world.
B. Yes, because this area produces oil and because of the political situation as well.

LESSON 49

Dialogue

	case	gaḍiyya	قضية
A.	I read in the paper about the Palestine matter ('case').	giriit fil-jariida 9an gaḍiyyat falasṭiin.	قريت في الجريدة عن قضية فلسطين.
	problem	muškila	مشكلة
	problems	mašaakil	مشاكل
	international	duwali	دولي
B.	This problem is [one] of the most important international political problems.	haadi l-muškila min ahamm al-mašaakil as-siyaasiyya d-duwaliyya.	هادي المشكلة من اهم المشاكل السياسية الدولية.
A.	They say that there may be ('arise') another war between the Arabs and Israel.	yiguulu innu mumkin tiguum Harb taanya been al-9arab w isra'iil.	يقولوا انه ممكن تقوم حرب ثانية بين العرب واسرائيل.
	at least	9ala l-agall	على الاقل
	fedayeen	fidaa'iyiin	فدائيين
	they fight	yiHaaribu	يحاربوا
	withdraws (f)	tinsaHib	تنسحب
	lands	araaḍi	اراضي
	occupied (f)	muHtalla	محتلة
B.	Or at least, the fedayeen will fight until Israel withdraws from the occupied territories.	aw 9ala l-agall, al-fidaa'iyiin Ha-yiHaaribu ileen isra'iil tinsaHib min al-araaḍi l-muHtalla.	او على الاقل الفدائيين حيحاربوا الين اسرائيل تنسحب من الاراضي المحتلة.
A.	Among them [are] the city of Jerusalem and Sinai and the West Bank.	minhum madiinat al-guds wu siina w aḍ-ḍiffa l-gharbiyya.	منهم مدينة القدس وسينا والضفة الغربية.

Structure Sentences

1.	The Second World War broke out in 1939..	gaamat al-Harb al-9aalamiyya t-taanya sanat tis9a wu talaatiin.	قامت الحرب العالمية الثانية سنة تسعة وثلاثين.
2.	And "the War of the Setback" was in 1967.	wu Harb an-naksa kaanat fi sanat sab9a wu sittiin.	وحرب النكسة كانت في سنة سبعة وستين.
3.	Keep that between me and you.	xalli haada beeni wu beenak.	خل هادا بيني وبينك.

4.	At least we solved the problem.	9ala l-agall, Halleena l-muškila.	على الاقل حلينا المشكله.
5.	Do you (p) want a political solution or a military solution?	tibghu Hall siyaasi walla Hall 9askari?	تبغوا حل سياسي ولا حل عسكري؟
6.	They discussed the Palestine matter in the United Nations.	atkallamu 9an gaḍiyyat falasṭiin fil-umam al-muttaHida.	اتكلموا عن قضية فلسطين في الامم المتحدة.
7.	There are negotiations between the two sides.	fii mufaawaḍaat been aṭ-ṭarafeen.	فيه مفاوضات بين الطرفين.

Grammatical Notes

1. To express 'one of the most' with an adjective, use /min/ with the comparative adjective:

min ahamm al-mašaakil	one of the most important problems
min akbar ar-rijaal	one of the oldest men

2. The verb /gaam/, 'to stand', is used idiomatically with /Harb/ to mean 'to break out', 'to arise', 'to occur'.

3. /been/, 'between', 'among', is sometimes used twice if two sides are mentioned. If pronouns are used, they are suffixed to the word:

beeni wu beenak	between me and you
beeni wu been aHmad	between me and Ahmad
been al-9arab wu isra'iil	between the Arabs and Israel
been al-9arab wu been isra'iil	between the Arabs and Israel

Vocabulary Notes

gaḍiyya, gaḍaaya	case, matter	قضية قضايا
muškila, mašaakil	problem	مشكلة مشاكل
arḍ, araaḍi*	land, territory	ارض اراضي
ḍiffa, ḍifaaf	bank (of a river)	ضفة ضفاف
umma, umam	nation	امة امم
fidaa'i, -iyya, -yiin	freedom fighter, commando	فدائي -يين
ṭaraf, aṭraaf	side	طرف اطراف
9askari, -iyya, -yiin	military	عسكري -يين
duwali -iyya	international	د ولي
Haarab, yiHaarib	fight	حارب يحارب
ansaHab, yinsaHib	withdraw	انسحب ينسحب

*This word is feminine.

Drills

1. I read in the paper about the Palestine matter.	ana giriit fil-jariida 9an gaḍiyyat falasṭiin.	انا قريت في الجريدة عن قضية فلسطين.

Substitute:

the Six-Day War ("War of the Setback")
the 1967 War
the negotiations between the Arabs and Israel
the occupied lands
the West Bank
the solution to ('of') the problem
World War II
the United Nations
the official policy

2. This problem is [one] of the most important problems.	haadi l-muškila min ahamm al-mašaakil.	هادي المشكلة من اهم المشاكل.

Substitute:

one of the biggest problems
one of the smallest problems
this matter
one of the most important matters
these negotiations
[some] of the longest meetings
[some] of the nicest meetings
[some] of the most important meetings
[some] of the most important problems
this problem

3. They say that there may be a war.	yiguulu innu mumkin tiguum Harb.	يقولوا انه ممكن تقوم حرب.

Substitute:

the negotiations may begin
the United Nations may have ('make') a meeting
the king may change the policy
the commandos may fight
Israel may withdraw from the occupied territories
the government may close the airport
the princes may travel to the Eastern Region
the director may ask for a translation
he may send the letter registered
a war may break out

4. The fedayeen will fight until Israel withdraws from the occupied territories.	al-fidaa'iyiin Ha-yiHaaribu ileen isra'iil tinsaHib min al-araaḍi l-muHtalla.	الفدائيين حيحاربوا الين اسرائيل تنسحب من الاراضي المحتلة.

Substitute:

until next year
will come to the meetings
will try
until they find a political solution
until they return to Jerusalem

will fight
until they take the West Bank
until Israel withdraws from the occupied territories

5. Keep that between me and you. — xalli haada beeni wu beenak. — خل هادا بيني وبينَك.

Substitute:

between him and her
between our family and yours ('your family')
between my side and your side
between the Palestinians and the Israelis
between the government and the people

Situations

1.
A. Who are the fedayeen?
B. They are Palestinians who are fighting against Israel.
A. Where are they fighting?
B. In many areas--in the West Bank and Jerusalem, in Syria, in Lebanon.
A. The Palestine issue is a big problem.
B. It's a problem for the Middle East and for the whole world ('all the world').

2.
A. Can you do me a favor ('service')?
B. Certainly, what?
A. I need the new 'Time' magazine but I'm in a hurry.
B. I'll buy it for you this afternoon.
A. I heard that there is an article about the fedayeen.
B. Good. I want to read it, too.

Cultural Notes

1. The subject of Israel is sensitive and rarely discussed socially. We have introduced the vocabulary words, but this is not to imply that the subject matter is appropriate for foreigners to use in initiating conversations.

LESSON 50

Review selected dialogues. Practice them using other persons, also changing tenses and changing the number of nouns.

Supplementary Drills

1. Given the following sentences, change the verbs to future tense:

giri l-jariida.	قري الجريدة.
ruHna li ṣaaHibna.	رحنا لصاحبنا.
akalat al-burtukaana.	أكلت البرتكانة.
aštareet saa9a jadiida.	اشتريت ساعة جديدة.
saafaru wu šaafu l-jabal.	سافروا وشافوا الجبل.
ana tarjamt al-jawaab.	انا ترجمت الجواب.
naḍḍafna s-sayyaara l-beeḍa.	نظفنا السيارة البيضا.
iidi waja9atni.	ايدي وجعتني.
aHmad sallam 9aleek.	احمد سلم عليكْ.
gafalu l-madrasa.	قفلوا المدرسة.
sa'al su'aal.	سأل سؤال.
raddeet 9ala l-mudarris.	رديت على المدرّس.
daxal wara l-9imaara.	دخل ورا العمارة.
as-si9r ma9guul.	السعر معقول.
al-ustaaz ma ǩaan mawjuud.	الاستاذ ما كان موجود.
aštaghal sawwaag taksi.	اشتغل سواق تكسي.

Repeat the drill, changing the nouns to plural.

2. Given the sentence, repeat it using an active participle instead of a verb:

axuuya raaH al-madrasa.	اخوي راح المدرسة.
ṣarafat fuluus katiir.	صرفت فلوس كثير.
šaaf an-naxil.	شاف النخل.
dafa9 al-Hisaab.	دفع الحساب.
simi9na l-kalaam.	سمعنا الكلام.
ṭalabt minnu musaa9ada.	طلبت منه مساعدة.
axuuya saag sayyaarati.	اخوي ساق سيارتي.
waṣalna l-Hafla badri.	وصلنا الحفلة بدري.
xaraju mit'axxiriin.	خرجوا متأخرين.
miši ma9aahum.	مشي معاهم.
al-awlaad naamu fi ghurfat an-noom.	الأولاد ناموا في غرفة النوم.

3. I have to rent a house. laazim <u>asta'jir beet</u>. لازم استأجر بيت.

Substitute:

buy a new sofa
import the fabric from America
find another refrigerator
see the oil wells some time
solve this problem
visit Jerusalem at Easter
rest all day
leave a tip for the waiter
study about communism and socialism in East Europe
travel to the Arabian Gulf
see my family during the summer vacation
buy medicine at the pharmacy
clean the curtains in the living room
take my daughter to the hospital
greet the guests
invite them to (/9ala/) dinner

4. I read in the paper about the matter.	giriit fil-jariida 9an al-gaḍiyya.	قريت في الجريدة عن القضية.

Substitute:

World War I
the oil embargo
the Hindu religion
Arab nationalism
the monarchist system
the minister's reception at the airport
the importing and exporting of goods in Arabia
the probability of another war
the new apparatus which the company bought
the meetings at the United Nations
the negotiations between the two sides
the five pillars of ('in') Islam
the occupied territories

5. We didn't go because we were tired.	ma ruHna li'ann kunna ta9baaniin.	ما رحنا لأن كنا تعبانين.

we forgot
my head hurt
we had gone before [that]
he didn't invite us
we had already bought fruits and vegetables
we didn't need anything
we didn't want to eat again
because of the rain
I wanted to sew
the children had to go to school
we didn't have a vacation this year

Narratives

1. Thank you, I'm honored to be here in your home. Your home is beautiful, here and in the garden. The food is delicious--bless your hands. That's enough--OK, only a little [more]. Thanks be to God. May your table always be thus. The fruit is [so] fresh--from where did you buy it? I was in the souk this morning but I didn't see fruit like this. The prices are so high now, maybe because it's winter and everything is imported from far [away].

2. This is the first time I've gone to a tailor to have a suit made ('make a suit'). He's very good. I asked for a cotton jacket like my old one ('the old one of mine'). Only I want the sleeves narrow--that's a good idea, isn't it? You should ('must') come with me the next time in order to meet the tailor. He also makes shirts and even ties. He's not expensive at all and his shop is near the center of town.

3. I read many international newspapers and magazines because I like to know about international politics, especially the politics of the Middle East. I have been working in Saudi Arabia for about two years, and I traveled to most of the Arab countries in this period. I don't understand the Palestine problem well, but I hope there is a solution soon, if possible. I agree with the government that after four wars in the area, a political solution and not a military [one] is best.

APPENDIX A

Specialized Vocabulary

1. Titles of Nobility

His Majesty (the King)	jalaalat al-malik	جلالة الملك
'owner of majesty'	ṣaaHib al-jalaala	صاحب الجلالة
Her Majesty (the Queen)	jalaalat al-malika	جلالة الملكة
'owner of majesty'	ṣaaHibat al-jalaala	صاحبة الجلالة
His Royal Highness (the Prince)	sumuww al-maliki al-amiir	سمو الملكي الامير
'owner of royal highness'	ṣaaHib as-sumuww al-maliki	صاحب السمو الملكي
His Highness (the Prince) (Princess)	sumuww al-amiir (amiira)	سمو الامير (اميرة)
'owner of highness'	ṣaaHib as-sumuww (ṣaaHiba)	صاحب السمو (صاحبة)
The Crown Prince	waliyy al-9ahd	ولي العهد
'[May God] lengthen your life' (said to royalty)	ṭaal 9umrak (9umrik)	طال عمرَك (عمرِك)
'[May God] lengthen his (her) life' (said about royalty)	ṭaal 9umru (9umraha)	طال عمره (عمرها)
His Excellency (the minister, the ambassador)	sa9aadat (al-waziir, as-safiir)	سعادة (الوزير، السفير)

2. Military

weapon, arms	silaaH, asliHa	سلاح اسلحة
training	tadriib	تدريب
soldier	9askari, 9asaakir	عسكري عساكر
officer	ẓaabiṭ, ẓubbaaṭ	ضابط ضباط
army	al-jeeš	الجيش
navy	al-baHariyya	البحرية
air force	silaaH aṭ-ṭayaraan	سلاح الطيران
ship	baaxira, bawaaxir	باخرة بواخر
port	miina, mawaani	مينا مواني
Saudi Arabian National Guard	al-Haras al-waṭani as-su9uudi	الحرس الوطني السعودي
The American Mission	al-bi9sa l-amrikiyya	البعثة الامريكية
The Corps of Engineers	silaaH al-muhandisiin	سلاح المهندسين

3. Political

president	ra'iis, ru'asa	رئيس رؤسا
Senate	majlis aš-šuyuux	مجلس الشيوخ
House of Representatives	majlis an-nuwwaab	مجلس النواب
election	intixaabaat	انتخابات
to elect	antaxab, yintixib	انتخب ينتخب
to win	kasab, yiksab	كسب يكسب
to lose	xisir, yixsar	خسر يخسر
candidate	muraššaH, -iin	مرشح -ين
citizen	muwaaṭin, -iin	مواطن -ين

citizenship	jinsiyya	جنسية
refugee	laaji', -iin	لاجئ -ين
majority	aktariyya	اكثرية
minority	aqalliyya	اقلية

4. Economic and Commercial

economic	iqtiṣaadi	اقتصادي
commercial	tujaari	تجاري
technology	tiknoloojiyya	تكنولوجية
technical	fanni	فني
industry	aṣ-ṣinaa9a	الصناعة
industrial	ṣinaa9i	صناعي
profit	fayda, fawaayid	فايدة فوايد
loss	xusaara, xasaayir	خسارة خساير
capitalism	ra'smaaliyya	رأسمالية
program	barnaamij, baraamij	برنامج برامج
advisor	mustašaar, -iin	مستشار -ين
permit	taṣriiH, taṣaariiH	تصريح تصاريح
work permit	taṣriiH 9amal	تصريح عمل
license	ruxṣa, ruxaṣ	رخصة رخص
driver's license	ruxṣat siwaaga	رخصة سواقة
factory	maṣna9, maṣaani9	مصنع مصانع
production	intaaj	انتاج
consumption	istihlaak	استهلاك
consumer	mustahlik, -iin	مستهلك -ين
progress	taqaddum	تقدم
rich	ghani, aghniya	غني اغنيا
poor	fagiir, fugara	فقير فقرا

5. Law

law	qanuun, qawaaniin	قانون قوانين
lawyer	muHaami, -iin	محامي -ين
court	maHkama, maHaakim	محكمة محاكم
judge	qaaḍi, qaḍaa	قاضي قضاة
crime	jariima, jaraayim	جريمة جرايم
criminal	mujrim, -iin	مجرم -ين
jail	sijn	سجن

6. Religion

mosque	jaami9, jawaami9*	جامع جوامع
church	kaniisa, kanaayis	كنيسة كنايس
temple	ma9bad, ma9aabid	معبد معابد
prophet	nabi, anbiya	نبي انبيا
'our master' (title for prophets)	sayyidna	سيدنا
religious authorities	9ulama	عُلما
religious police	muṭawwi9, -iin	مطوع -ين
The Holy Koran	al-qur'aan al-kariim	القرآن الكريم
Holy Mecca ('the venerated')	makka l-mukarrama	مكة المكرمة
Holy Medina ('the lighted')	al-madiina l-munawwara	المدينة المنورة
lesser pilgrimage	al-9umra	العمرة

*This word alternates with /masjid/.

7. Health

disease	maraḍ, amraaḍ	مرض امراض
accident	Haadisa, Hawaadis	حادثة حوادث
wound	jurH, jiraaH	جرح جراح
clinic	9iyaada, -aat	عيادة -ات
operation	9amaliyya, -aat	عملية -ات
analysis	taHliil, taHaaliil	تحليل تحاليل
checkup	kašf	كشف
shot	Hugna, Hugan	حقنة حقن
nurse	mumarriḍa, -aat	ممرّضة -ات
vaccination	talgiiH	تلقيح
blood	damm	دم
liver	kabd	كبد
kidney	kulya, kalaawi	كلية كلاوى
stomach	mi9da	معدة
lung	ri'a, -aat	رئة -ات
diarrhea	ishaal	أسهال
dysentery	dizanṭaarya	دزنطاريا
fever	Humma	حمة
measles	al-Haṣba	الحصبة
mumps	an-nukaaf	النكاف
cancer	saraṭaan	سرطان
tuberculosis	as-sull	السل
cholera	al-kuliraa	الكوليرا

8. Household Words

houseboy	ṣabi	صبي
maid	xaddaama	خدامة
to cook	ṭabax, yuṭbux	طبخ يطبخ
refrigerator	tallaaja	ثلاجة
stove	butagaaz	بتكاز
oven	furn	فرن
cupboard	dulaab, dawaaliib	دولاب دواليب
dish, dishes	ṣaHan, ṣuHuun	صحن صحون
washer	ghassaala	غسالة
dryer	naššaafa	نشافة
electricity	kahraba	كهربا
pan, pans (pots)	gidir, guduur	قدر قدور
platter, tray	ṣiniyya, ṣawaani	صنية صواني
knife	sikkiina, sakaakiin	سكينة سكاكين
fork	šooka, šuwak	شوكة شوك
spoon	ma9laga, ma9aalig	معلقة معالق
to wash	ghassal, yighassil	غسل يغسل
to shine	massaH, yimassiH	مسح يمسح
to break	kassar, yikassir	كسّر يكسّر
clean	naḍiif, nuḍaaf	نظيف نظاف
dirty	wisix, -iin	وسخ -ين
tablecloth, bedspread	mafraš, mafaariš	مفرش مفارش
sheet	milaaya, -aat	ملاية -ات
blanket	baṭaniyya, baṭaaṭiin	بطنية بطاطين
towel	manšafa, manaašif	منشفة مناشف
soap	ṣabuun	صابون

APPENDIX B

Social Expressions

In addition to expressions given in the text, there are many other occasions on which speech formulas are used, and some familiar expressions can also be elaborated upon. Most of these are religious in content. All the formulas will be presented in the masculine or plural form.

1. Hello and Goodby

Good evening. (men only)	masaak aḷḷaah bil-xeer.	مساك الله بالخير.
Goodby. ('God with you')	aḷḷaah ma9aak.	الله معاك.

2. Speaking of a Future Plan

May our Lord make it easy.	rabbana yisahhil.	ربنا يسهّل.
Our Lord with you.	rabbana ma9aak.	ربنا معاك.
God with you.	aḷḷaah ma9aak.	الله معاك.
With the permission of God.	b-izn illaah.	باذن الله.

3. Giving Thanks

May God keep you for us. (usually said to a superior)	aḷḷaah yixalliik lana.	الله يخليك لنا.
[May God] increase your goodness.	kattar xeerak.	كثر خيرك.
May God preserve you.	aḷḷaah yiHfaẓak.	الله يحفظك.

4. Blessings

[It is] what God wills.	ma šaa' aḷḷaah.	ما شاء الله.
May God bless.	tabaarak aḷḷaah.	تبارك الله.
The name of God.	ism aḷḷaah.	اسم الله.
(At birth) May God keep him.	aḷḷaah yixallii.	الله يخليه.
(To the mother) Thank God for [your] safety.	al-Hamdu lillaah 9ala s-salaama.	الحمد لله على السلامة.

5. Offering Food

Have some.	atfaḍḍal.	اتفضل.
(Response) To [your] strength.	bil-9aafiya.	بالعافية.

6. <u>When Someone Compliments Your Food</u>

To [your] happiness and health.	bil-hana wu š-šifa.	بالهنا والشفا.

7. <u>After Someone Drinks</u>

Healthful.	hanii'an.	هنيئا.
(Response) May God give you happiness.	hanaak aḷḷaah.	هناك الله.

8. <u>When Seeing Someone Working, or After He Has Completed A Task</u>

May God give you strength.	aḷḷaah ya9ṭiik al-9aafiya.	الله يعطيك العافية.
(Response) May God stregthen you.	aḷḷaah yi9aafiik.	الله يعافيك.

9. <u>Before Someone Takes a Trip</u>

Bon voyage. ('With safety, if God wills')	bis-salaama in šaa' aḷḷaah.	بالسلامة ان شاء الله.
[May you] go and return with safety.	tisaafir wu tirja9 bis-salaama.	تسافر وترجع بالسلامة.
(Response) May God make you safe.	aḷḷaah yisallimak.	الله يسلمك.

10. <u>Asking Pardon</u>

No offense.	la mu'axza.	لا مؤاخذة
(Response) Never mind.	ma9aleeš.	معليش.

11. <u>When Someone Says "I have news for you" or "Guess what?"</u>

[Let it be] good, if God wills.	xeer, in šaa' aḷḷaah.	خير ان شاء الله

12. <u>When Something is Broken</u>

[It is] evil [which] was broken.	ankasar aš-šarr.	انكسر الشر.

13. <u>Before Engaging in a Dangerous Task, or Waking Someone</u>

In the name of God, the Merciful, the Compassionate.	bism ilaah ar-raHmaan ar-raHiim.	بسم الله الرحمن الرحيم.

14. <u>Expressing Uncertainty</u>

[only] God knows. ('God is the most-knowing')	aḷḷaahu a9lam.	اللهُ اعلم.

15. <u>Wedding</u>

Congratulations ('blessed').	mabruuk.	مبروك.
[We await] the first-born.	9ugbaal al-bakaari.	عقبال البكاري.

16. <u>During Ramadan</u>

Ramadan is generous.	ramaḍaan kariim.	رمضان كريم.

17. <u>When Someone is Going on Pilgrimage</u>

Blessed pilgrimage.	Hajj mabruur.	حج مبرور.

18. <u>Speaking of Something Bad</u>

May God not permit it.	la samaH aḷḷaah.	لا سمح الله .
[May it be] outside and distant.	barra wu ba9iid.	برا وبعيد.

19. <u>When Facing a Difficult Situation</u>

I take refuge in God.	a9uuzu billaah.	اعوذُ بالله .
(Response) May God give you aid.	aḷḷaah yikuun b-9uunak.	الله يكون بعونَك.

20. <u>Condolences for a Death</u>

May God greaten your reward.	9aẓẓam aḷḷaah ajrak.	عظّم الله اجرَك.
(Response) May God compensate you with good.	jazaak aḷḷaah xeer.	جزاك الله خير.
[May] the remainder [be added] to your life.	al-baagiya fi Hayaatak.	الباقية في حياتك.
(Response) And your life.	wu fi Hayaatak.	وفي حياتك.

21. <u>When Speaking of a Dead Person</u>

(Name), may God have mercy on him.	aḷḷaah yirHamu.	الله يرحمه .
The late (name).	al-marHuum.	المرحوم.

APPENDIX C

Gestures

Gestures are used in all societies to register reactions to people and events and to communicate messages silently. The gestures described below are used in the Hijaz region of Saudi Arabia, and represent only the most common ones. They include only those which are different from gestures used by Americans. (You will observe many other gestures identical for both Americans and Arabians.)

Much of this material was based on an article, "Arabic Gestures", by Robert A. Barakat, which appeared in the Journal of Popular Culture, Spring, 1973 (reprinted with permission).

1. Move the head slightly back and raise eyebrows: no.
   Move the head back and chin upward: no.
   Move the chin slightly back and make a clicking sound with the tongue: no.
   Open the right palm toward the other person, moving it from right to left: no.
2. After shaking hands, place the right hand to the heart: greeting with respect or sincerity.
   (Among women: place the right hand to the heart after offering food or drink: offering with sincerity.)
3. Kiss forehead, nose, or right hand of person who is being greeted: extreme respect.
4. Place the right hand on the heart, or pat the heart a few times: that's enough, thank you.
5. Hold the right hand out stiff, with palm down, and move it from left to right: never.
6. Hold open palms facing the other person: excellent.
7. Touch outer edge of eyes with fingertips: OK.
8. Hold right hand up and shake it: go away.
9. Touch tip of nose with tip of right forefinger: promise to do something.
10. Hold out right hand with palm down, move up and down slowly: quiet down.
11. Hold right forefinger in front of mouth and blow on it: be quiet.
12. Bite right forefinger which is placed sidewards in mouth: shame!
13. Flick right thumbnail on front teeth: I have no money.

APPENDIX D

Saudi Names

The Arab countries follow several systems in arriving at the composition of a person's name. And within one country, different social classes and religious groups may use different systems. In Saudi Arabia, the system is quite traditional and consistent.

Arab names reflect the geneology on the father's side. Each person has a given name, and his (or her) "middle name" is that of the father. Thus, women have masculine middle names. The person's name may be followed by "ibn" (son) or "bint" (daughter) with the father's name (this is especially common in the eastern Arabian peninsula). Thus, a person's name may be recited as Muhammad ibn Ahmad ibn Mahmoud, or Habiba bint Ahmad.[1]

Each family has its "family" name. This name identifies the large extended family whose members consider themselves tied by bonds of kinship and honor and who see the group as their main source of identification. Family names are often geographical: Al-Halaby (from Aleppo), Al-Makkawi (Meccan), Shami (Syrian); denote an occupation: Haddad (blacksmith), Najjar (carpenter); descriptive: Al-Asmar (dark-complected), Al-Badawi (Bedouin); tribal: Al-Harbi (from the Harb tribe), Al-Qahtani (from the Qahtan tribe); or sound like a personal name because they are the name of a common ancestor: Ibrahim, Hussein.

In the full form of a name, as used for legal purposes, a person may have more than one name in the middle, those of the grandfather, great-grandfather, etc., but these are omitted in daily use. For example, if a man's full name is:

Muhammad	Hasan	Ahmad	Al-Makkawi
(given)	(father)	(grandfather)	(family)

he may be called Muhammad Hasan on one occasion, or Muhammad Hasan Ahmad, as well as Muhammad Al-Makkawi.

To further complicate the picture, some people are given double names as their first name. In this case, the person usually chooses to "go by" one of his names, and the other shows up only in legal situations. A man known as Hussein Ibrahim could be really named Muhammad-Hussein Ibrahim (the name Muhammad is especially common as the first element of a doubled name). Most American employers double-check the names given by employees to be sure that they are complete, and they decide on a consistent naming practice.

In Saudi Arabia, it is common to address someone you have just met by his first name. (Notice that Saudis will often address you as Mr. John, Mr. Bill, etc.) Arabs often find it odd that Americans refer to each other by their last names.

A woman's name does not change after marriage, since she cannot, of course, take her husband's geneology, which is what it would entail. Names, therefore, may give no clue whatsoever that two people are husband and wife. Socially, she may be referred to as "the wife of", using her husband's first name. For this reason, Saudis frequently refer to foreign women as Mrs. John, Mrs. Bill, etc.

After having children, parents are often referred to as "Abu" (father) and "Umm" (mother) of their eldest son. For example, a man may be called "Abu Hasan", if this is the name of his eldest son (he will be called after his eldest daughter it he has no sons). This is, of course, non-official. If such a name is used throughout a person's lifetime, it may become a family name in

1. For ease in reading, most names are spelled in a modified phonemic system, approximately the way Arabs spell their names in English.

time, referring to this ancestor, and this is sometimes heard as a form of family name. The use of "Umm" is very common for women, and it provides a more proper, less personal way of addressing a lady than by using her own name.

Arabs make frequent use of nicknames as well. The most common type of nickname is formed by repeating a consonant sound in the person's name, using a double syllable. Common nicknames may be Fifi, Susu, Bobo, Mimi, etc. These are most often used for women and small children, but not always. There is another set of "equivalent" nicknames (like William = Bill, Elizabeth = Betty in English), substituting a name with "Abu" plus another name (in this case, this does not describe a father-son relationship), for example: Hasan = Abu Ali, Omar = Abu Siraj.

There is also the use of titles. Common titles are Duktoor (doctor), Ustaaz (professor), Muhandis (engineer). Other titles frequently used are Hajj (for someone who has made the pilgrimage to Mecca), and titles of nobility.

A person's name can also be a clue to certain facts about him. Names may indicate religion, country or area of origin, and often, social status. This explains why persons may introduce themselves with various long combinations of names.

Most Arabic names are not religiously restricted, but some are, and may not be all that obvious. While all Saudis are Moslem, there are some non-Moslem Arabs living in the country. Only a few patterns emerge as guidelines:

(1) If the name sounds Western (George, Michael, Marie), it marks a Christian name.

(2) Moslems use names hyphenated with Abdel-, plus the attributes of God (Abdel-Rahman, Abdel-Karim, etc.).[2] Other names are in combination with the word Din (religion), or built on the roots H-m-d, H-s-n, and Sh-r-f (Ahmad, Hamid, Hasan, Sharif).

(3) Most names which refer to personal qualities or attributes are shared by all groups, such as Jamil (beautiful), Zaki((intelligent), Karim (generous).

The following lists of names are by no means exhaustive; they are some of the more common names.

---

2. Christians use this pattern with a few names: Abdel-Massih, Abdel-Malik, Abdel-Shahid.

Common Names

Men

Abdel- Names

Abdallah
Abdel-Aziz
Abdel-Fattah
Abdel-Ghani
Abdel-Hadi
Abdel-Hakim
Abdel-Halim
Abdel-Jabbar
Abdel-Karim
Abdel-Latif
Abdel-Majid
Abdel-Rahman
Abdel-Rauf
Abdu

"Din" Names

Ala-Eddin
Badr-Eddin
Izz-Eddin
Mohie-Eddin
Salah-Eddin
Shams-Eddin
Sharaf-Eddin

H-m-d Names

Ahmad
Hamad
Hamid
Hammady
Hamud
Mahmoud
Muhammad

H-s-n Names

Hasan
Hasanein
Hassuna
Hosny
Hussein
Mohsen

Sh-r-f Names

Ashraf
Sharaf
Sharif

Koranic, Biblical

Ayoub (Job)
Daud (David)
Ibrahim (Abraham)
Isa (Jesus)
Ishaq (Isaac)
Musa (Moses)
Suleiman (Solomon)
Yacoub (Jacob)
Yehya (John)
Younis (Jonah)
Yousef (Joseph)

Other Names

Abbas
Adel
Adnan
Akram
Ali
Amin
Arif
Bakri
Bashir
Basim
Fahd
Fakhri
Faraj
Farid
Farouk
Fawzi
Fayez
Faysal
Fuad
Ghasan
Habib
Hadi
Hani
Hashim
Hatim
Hisham
Husam
Ihab
Isam
Ismail
Jabir
Jafar
Jalal
Jamal
Jamil
Juma
Kamal
Karim
Khalid
Khalil
Labib
Mahir
Majid
Mamduh
Mamoun
Mansour
Mounib
Mounir
Muammar
Mustafa
Muwaffaq
Nabil
Naim
Nasir
Nuri
Omar
Qays
Rafiq
Ramadan
Ramez
Rashid
Rauf
Ridwan
Rizk
Saad
Sadek
Said
Salah
Salih
Salim
Sami
Samir
Saud
Shafik
Shukri
Suhail
Taha
Tahir
Talal
Tariq
Usama
Wahib
Wajih
Yasin
Yasir
Zaki
Zayad
Zayd

Women

Often men's names are used, with /-a/ added to the end. Other names describe personal attributes, or are the names of historical persons.

-a Names	Other Names	
Amina	Abla	Lubna
Aziza	Afaf	Maha
Badia	Ahlam	Mayy
Bahija	Aida	Miryam
Basma	Amal	Muna
Farida	Ayesha	Nadia
Habiba	Azza	Najwa
Hadia	Dalal	Nawal
Jalila	Fatma	Nuha
Jamila	Fayruz	Raja
Karima	Hala	Raqiya
Majida	Hana	Sabah
Mounira	Hanan	Safiya
Nadira	Hawa	Sahar
Nura	Hind	Sakina
Rabia	Hosna	Salma
Samia	Huda	Salwa
Samiha	Ibtisam	Sana
Samira	Inam	Sara
Sharifa	Insaf	Suad
Wahiba	Khadija	Shadiya
Zakiya	Layla	Thoraya
		Wafa
		Zahra
		Zaynab

GLOSSARY

Items in this glossary are arranged according to English alphabetical order, with the special symbols included as follows: a, b, d, ḍ, e, f, g, gh, h, H, i, j, k, l, m, n, q, r, s, ṣ, š, t, ṭ, u, w, x, y, z, ẓ, 9.

Nouns and adjectives are presented in the masculine singular form, and the plural forms are parenthesized. A few nouns are given in the singular or plural form only, if the other is rare. Nouns which are usually used in the collective plural (foods, for example), are listed under this form.

The feminine form is regular, so it is not shown except for adjectives of color. If a noun is usually used with the article /al-/, it will be listed under the noun (for example, /as-suudaan/). Phrases are listed under the first item (for example, /ma9a l-asaf/). Some proper nouns are given, such as the names of countries, but names of cities are not given unless their pronunciation is very different from that of English.

Verbs are given in the 'he' form of the perfect tense, followed by the imperfect tense. If a verb is usually used with a preposition, this is given in parentheses.

ARABIC -ENGLISH

aadaab	literature, humanities
aanisa	Miss
aasif (-iin)	sorry
aasya	Asia
aaxir (-iin)	last; end
abadan	never
abb	father
abriil	April
abyaḍ (beeḍa)(beeḍ)	white
ab9ad	further, more distant
adda, yiddi	to give
afriqya	Africa
agall	less
agdam	older
agrab	nearer
agṣar	shorter
aghla	more expensive
ahamm	more important
ahl	family, relatives, people

ahlan	welcome; hi
ahlan wu sahlan	welcome
aHad	someone
al-aHad	Sunday
aHla	prettier
aHmar (Hamra) (Humur)	red
aHsan	better
ajadd	newer
ajmal	more beautiful
ajnabi (ajaanib)	foreigner
akal, yaakul	to eat
akbar	bigger
akl	food
aktar	more
alf (aalaaf)	thousand
al-Hiin	now
aḷḷaah	God
alli	which (non-interrogative)
almaani (almaan)	German (language, nationality)
almaanya	Germany
alṭaf	nicer, more pleasant
amaan	safety
amiir (umara)	prince
amiira (-aat)	princess
amma	either; as for
amriika	America
amrikaani (amrikaan)	American
amriiki (-yiin)	American
ams	yesterday
ana	I
ansaHab, yinsaHib (min)	to withdraw
antaj, yintij	to produce

antaẓar, yintaẓir	to wait for
arba9a	four
arba9iin	forty
arba9ṭa9š	fourteen
arḍ (araaḍi)	land
arsal, yirsil	to send
arxaṣ	cheaper
asbaani (asbaan)	Spaniard, Spanish
asbaanya	Spain
asta'jar, yista'jir	to rent
asta'zan, yista'zin	to take leave; ask permission
astanna, yistanna	to wait for
astaraaH, yistariiH	to rest
astawrad, yistawrid	to import
asta9jal, yista9jil	to hurry
asta9mal, yista9mil	to use
aswad (sooda) (suud)	black
as9ad	happier
aṣfar (ṣafra) (ṣufur)	yellow
aṣghar	smaller
aštaghal, yištaghil	to work
aštara, yištari	to buy
at'axxar, yit'axxir	to be late, delayed
atfaḍḍal	go ahead; sit down; have some
atgal	heavier
atkallam, yitkallam	to speak
atmarran, yitmarran	to practice
atšarraf, yitšarrif	to be honored
at9allam, yit9allim	to be educated
at9arraf, yit9arrif (9ala)	to be introduced
at9awwad, yit9awwid (9ala)	to become accustomed

aṭwal	longer
aṭyab	better
aw	or
awHaš	worse; uglier
awsa9	wider
awwal	first; beginning
al-awwal	firstly
awwal ams	the day before yesterday
awwal-ma (+ verb)	as soon as
axad, yaaxud	to take
axaff	more lightweight
axḍar (xaḍra) (xuḍur)	green
axx (axwaan)	brother
ayy?	which?
ayy	any
azrag (zarga) (zurg)	blue
a9taqad, ya9taqid	to believe
a9ṭa, yi9ṭi	to give
baab (abwaab)	door
al-baagi	the rest, remainder
baarid	cold
baa9, yibii9	to sell
bada', yibda'	to begin
badawi (badu)	Bedouin
badla (bidal)	suit
badri	early
bagar	cattle; beef
baggaal (-iin)	grocer
baglaawa	baklava pastry
baHr (buHuur)	sea
al-baHreen	Bahrein
bakaluryoos	Bachelor's degree

bala	without
balad (bilaad; buldaan)	country
balaH	red dates
balakoona (-aat)	balcony
balyoon (balaayiin)	billion
banafsaji	purple, violet
banṭaloon (-aat)	trousers
banziin	gasoline
bard	cold
bardaan (-iin)	cold
bariid	mail; post office
bariid `jawwi	air mail
barmiil (baraamiil)	barrell
barra	outside; abroad
basboor (-ṭaaṭ)	passport
bass	only
baṣal	onions
baṭaaṭis	potatoes
baṭn	stomach, abdomen
baṭrool	petroleum
baṭṭaal (-iin)	bad
baxšiiš	tip
bazaaliya	peas
ba9d	after
ba9d kida	after that
ba9deen	later
ba9ḍ	each other
ba9iid	far, distant
beeḍ	eggs
been	between
beet (buyuut)	house
bidinjaan	eggplant

biduun	without
biḍaa9a	goods
biir (aabaar)	(oil) well
bil-Heel	very much, extremely
bil-marra	very much, extremely
bint (banaat)	girl
bissa (bisas)	cat
biẓ-ẓabt	exactly
bluuza (-aat)	blouse
b-sur9a	quickly
b-šweeš	slowly
bukra	tomorrow
bunni	brown
burtukaan	oranges
burtukaani	orange (color)
buudi (-yiin)	Buddhist
buuṣa	inch
daaxili	interior, inner
daayim	eternal
dafa9, yidfa9	to pay
daftar (dafaatir)	notebook
dagiiga (dagaayig)	minute
daHHiin	now
dajaaj	chicken
daras, yidrus	to study
darras, yidarris	to teach
dars (duruus)	lesson
dasta (-aat)	dozen
dawa (adwiya)	medicine
dawwar, yidawwir (9ala)	to look for
daxal, yudxul	to enter
daxxal, yidaxxil	to cause to enter, bring in

daxxan, yidaxxin	to smoke
dayman	always
diblumaasi (-yiin)	diplomatic, diplomat
difaa9	defense
diin (adyaan)	religion
dimišq	Damascus
dimuqraaṭi (-yiin)	democrat, democratic
ad-dimuqraaṭiyya	democracy
diraasa (-aat)	study
diraa9 (-een)	arm
diri, yidri	to be aware
disambar	December
dukkaan (dakaakiin)	shop
duktoor (dakaatra)	doctor
dukturaa	Doctor's degree
dulaab (dawaaliib)	closet, cupboard
dulaar (-aat)	dollar
dunya	world
duub- (+ verb)	just
duwali	international
duxuul	entering
ḍahr	back
ḍariiba (ḍaraayib)	tax
ḍayyig	narrow
ḍeef (ḍuyuuf)	guest
ḍidd	against
ḍiffa (ḍifaaf)	bank (of river)
ḍuhur	noon
eeš	what?
faaḍi (-yiin)	free, empty
faṣuuliyya	beans
faḍḍal, yifaḍḍil	to prefer

fahham, yifahhim	to explain, help to understand
fajr	dawn
fakha (fawaakih)	fruit
fakk, yifukk	to take apart; change money
fakka	change (money)
falasṭiin	Palestine
fallaaH (-iin)	peasant farmer
faraansa	France
faransaawi (-yiin)	French (language, nationality)
faṣl (fuṣuul)	season, class
fataH, yiftaH	to open
faṭuur	breakfast
feen?	where?
fi	in
fibraayir	February
fidaa'i (-yiin)	freedom fighter, commando
fii	there is, are
fikra (afkaar)	idea
filfil	pepper
fil-miyya	per cent
finjaan (fanaajiin)	cup
foog	up, above, upstairs
fundug (fanaadig)	hotel
furn	oven
furṣa (furaṣ)	opportunity, occasion
fustaan (fasaatiin)	dress
gaabal, yigaabil	to meet
gaal, yiguul	to say
gaam, yiguum	to get up, stand up
gaas, yigiis	to measure
gabl	before; since; ago

gabl kida	before that
gadam (agdaam)	foot (measurement)
gaddeeš?	how much?
gadiim (gudum)	old
gaḍiyya (gaḍaaya)	case, matter
gafal, yigfil	to close
gahwa	coffee
galam (aglaam)	pen
galiil (-iin)	few
gamiiṣ (gumṣaan)	shirt
garaaj	garage
gariib (-iin)	near; soon
garš (guruuš)	piastre
gaṣiir (guṣaar)	short
ga9ad, yug9ud	to sit
gidir, yigdar	to be able
giid- (+ verb)	already
giri, yigra	to read
gism (agsaam)	department
guddaam	in front of
al-guds	Jerusalem
gumaaš (agmiša)	fabric
gunṣuliyya (-aat)	consulate
guṭun	cotton
guzaaz	glass
ghaali (-yiin)	expensive
ghada	lunch
ghalaṭ	wrong
ghalṭaan (-iin)	wrong
gharb	west
ghayyar, yighayyir	to change
gheer kida	other than that

ghraam	gram
ghurfa (ghuraf)	room
ghurfat al-intiẓaar	lobby, reception room
ghurfat al-juluus	living room
ghurfat an-noom	bedroom
ghurfat as-sufra	dining room
haada	this (m)
haadi	this (f)
hadaak	that (m)
hadiik	that (f)
hadolaak	those
hadool	these
halala	(unit of money)
handasa	engineering
hina	here
hinaak	there
hinduusi (-yiin)	Hindu
hiyya	she
humma	they
huwwa	he
Haaḍir	very well, OK; ready
Haaja (-aat)	thing; need, necessity
Haal (aHwaal)	situation, condition
Haarab, yiHaarib	to fight, go to war
Haawal, yiHaawil	to try
Habb, yiHubb	to like, love; to want to
Habba	a piece, one
Haḍaana	nursery school, kindergarten
Haḍratak	you (honorific)
Hafla (Hafalaat)	party
Hagg (-oon)	belonging to

Hajj	the pilgrimage to Mecca
Hajz	reservation
Haliib	milk
Hamd	glory
Hammaal (-iin)	porter
Hammaam (-aat)	bathroom
Harb (Huruub)	war
Harr	hot; heat
Harraan (-iin)	hot
Hatta	even; until
Haṭṭ, yiHuṭṭ	to put
Hawaali	about, approximately
Hijaazi (-yiin)	Hijazi
Hijri	A.H. (Islamic calendar)
Hilu (-wiin)	pretty; sweet
Hisaab (-aat)	check, bill, account
Hizaam	belt
Hizb (aHzaab)	party (political)
Hood	sink
Hooš	garden
Hukuuma (-aat)	government
ibšer	gladly, certainly
ibtidaa'i	elementary
iHḍa9š	eleven
iHna	we
iHtimaal	probability
iid (yadeen)	hand
iijaar	rent
iiwa	yes
ijtimaa9 (-aat)	meeting
ijtimaa9i	social

ileen	until
illa	yes; minus
al-imaaraat	the Emirates
imtiHaan (-aat)	examination, test
in šaa' aḷḷaah	if God wills
ingiliizi (ingiliiz)	English (language, nationality)
ingiltera	England
innu	that (conjunction)
inta	you (m)
inti	you (f)
intu	you (p)
iqtiṣaad	economics
islaami	Islamic
ism (asaami)	name
isra'iil	Israel
isra'iili (-yiin)	Israeli
istiiraad	importing
istigbaal (-aat)	reception
išaara (-aat)	signal, traffic signal
ištiraaki	socialist
al-ištiraakiyya	socialism
itna9š	twelve
itneen	two
al-itneen	Monday
ittifaag (-aat)	agreement
iṭaali (-yiin)	Italian
iza	if
izn	permission
i9daadi	intermediate
i9laam	information
jaab, yijiib	to bring
jaam9a (-aat)	university

jabal (jibaal)	mountain
jadiid (judud)	new
jadur (judraan)	wall
jakitta (-aat)	jacket
jalas, yijlis	to sit
jamb	beside
jamiil	beautiful
januub	south
jariida (jaraayid)	newspaper
jarraaH (-iin)	surgeon
jarrab, yijarrib	to try out
jawaab (-aat)	letter; answer
jawaaz (-aat) as-safar	passport
jawaazaat	passport control
jaww	weather
jayy (-iin)	coming, next
al-jazaayir	Algeria, Algiers
jazma (jizam)	shoes
jazzaar (-iin)	butcher
jeeš (juyuuš)	army
jiddan	very
jihaaz (ajhiza)	equipment, appliance, apparatus
jii9aan (-iin)	hungry
jild	leather, skin
jineena (janaayin)	garden
jughrafya	geography
jumhuuri	republican
jumhuuriyya	republic
jumla (jumal)	sentence
al-jum9a	Friday
juwwa	inside
kaafir (-iin)	unbeliever

kaan, yikuun	to be
kabaab	shish kabob
kabiir (kubaar)	big
kalaam	speech
kalb (kilaab)	dog
kallaf, yikallif	to cost
kallam, yikallim	to talk to
kam?	how many?
kamaan	too, also
kammal, yikammil	to finish
kanaba (-aat)	sofa
karafiṭṭa (-aat)	necktie
kart (kuruut)	card
katab, yiktub	to write
katiir	much, many
kazaalik	thus, as well
keef?	how?
kida	like that
kifaaya	enough
kiilu	kilo
kiimya	chemistry
kilma (kalimaat)	word
kitaab (kutub)	book
kitaaba	writing
kubbaaya (-aat)	drinking glass
kubri (kabaari)	bridge
kufta	ground spiced meat
kull	each, every
kull-ma (+ verb)	whenever
kulliyya (-aat)	college
kumm (akmaam)	sleeve

kursi (karaasi)	chair
kuusa	squash
al-kuweet	Kuwait
kwayyis (-iin)	good
la'	no
laa (+ verb)	do not (negative command)
laakin	but
laazim (+ verb)	must
laff, yiluff	to turn
laga, yilaagi	to find
laHam	meat
lamman	when (non-interrogative)
laţiif (luţaaf)	nice, pleasant
law	if
law samaHt	if you please
leel	night
leemuun	lemons
leeš?	why?
li'ann	because
libnaan	Lebanon
liHadd-ma (+ verb)	until
liibya	Libya
lillaah	to God
li muddat	for a period of
lissa9	still; not yet
lista (lisat)	list
litir	liter
lugha (-aat)	language
ma (+ verb)	not
ma fii	there is not, are not
maaḍi	last, past

maali	financial
maaris	March
maaṣa (-aat)	desk
maayu	May
mabni (-yiin)	built
mabruuk (-iin)	blessed; "congratulations"
mabsuuṭ (-iin)	happy
madiina (mudun)	city
madrasa (madaaris)	school
madxal (madaaxil)	entrance
mafhuum (-iin)	understood
maftuuH (-iin)	opened
magaas (-aat)	size
magfuul (-iin)	closed
maghrib	sunset
al-maghrib	Morocco
maHad	nobody
maHall (-aat)	place, store
maHaṭṭa (-aat)	station, stop
maHbuub (-iin)	beloved
maHduud (-iin)	limited, fixed
maHši	stuffed
majalla (-aat)	magazine
majisteer	Master's degree
majlis (majaalis)	majlis session
makaan (amaakin)	place
maktab (makaatib)	office
maktaba (-aat)	library, bookstore
maktuub (-iin)	written
malik (muluuk)	king
malika (-aat)	queen

maliki	monarchist, monarchistic
malikịyya	monarchy
malla, yimalli	to fill, fill out
malyoon (malaayiin)	million
mamlaka (-aat)	kingdom
mamnuu9 (-iin)	forbidden
manṭiga (manaaṭig)	region, area
manzil (manaazil)	house
man9	embargo, prevention
maqaala (-aat)	article (magazine, newspaper)
maṛHaba	welcome
marra	very; occasion; some time
masa	p.m., evening
masaa'	evening
masalan	for example
masiiHi (-yiin)	Christian
masjid (masaajid)	mosque
mas'uul (-iin)	responsible; official (person)
maṣur	Egypt
mašghuul (-iin)	busy
maškuur (-iin)	thanked
mašruu9 (mašaarii9)	project
mašwi	grilled
maṭaar (-aat)	airport
maṭar	rain
maṭbax	kitchen
maṭ9am (maṭaa9im)	restaurant
mawgif (mawaagif)	stop, stand (bus, taxi)
mawlid an-nabi	the Prophet's Birthday
mawjuud (-iin)	present, found
mawluud (-iin)	born
maw9ad (mawaa9iid)	appointment

maxṭuub (-iin)	engaged (to be married)
maẓbuuṭ (-iin)	correct, precise
ma9a	with
ma9a kida	in spite of that, nevertheless
ma9a l-asaf	unfortunately
ma9aleeš	never mind, it doesn't matter
ma9dan (ma9aadin)	metal
ma9guul (-iin)	believable, reasonable
ma9had (ma9aahid)	institute
ma9muul (-iin)	done
ma9ruuf (-iin)	known, well-known
ma9rifa	acquaintance
miHtaaj (-iin)	needing, in need of
miilaadi	A.D. (Christian calendar)
miin?	who?
milH	salt
min	from; ago
min faḍlak	please
min gheer	without
minHa (minaH)	scholarship, grant
mintaẓir (-iin)	waiting
mistanni (-yiin)	waiting
mista9jil (-iin)	in a hurry
miši, yimši	to walk; leave
mita?	when?
mit'akkid (-iin)	sure, certain
mit'assif (-iin)	sorry
mit'axxir (-iin)	late, delayed
mitir (amṭaar)	meter
mitzawwij (-iin)	married
mit9allim (-iin)	educated
miyya (-aat)	hundred

mooz	bananas
moyya	water
mubii9aat	sales
mudarris (-iin)	teacher
mudda	period of time
mudiir (-iin)	director, boss
mudiir maktab	appointments secretary
mufaawaḍaat	negotiations
mugaabil	facing
muhandis (-iin)	engineer
muhimm (-iin)	important
muHtall	occupied
mumkin	possible
mumtaaz (-iin)	excellent
musajjil (-aat)	recorder
musaa9ada	help, aid
musaa9id	assistant
musajjal	registered
muslim (-iin)	Moslem
mustašfa (-yaat)	hospital
musta9mal (-iin)	used
muškila (mašaakil)	problem
mušrif (-iin)	supervisor; inspector
muštarawaat	purchases
mutarjim (-iin)	translator, interpreter
muttaHid	united
muu	not
muu kida?	Isn't that so?
muwaafig (-iin)	in agreement
muwaaṣalaat	transportation, communication
muwaẓẓaf (-iin)	employee
mu9tadil	moderate

mu9ẓam	majority
naam, yinaam	to sleep
naas	people
naayib (nuwwaab)	deputy, representative
naḍḍaf, yinaḍḍif	to clean
naḍiif (nuḍaaf)	clean
nafs	same; oneself
nafṭ	oil
nahaar	daytime
nahr (anhaar)	river
najdi (-yiin)	Najdi
najjaar (-iin)	carpenter
naksa	setback
naxil	palmtrees
nazal, yinzal	to descend, stay
nazzal, yinazzal	to cause to descend, take down
na9am?	pardon?
na9am	yes
nimra (nimar)	number
nisi, yinsa	to forget
niẓaam (nuẓum)	system
noom	sleep
nufambar	November
nuṣṣ	half
nuur	light
nuu9 (anwaa9)	type, kind
al-qaahira	Cairo
qaṭar	Qatar
qawmi	national, nationalistic
al-qawmiyya	nationalism
raabi9	fourth
raadyu (rawaadi)	radio

raaH, yiruuH	to go
raas	head
rabbana	our Lord
rabii9	spring (season)
ar-rabuu9	Wednesday
radd, yirudd (9ala)	to answer
ragam (argaam)	number
rajja9, yirajji9	to return (something)
raml	sand
rasmi	official
raṭl (arṭaal)	pound (measurement)
raxiiṣ (ruxaaṣ)	cheap
riji9, yirja9	to return
rijjaal (rijaal)	man
rijl (rujuul)	foot
risaala (rasaayil)	message, letter
riyaaḍa	mathematics
riyaal (-aat)	riyal
rub9	quarter, one fourth
rukn (arkaan)	pillar
rumaadi	gray
ruusi (ruus)	Russian (language, nationality)
ruusya	Russia
ruzz	rice
sa'al, yis'al	to ask
saab, yisiib	to leave behind
saabi9	seventh
saadis	sixth
saafar, yisaafir	to travel
saag (-een)	leg
saag, yisuug	to drive
saakin (-iin)	living, residing

saanawi	secondary; yearly
saaniya (sawaani)	second (unit of time)
saa9a (-aat)	hour; watch
saa9ad, yisaa9id (fi)	to help
sa'al, yis'al	to ask
as-sabt	Saturday
saba9ṭa9š	seventeen
sab9a	seven
sab9iin	seventy
safaara (-aat)	embassy
safiir (sufara)	ambassador
sahl	easy
salaam	peace
salaama	safety
saliig	rice cooked with milk and meat
sallam, yisallim (9ala)	to greet; make safe
samaH, yismaH	to permit
samak (asmaak)	fish
sana (siniin, sanawaat)	year
sariir (surur)	bed
sawa	together
sawwa, yisawwi	to make, do
sawwaag (-iin)	driver
sayyaara (-aat)	car
sayyid	Mr.
sayyida	Mrs.
sa9iid (su9adaa')	happy
sibtambar	September
sideeri	vest
siib (asyaab)	hall, hallway
siina	Sinai
sikirteer (-iin)	secretary

simi9, yisma9	to hear
sitaara (sataayir)	curtain, drape
sitt (-aat)	woman, lady
sitta	six
sittiin	sixty
siṭṭa9š	sixteen
siyaasa (-aat)	policy
si9r (as9aar)	price
su'aal (as'ila)	question
sujjaada (sajaajiid)	rug, carpet
sukkar	sugar
as-suudaan	Sudan
suug (aswaag)	souk
suuriya	Syria
su9uudi (-yiin)	Saudi
as-su9uudiyya	Saudi Arabia
ṣaala	entrance area in a home
ṣaam, yiṣuum	to fast
ṣaar, yiṣiir	to happen
ṣabaaH	morning
ṣaddar, yiṣaddir	to export
ṣaghiir (ṣughaar)	small
ṣahyuuni (-yiin)	Zionist
aṣ-ṣahyuuniyya	Zionism
ṣaHH	right, correct
ṣaHiiH	true
ṣaHra (ṣaHaari)	desert
ṣalaa	prayer
ṣalla, yiṣalli	to pray
ṣalaṭa	salad
ṣaloon	guests' receiving room

ṣanduug (ṣanaadiig)	box, trunk
ṣanti	centimeter
ṣaraf, yiṣruf	to spend
ṣarraaf (-iin)	moneychanger
ṣayaaḍiyya	dish of fish, onions, and rice
ṣaydala	pharmacy (subject)
ṣaydaliyya	pharmacy (store)
ṣa9b	difficult
ṣeef	summer
ṣifir	zero
ṣiHHa	health
ṣinaa9a	industry
ṣoom	fasting
ṣubuH	a.m., morning
ṣufra	table of food
ṣufraji (-yiin)	waiter
ṣuuf	wool
ṣaaHib (aṣHaab)	friend
šaaf, yišuuf	to see
šaahi	tea
šaal, yišiil	to carry
šaari9 (šawaari9)	street
šaaṭi' (šawaaṭi')	coast
šagga (šugag)	apartment
šahar (šuhuur)	month
šajara (ašjaar)	tree
šakar, yuškur	to thank
šamaal	north
šams	sun
šanṭa (šunaṭ)	suitcase, purse, briefcase
šarg	east
šarika (-aat)	company

aš-šarq al-awsaṭ	the Middle East
šarraf, yišarrif	to honor
šayy (ašyaa')	thing
šayyal, yišayyil	to load, cause to carry
šeex (šuyuux)	sheikh
šihaada (-aat)	declaration of faith; certificate
šimaal	left
širib, yišrab	to drink
šita	winter
šloonak?	How are you?
šubbaak (šabaabiik)	window
šughul (ašghaal)	work
šukr	thanks
šukran	thank you
šurb	drinking
šuyuu9i (-yiin)	communist
aš-šuyuu9iyya	communism
šwayya	a little bit
taajir (tujjaar)	merchant
taalit	third
taamin	eighth
taani (-yiin)	second; another, other
taani (+ verb)	again
taariix	history
taasi9	ninth
tagiil (tugaal)	heavy
tagriiban	approximately
taHat	under, below, downstairs
taksi (-yaat)	taxi
takyiif	air conditioning
talaata	three

talaatiin	thirty
talaţa9š	thirteen
talj	ice, snow
tallaaja (-aat)	refrigerator
at-taluut	Tuesday
tamaniin	eighty
tamanţa9š	eighteen
tamanya	eight
tamriin (tamaariin)	drill
tamur	dried dates
tarbiya	education, upbringing
tarjama	translation
tarjam, yitarjim	to translate
taşdiir	exporting
taşmiim (-aat)	design
ta'šiira (-aat)	visa
taww- (+ verb)	just
tazkira (tazaakir)	ticket
ta9aal (irregular)	come!
ta9b	trouble, bother
ta9baan (-iin)	tired
ta9liim	education
ta99ab, yita99ib	to trouble, tire
tijaara	commerce
tilifizyoon (-aat)	television
tilifoon (-aat)	telephone
tisa9ţa9š	nineteen
tis9a	nine
tis9iin	ninety
tuffaaH	apples
tult	one third

turki (atraak)	Turk
tuunis	Tunisia, Tunis
ţaaba9 (ţawaabi9)	stamp
ţaalib (ţalaba, ţullaab)	student
ţaaza	fresh
ţabbaax (-iin)	cook
ţab9an	of course
ţaHiina	sesame dip
ţalab (-aat)	order, request
ţalab, yuţlub	to ask for, request, order
ţalla9, yiţalli9	to carry up, out
ţamaaţim	tomatoes
ţarabiiza (-aat)	table
ţarablus	Tripoli
ţaraf (aţraaf)	side
ţard (ţuruud)	package
ţariig (ţurug)	way, road
ţawiil (ţuwaal)	tall
ţayaraan	airlines
ţayyaara (-aat)	airplane
ţayyib (-iin)	good, OK
ţibb	medicine (subject)
ţili9, yiţla9	to go up, ascend
ţi9im	delicious
ţuul	length
ughusţus	August
uktuubar	October
umma (umam)	nation
umm	mother
al-urdun	Jordan
urubba	Europe

usbuu9 (asaabii9)	week
ustaaz (asaatiza)	professor
utubiis (-aat)	bus
uula (irregular)	first (f)
uxt (axwaat)	sister
waafag, yiwaafig (9ala)	to agree
waaHa (-aat)	oasis
waaHid	one
waajib (-aat)	duty
waalid	father
waalida	mother
waasi9 (-iin)	wide
wagf (awgaaf)	wagf (religious endowment)
waggaf, yiwaggif	to stop, make stop
wagt (awgaat)	time
waHaš	to miss
waja9, yuja9	to hurt
'wala	or else
walad (awlaad)	boy, child
walla	or
waḷḷah	by God (oath)
wara	behind
warag	paper
warda (wuruud)	flower
warra, yiwarri	to show
waṣal, yiwṣal	to arrive
wasaṭ	middle, center
waṣṣal, yiwaṣṣil	to deliver, take to a destination
waṭani	national, patriotic
waziir (wuzara)	minister

wazn (awzaan)	weight
wigif, yiwgaf	to stand, stop
wiHiš (-iin)	bad
wilaaya (-aat)	state (of the U.S.A.)
wizaara (-aat)	ministry
wuguuf	stopping, standing
wujuud	existence, presence
wusṭ	waist
xaariji	external, foreign
xaaṭir	sake
xabbaaz (-iin)	baker
xaddaam (-iin)	servant
xafiif (xufaaf)	lightweight
xalaṣ	finished
xaliij	gulf
xalla, yixalli	to let, leave, allow
xallaṣ, yixaḷḷis	to finish
xamasṭa9š	fifteen
al-xamiis	Thursday
xamsa	five
xamsiin	fifty
xaraj, yuxruj	to go out
xarbaan (-iin)	out of order
xariif	autumn
xarraj, yixarrij	to expel
xaruuf (xirfaan)	lamb
xass	lettuce
xaṭṭ (xuṭuuṭ)	line
xayyaaṭ (-iin)	tailor
xayyaṭ, yixayyiṭ	to sew
xeer	goodness

xidma (xadamaat)	service, favor
xilaal	during
xiyaar	cucumbers
xubz	bread
xuḍaar	vegetables
xuruuj	exit
xuṣuuṣan	especially
xuṭṭa (xuṭaṭ)	plan
ya hala	welcome
al-yabaan	Japan
yabaani (-yiin)	Japanese
yahuudi (-yiin, yahuud)	Jew
yaḷḷa	let's go
al-yaman	Yemen
yamaani (-yiin)	Yemeni
yamiin	right (direction)
yanaayir	January
yarda (-aat)	yard (measurement)
ya9ni	that means, that is to say
yibgha	to want
yimkin	maybe
yoom (ayyaam)	day
al-yoom	today
yuulya	July
yuunya	June
zaakar, yizaakir	to study
zaar, yizuur	to visit
zaayid	plus
zakaa	alms
zamaan	long ago
zawj	wife
zayy	like, similar to

zayy kida	like that
zeen	good
zeet	oil
ziraa9a	agriculture
ziraa9i	agricultural
ziyaada	more, extra
ẓann, yiẓunn	to think
ẓarf (ẓuruuf)	envelope
9aad, yi9iid	to repeat
9aadatan	usually
9aadi (-yiin)	ordinary
9aafiya	strength
9aalam	world
9aalami	international
9aam	year
9aamir	filled
9aašir	tenth
9aaṣima (9awaaṣim)	capital (city)
9aayiš (-iin)	living, alive
9adas	lentils
9add, yi9idd	to count
9adda, yi9addi	to cross
9adl	justice
9afš	luggage
9afwan	you're welcome; pardon me
9ajab, yi9jib	to please
9ala (9a)	on
9ala Hisaab	at the expense of
9ala keefak	you wish
9ala l-agall	at least
9ala mahl-	carefully

9ala ṭuul	straight ahead
9amal, yi9mil	to do, work
9amal	work
9ammaal (+ verb)	in the process of
9an	about, regarding
9arabi (9arab)	Arab
9arabi	Arabic
9arḍ	width
9arraf, yi9arrif (9ala)	to introduce, inform
9asa	it is hoped, possibly
9askari	military
9askari (9asaakir)	soldier
9asa	dinner
9ašaan	because, in order to
9aṣiir	juice
9aṣur	late afternoon
9ašara	ten
9aṭšaan (-iin)	thirsty
9azam, yi9zim	to invite
9eela (9awaayil)	family
9een (9uyuun)	eye
9ibaara 9an	composed of
9iid (a9yaad)	holiday
9iid al-giyaama	Easter
9iid al-istiqlaal	Independence Day
9iid al-miilaad	Christmas
9iid miilaad	birthday
9iid aš-šukr	Thanksgiving
9ilm (9uluum)	science
9imaara (-aat)	building
9inab	grapes
9ind	to have; at the home of

9inwaan (9anaawiin)	address
al-9iraag	Iraq
9irif, yi9rif	to know
9iša	evening prayer
9išriin	twenty
9uluum siyaasiyya	political science
9umaan	Oman
9umr	life
9uṭla (9uṭal)	vacation

GRAMMATICAL INDEX